UNMANNED SPACE MISSIONS

AN EXPLORER'S GUIDE TO THE UNIVERSE

UNMANNED SPACE MISSIONS

EDITED BY ERIK GREGERSEN, ASSOCIATE EDITOR, ASTRONOMY AND SPACE EXPLORATION

Britannica®
Educational Publishing

IN ASSOCIATION WITH

ROSEN
EDUCATIONAL SERVICES

Published in 2010 by Britannica Educational Publishing
(a trademark of Encyclopædia Britannica, Inc.)
in association with Rosen Educational Services, LLC
29 East 21st Street, New York, NY 10010.

Distributed exclusively by Rosen Educational Services.
For a listing of additional Britannica Educational Publishing titles, call toll free (800) 237-9932.

First Edition

Britannica Educational Publishing
Michael I. Levy: Executive Editor
Marilyn L. Barton: Senior Coordinator, Production Control
Steven Bosco: Director, Editorial Technologies
Lisa S. Braucher: Senior Producer and Data Editor
Yvette Charboneau: Senior Copy Editor
Kathy Nakamura: Manager, Media Acquisition
Erik Gregerson: Associate Editor, Astronomy and Space Exploration

Rosen Educational Services
Jeanne Nagle: Senior Editor
Nelson Sá: Art Director
Nicole Russo: Designer
Introduction by Corona Brezina

Library of Congress Cataloging-in-Publication Data

Unmanned space missions / edited by Erik Gregersen.—1st ed.
    p. cm.—(An explorer's guide to the universe)
Includes index.
ISBN 978-1-61530-018-1 (lib. bdg.)
1. Space probes—Popular works. 2. Space flights—Popular works. I. Gregersen, Erik.
TL795.3.U56 2010
629.43'5—dc22

2009036103

Manufactured in the United States of America

On the cover: The ability to collect samples and take photographs in inhospitable
environments makes unmanned spacecraft, such as NASA's Mars rovers, highly valuable
when exploring the universe. *AFP/Getty Images*

CONTENTS

22

71

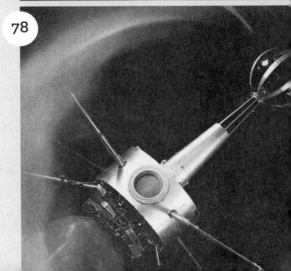

78

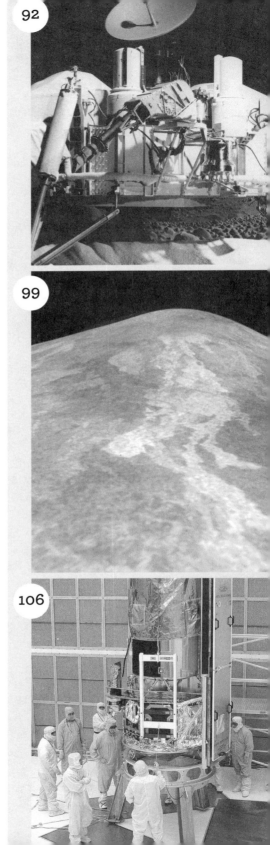

92

99

106

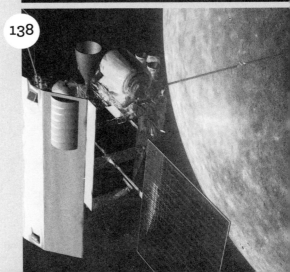

CHAPTER 4: SCIENCE IN SPACE 156

CHAPTER 5: SPACE APPLICATIONS 168

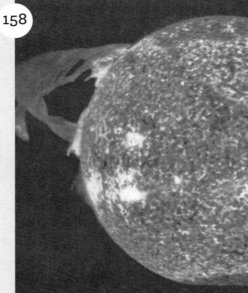

182

183

188

INTRODUCTION

Current estimates indicate there are more than 900 functioning satellites orbiting Earth, collecting information and improving telecommunications around the globe on a continuous basis. In a way, these satellites are the enduring legacy of all the unmanned space missions that have come before, when humans sent technology out into the universe in their stead.

This book examines unmanned space missions, from the launching of the former Soviet Union's Sputnik in the 1950s to the extensive exploration of the solar system's planets conducted by Voyager spacecraft and the Mars Exploration Rovers. These pages describe the history of unmanned spaceflight, speculate about what the future holds, examine the scientific and practical applications of unmanned spaceflight, and profile some of the missions that have been launched into Earth's orbit and that have navigated the solar system.

The story of unmanned spaceflight begins with the fundamental achievement of transporting a craft into Earth's orbit, beyond the pull of gravity. There is only one vehicle that delivers the necessary thrust and that also operates both in the atmosphere and in space—the rocket. The first rockets were fired by the Chinese in the 13th century. Rocketry was later refined using a propulsion system based on the fundamental physical principles outlined in the 17th century by Sir Isaac Newton. By the 19th century, rockets were being used in warfare, as the delivery system for exploding warheads.

The development of a rocket capable of space travel proved to be a lengthy and costly process, interrupted by frequent setbacks. The first person to propose rockets as a means of space travel was Konstantin Tsiolkovsky, a Russian teacher and visionary. His groundbreaking theories on spaceflight, especially the 1903 work *Investigation of Outer Space by Reaction Devices*, outlined the potential advantages and disadvantages of rockets operating in space. His theories were proved by American physicist and inventor Robert Goddard who, like Tsiolkovsky, recognized that in order to reach space, a rocket must be propelled by a liquid form of fuel. In 1926, Goddard successfully launched the first liquid-fuelled rocket, an event credited as marking the beginning of the Space Age.

The U.S. government showed little interest in supporting Goddard's work on rockets, but the situation was different in Germany. During the 1940s, the rocket engineer Werner von Braun led a team that developed a series of experimental rockets. The project culminated with the V-2 rocket, which was used as a weapon during World War II.

The development of rocket launchers—a later version of which propelled this United States Gemini mission—made sending unmanned spacecraft into orbit a reality as early as the 1950s.
Space Frontiers/Hulton Archive/Getty Images

After the war ended in 1945, political tensions shifted as United States and the Soviet Union entered the Cold War. Both nations began an arms race and established massive programs to develop new weapons arsenals. Both nations recruited German rocket scientists, and within two years, they each had tested their own V-2 rockets.

In 1957 the Soviets launched Sputnik, the first artificial satellite to orbit Earth. Launched using a modified intercontinental ballistic missile, Sputnik was an 83-kilogram (184-pound) sphere that communicated information such as temperature readings to a ground station by shortwave radio. The launch became a symbol of Soviet technological progress in the Cold War. In response, the United States scrambled to accelerate its own space program. In 1958, a Jupiter-C rocket designed by von Braun's team blasted into space with the first American satellite, the Explorer 1.

One ambitious goal followed for both countries—sending humans into space. In order to prepare for a manned spaceflight, the United States and the Soviet Union flew unmanned missions that were launched to test equipment and procedures. A number of test flights also studied the effects of space travel on animals.

Unmanned space missions also played a key role in the race to put a man on the Moon. The United States initiated Project Gemini to develop and test the spacecraft and procedures that could achieve this goal. The first two Gemini missions were unmanned test flights that demonstrated the success of the rocket, heat shield, landing system, and ocean recovery. In order to prepare for a Moon landing, NASA also launched unmanned Lunar Orbiters, which photographed the lunar surface. The images were used to select possible landing sites for a manned mission. Unmanned Lunar Surveyors also landed on the Moon, to obtain physical data. The Soviet Union also sent probes to the Moon.

In general, there are four types of unmanned scientific missions: orbital (the probe circles a planet or other body), flyby (the craft flies past a celestial body and continues on), landing (the vehicle lands on the surface of a planet or moon and sends back pictures), and sample return missions (the vehicle returns with samples from the planet or moon). In 1962, NASA's Mariner II became the first probe to reach another planet. During a flyby mission, it proved that under Venus's cloud cover, the surface temperature averaged 860 °F (460 °C). Subsequent Mariner missions yielded new breakthroughs. In 1971, Mariner 9 reached Mars and became the first craft to orbit another planet. Mariner 10 explored Mercury for the first time in 1974. Two Viking spacecraft reached Mars in 1976, landing on the surface and taking enough photographs from orbit to map most of the planet.

Exploration of Mars continues in the new millennium with the Mars rovers Spirit and Opportunity, a pair of vehicles that landed on opposite sides of the planet in

NASA's Spirit rover took this image of a large, continuous rocky outcrop on a cratered Martian plain. NASA/JPL

2004. They explored the geology of Mars, taking soil samples and sending back photographs—images of an alien planet that captivated the world. The two rovers long outlasted their expected functional lifetime, and their outstanding success bodes well for other possible robot explorers in the future.

These and many other successful unmanned space missions have been directed by NASA, but the Soviet Union, the European Space Agency (ESA), and Japan have also conducted successful missions. Today, many projects are collaborations among multiple agencies and nations.

There are several advantages to unmanned space missions. Foremost in importance is that they do not put human life at risk. Even if a mission utterly fails, it is not a tragedy on the same level as the loss of the *Challenger* or *Columbia* space shuttles, each of which carried crews of seven people. For instance, on Feb. 10, 2009, 790 km (491 miles) above the surface of the earth, two communication satellites collided over Siberia. One of the satellites involved in the collision was an American Iridium satellite, launched in 1997. The other was a larger Russian Cosmos, a non-operational satellite launched in 1994. The satellites collided at a 90-degree angle and broke apart into a cloud of debris. Aside from some pieces of debris that posed a threat to other satellites, there were no repercussions from the collision, and certainly no risk to human life.

Unmanned space missions are also less expensive than manned spaceflight, in part because they do not require life support systems or cargo such as food and other necessities. Unmanned probes can travel greater distances over longer stretches of time than manned missions, sometimes taking years to reach their destination. Because of the vast distances, only a handful of missions have reached Jupiter, Saturn, Uranus, Neptune, and their moons. The most famous missions were Voyager 1 and Voyager 2, launched in 1977 to make a "Grand Tour" of the outer planets. The two craft returned a wealth of data and images and continued their outward journey toward the edge of the solar system.

Unmanned space missions have obtained scientific information about Earth, the solar system, and the outer reaches of the universe. Probes have examined every one of the planets and many of the moons in the solar system. Unmanned space missions have produced many spectacular successes that have captured the imagination of the public and inspired a passion for science in many young people.

Although public attention has remained focused on high-profile manned spaceflight programs, extraordinary scientific breakthroughs have been achieved via unmanned missions. Sensors and detectors on satellites sent back information on the properties of the upper atmosphere and on the dynamics of the Sun. The importance of satellites in people's everyday lives cannot be understated. Satellites facilitate communication technology, such as mobile devices and television. Satellites provide navigation services such as global positioning systems (GPS). Satellites are essential in meteorology—the branch of science dealing with the atmosphere and the weather—and observations of events occurring on the earth such as geological disturbances. For the military, satellites are a valuable tool in guaranteeing national security.

Unmanned space missions also have been responsible for the creation of space-based observatories, the most famous being the Hubble Space Telescope launched in 1990. Unlike ground based observatories, space telescopes offer a view of the universe that is not

Released after having its main mirror repaired in 1993, the Hubble Space Telescope continued on its lonely journey, documenting the outer reaches of the solar system. NASA/Hulton Archive/Getty Images

obscured by the earth's atmosphere. Despite early setbacks—a problem in the mirror required a 1993 repair mission to bring it to full performance—Hubble has provided valuable information on the solar system and universe. It has revealed the furthest reaches of the universe, spotted active volcanoes on Jupiter's moon Io, and identified new planets orbiting faraway stars. Hubble's successor, the James Webb Space Telescope, is scheduled to be launched in 2013.

What does the future hold for unmanned spaceflight? Satellites will continue to make the world more interconnected. Technologically advanced space probes and observatories will return new data on the Sun and neighboring planets and moons. There has been discussion of a return to the Moon, and manned missions to Mars. If the latter goal becomes reality, unmanned space missions undoubtedly will lead the way for human exploration. And from there? The possibilities are limitless, brought into closer view by the achievements of unmanned space missions.

CHAPTER 1

GETTING TO SPACE

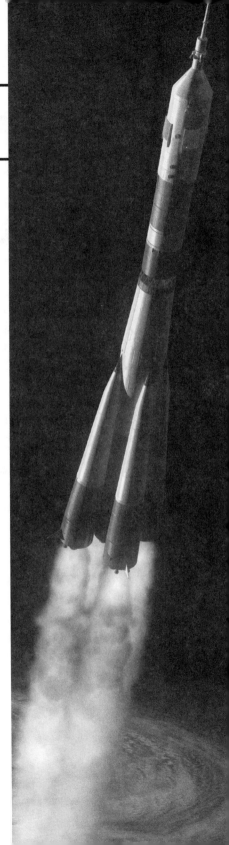

Although the possibility of exploring space has long excited people in many walks of life, for most of the latter 20th century only national governments could afford the very high costs of launching people and machines into space. This reality meant that space exploration had to serve very broad interests, and it indeed has done so in a variety of ways. Government space programs have increased knowledge, served as indicators of national prestige and power, enhanced national security and military strength, and provided significant benefits to the general public. In areas where the private sector could profit from activities in space, most notably the use of satellites as telecommunication relays, commercial space activity has flourished without government funding.

In the years after World War II, governments assumed a leading role in the support of research that increased fundamental knowledge about nature, a role that earlier had been played by universities, private foundations, and other non-governmental supporters. This change came for two reasons. First, the need for complex equipment to carry out many scientific experiments and for the large teams of researchers to use that equipment led to costs that only governments could afford. Second, governments were willing to take on this responsibility because of the belief that fundamental research would produce new knowledge essential to the health, security, and quality of life of their citizens. Thus, when scientists sought government support for early space experiments, it was forthcoming. Since the start of space efforts in the United States, the Soviet Union, and Europe, national governments have given high priority to the support of science done in and from space. From modest beginnings, space exploration has expanded under government support to include multibillion-dollar exploratory missions in the solar system and to major space-based astronomical observatories, such as the Hubble Space Telescope.

In 1957, Soviet leader Nikita Khrushchev used the fact that his country had been first to launch a satellite, Sputnik 1, as evidence of the technological power of the Soviet Union and of the superiority of communism. He repeated these claims after Yury Gagarin's orbital flight in 1961. Although U.S. Pres. Dwight D. Eisenhower had decided not to compete for prestige with the Soviet Union in a space race, his successor, John F. Kennedy, had a different view. On April 20, 1961, in the aftermath of the Gagarin flight, he asked his advisers to identify a "space program which promises dramatic results in which we could win." The response came in a May 8, 1961, memorandum recommending that the United States commit to sending people to the Moon, because "dramatic achievements in space...symbolize the technological power and organizing capacity of a nation" and because the ensuing prestige would be "part of the battle along the fluid front of the cold war." From 1961 until the collapse of the Soviet Union in 1991, competition between the United States and the Soviet Union was a major

influence on the pace and content of their space programs. Other countries also viewed having a successful space program as an important indicator of national strength.

Even before the first satellite was launched, U.S. leaders recognized that the ability to observe military activities around the world from space would be an asset to national security. Following on the success of its photoreconnaissance satellites, which began operation in 1960, the United States built increasingly complex observation and electronic-intercept intelligence satellites. The Soviet Union also quickly developed an array of intelligence satellites, and later a few other countries instituted their own satellite observation programs. Intelligence-gathering satellites have been used to verify arms-control agreements, provide warnings of military threats, and identify targets during military operations, among other uses.

In addition to providing security benefits, satellites offered military forces the potential for improved communications, weather observation, navigation, and position location. This led to significant government funding for military space programs in the United States and the Soviet Union. Although the advantages and disadvantages of stationing force-delivery weapons in space have been debated, as of the early 21st century, such weapons have not been deployed, nor have space-based antisatellite systems—that is, systems that can attack or interfere with orbiting satellites. The stationing of weapons of mass destruction in orbit or on celestial bodies is prohibited by international law.

Governments realized early on that the ability to observe Earth from space could provide significant benefits to the general public apart from security and military uses. The first application to be pursued was the development of satellites for assisting in weather forecasting. A second application involved remote observation of land and sea surfaces to gather imagery and other data of value in crop forecasting, resource management, environmental monitoring, and other applications. The U.S. and Soviet governments also developed their own satellite-based global positioning systems, originally for military purposes, that could pinpoint a user's exact location, help in navigating from one point to another, and provide very precise time signals. These satellites quickly found numerous civilian uses in such areas as personal navigation, surveying and cartography, geology, air traffic control, and the operation of information-transfer networks. They illustrate a reality that has remained constant for the past half century—as space capabilities are developed, they often can be used for both military and civilian purposes.

Another space application that began under government sponsorship but quickly moved into the private sector is the relay of voice, video, and data via orbiting satellites. Satellite telecommunications has developed into a multibillion-dollar business and is the one clearly successful area of commercial space activity. A related commercial space business is the provision of launches for private and government satellites. Suggestions have been made that in the future other areas of space activity, including remote sensing and the capture of solar energy to provide electric power on Earth, could become successful businesses.

Building the systems and components needed to carry out both government and commercial space programs has required the participation of private industry, and a number of firms now have substantial space involvement. Often these firms have also been major suppliers of aviation and defense products, a reflection of the common technological foundation for what has become known as the aerospace industry.

Most space activities have been pursued because they serve some utilitarian purpose, whether increasing knowledge or making a profit. Nevertheless, there remains a powerful underlying sense that it is important for humans to explore space for its own sake, "to see what is there." Since the launch of Sputnik 1 in 1957, Earth-orbiting satellites and robotic spacecraft journeying away from Earth have gathered valuable data about the Sun, Earth, other bodies in the solar system, and the universe beyond. Robotic spacecraft have landed on the Moon, Venus, Mars, and the asteroid Eros, have visited the vicinity of all the major planets, and have flown by the nuclei of comets, including Halley's Comet, traveling in the inner solar system. Scientists have used space-derived data to deepen human understanding of the origin and evolution of galaxies, stars, planets, and other cosmological phenomena. Although the only voyages that humans have made away from the near vicinity of Earth—the Apollo flights to the Moon—were motivated by Cold War competition, there have been recurrent calls for humans to return to the Moon, travel to Mars, and visit other locations in the solar system and beyond. Until humans resume such journeys of exploration, robotic spacecraft will continue to serve in their stead to explore the solar system and probe the mysteries of the universe.

As the many benefits of space activity have become evident, other countries have joined the Soviet Union and the United States in developing their own space programs. They include a number of western European countries operating both individually and, after 1975, cooperatively through the European Space Agency (ESA), as well as China, Japan, Canada, India, Israel, and Brazil. By the

THE SPACE ENVIRONMENT

Space, as considered here, is defined as all the reaches of the universe beyond Earth's atmosphere. There is no definitive boundary above Earth at which space begins, but, in terms of the limiting altitude for vehicles designed for atmospheric flight, it may be considered to be as low as 45 km (28 miles). The lowest practical orbit for an artificial satellite around Earth is about 160 km (100 miles). By comparison, Earth's natural satellite, the Moon, orbits the planet at a mean distance about 2,400 times greater—at 384,400 km (239,000 miles). Even this distance, however, is small compared with the size of the solar system, where spacecraft must traverse interplanetary distances measured in the hundreds of millions to billions of kilometres, and it is infinitesimal compared with the size of the universe. Earth's nearest neighbouring stars lie more than 40 trillion km (25 trillion miles) away.

The space that separates cosmic objects is not entirely empty. Throughout this void, matter—mostly hydrogen—is scattered at extremely low densities. Nevertheless, space constitutes a much greater vacuum than has been achieved on Earth. Additionally, space is permeated by gravitational and magnetic fields, a wide spectrum of electromagnetic radiation, and high-energy cosmic ray particles. Until the end of World War II, all deductions about space had been made from observations through the distorting atmosphere of Earth. With the advent of sounding rockets in the late 1940s and then of instrumented satellites, space observatories, probes, and manned spacecraft, it became possible to directly explore the complexities of space phenomena.

Another important environmental attribute of space is microgravity, a condition achieved by the balance between the centrifugal acceleration of an Earth-orbiting spacecraft and Earth's gravity. This condition, in which there is no net force acting on a body, can be simulated on Earth only by free fall in an evacuated "drop tower."

start of the 21st century, more than 30 countries had space agencies or other government bodies with substantial space activities.

ROCKETS

Getting into space requires an enormous amount of power to overcome the pull of Earth's gravity. Such power is supplied by the intense burning of fuel and the subsequent emission of the exhaust of a rocket engine. A rocket is any of a type of jet-propulsion device carrying either solid or liquid propellants that provide both the fuel and oxidizer required for combustion. (The term is also commonly applied to any of various vehicles, including

LIQUID PROPELLANTS IN VARIOUS FLIGHT VEHICLES		
ROCKET	OXIDIZER	FUEL
German V-2	liquid oxygen	ethyl alcohol-water (75%–25%)
Atlas ICBM	liquid oxygen	RP-1 (kerosene)
Delta		
first stage	liquid oxygen	RP-1 (kerosene)
second stage	nitrogen tetroxide	hydrazine-UDMH* (50%–50%)
Saturn		
first stage	liquid oxygen	RP-1 (kerosene)
second stage	liquid oxygen	liquid hydrogen
third stage	liquid oxygen	liquid hydrogen
Apollo Lunar Module	nitrogen tetroxide	hydrazine-UDMH* (50%–50%)
Space Shuttle		
main engines	liquid oxygen	liquid hydrogen
Orbital Maneuvering System	nitrogen tetroxide	monomethyl hydrazine
Ariane 4, first stage	nitrogen tetroxide	UDMH*
Energia, first stage		
core	liquid oxygen	liquid hydrogen
cluster	liquid oxygen	kerosene

*Unsymmetrical dimethylhydrazine.

Rocket engines of the Soviet launch vehicle that was used to place manned Vostok spacecraft into orbit. Based on the R-7 intercontinental ballistic missile, the launcher had four strap-on liquid-propellant boosters surrounding the liquid-propellant core rocket. Novosti Press Agency

combustion products of "propellants" that are carried on board. While the turbojet engine requires air pulled in from the outside, the rocket does not. But like the turbojet engine, the rocket develops thrust through the rearward ejection of mass at very high velocity.

The fundamental physical principle involved in rocket propulsion was formulated by Sir Isaac Newton. According to his third law of motion, the rocket experiences an increase in momentum proportional to the momentum carried away in the exhaust,

$$M\Delta v_{R} = \overset{\circ}{m} v_{e} \Delta t = F \Delta t,$$

where M is the rocket mass, Δv_{R} is the increase in velocity of the rocket in a short time interval, Δt, $\overset{\circ}{m}$ is the rate of mass discharge in the exhaust, v_{e} is the exhaust velocity (relative to the rocket), and F is force. The quantity $\overset{\circ}{m} v_{e}$ is the propulsive force, or thrust, produced on the rocket by exhausting the propellant,

$$F = \overset{\circ}{m} v_{e}. \qquad (2)$$

firework skyrockets and guided missiles as well as spacecraft launch vehicles, driven by such a propulsive device.)

How Rockets Work

The rocket differs from the turbojet and other "air-breathing" engines in that all of the exhaust jet consists of the gaseous

Evidently, thrust can be made large by using a high mass discharge rate or high exhaust velocity. Employing high $\overset{\circ}{m}$ uses up the propellant supply quickly (or requires a large supply), and so it is preferable to seek high values of v_e. The value of v_e is limited by practical considerations, determined by how the exhaust is accelerated in the engine and what energy supply is available for the purpose.

Most rockets derive their energy in thermal form by combustion of condensed-phase propellants at elevated pressure. The gaseous combustion products are exhausted through a nozzle that converts part of the thermal energy to kinetic energy. The maximum amount of energy available is limited to that provided by combustion or by practical considerations imposed by the high temperature involved. Higher energies are possible if other energy sources (e.g., electric arc or microwave heating) are used in conjunction with the chemical propellants on board the rockets. Extremely high energies are achievable when the exhaust is accelerated by electromagnetic means. As yet, these more exotic systems have not found application because of technical reasons but probably will be used in some future space missions where requisite electrical power sources can be shared by propulsion and other mission requirements.

The exhaust velocity is a figure of merit for rocket propulsion because it is a measure of thrust per unit mass of propellant consumed—i.e.,

$$\frac{F}{\overset{\circ}{m}} = v_e .\qquad(3)$$

Values of v_e are in the range 2,000 to 5,000 metres (6,562 to 16,404 feet) per second for chemical propellants, while values two or three times that are claimed for electrically heated propellants. Values up to 40,000 metres (131,233 feet) per second are predicted for systems using electromagnetic acceleration. In engineering circles, notably in the United States, the exhaust velocity is widely expressed in units of pound thrust per pound weight per second, or seconds, which is referred to as specific impulse. (In the International System of Units [SI], the unit of specific impulse is newton-seconds per kilogram.) Values in the range 185 to 465 seconds are analogous to the range of exhaust velocities noted above for chemical propellants.

In a typical chemical-rocket mission, anywhere from 50 to 95 percent or more of the takeoff mass is propellant. This can be put in perspective by the equation for burnout velocity (gravity-free flight),

$$v_b = v_e \ln \frac{M_o}{M_s + M_{pay}}$$

$$= v_e \ln \frac{1}{\left(\frac{M_s}{M_p}\right)\left(\frac{M_p}{M_o}\right) + \left(\frac{M_{pay}}{M_o}\right)} .\qquad(4)$$

In this expression, M_s/M_p is the ratio of propulsion system and structure weight to propellant weight, with a typical value of 0.09 (the symbol ln represents natural logarithm). M_p/M_o is the ratio of propellant weight to all-up takeoff weight, with a typical value of 0.90. A typical value for v_e for a hydrogen-oxygen system is 3,536 metres (11,601 feet) per second. From the above equation, the ratio of payload mass to takeoff mass (M_{pay}/M_o) can be calculated. For a low Earth orbit, v_b is about 7,544 metres (24,751 feet) per second, which would require M_{pay}/M_o to be 0.0374. In other words, it would take a 1,337,000-kg (2,947,580-pound) takeoff system to put 50,000 kg (110,231 pounds) in a low orbit around Earth. This is an optimistic calculation because equation

$$v_b = v_e \ln \frac{M_o}{M_s + M_{pay}}$$

$$= v_e \ln \frac{1}{\left(\frac{M_s}{M_p}\right)\left(\frac{M_p}{M_o}\right) + \left(\frac{M_{pay}}{M_o}\right)}. \qquad (4)$$

does not take into account the effect of gravity, drag, or directional corrections during ascent, which would double the takeoff mass. From equation

$$v_b = v_e \ln \frac{M_o}{M_s + M_{pay}}$$

$$= v_e \ln \frac{1}{\left(\frac{M_s}{M_p}\right)\left(\frac{M_p}{M_o}\right) + \left(\frac{M_{pay}}{M_o}\right)}. \qquad (4)$$

it is evident that there is a direct trade-off between M_s and M_{pay}, so that every effort is made to design for low structural mass, and M_s/M_p is a second figure of merit for the propulsion system. While the various mass ratios chosen depend strongly on the mission, rocket payloads generally represent a small part of the takeoff weight.

A technique called multiple staging is used in many missions to minimize the size of the takeoff vehicle. A launch vehicle carries a second rocket as its payload, to be fired after burnout of the first stage (which is left behind). In this way, the inert components of the first stage are not carried to final velocity, with the second-stage thrust being more effectively applied to the payload. Most spaceflights use at least two stages. The strategy is extended to more stages in missions calling for very high velocities.

The unique features of rockets that make them useful include the following:

1. Rockets can operate in space as well as in the atmosphere of Earth.
2. They can be built to deliver very high thrust (a modern heavy space booster has a takeoff thrust approaching 4.5 million kg [992 million pounds]).
3. The propulsion system can be relatively simple.
4. The propulsion system can be kept in a ready-to-fire state (important in military systems).
5. Small rockets can be fired from a variety of launch platforms, ranging from packing crates to shoulder launchers to aircraft since there is no recoil.

These features explain not only why all speed and distance records are set by rocket systems (air, land, and space) but also why rockets are the exclusive choice for spaceflight. They also have led to a transformation of warfare, both strategic and tactical. Indeed, the emergence and advancement of modern rocket technology can be traced to weapon developments during and since World War II, with a modest but growing portion being funded through "space agency" initiatives such as the Ariane, Apollo, and Space Shuttle programs.

Chemical Rockets

Rockets that employ chemical propellants come in different forms, but all share analogous basic components. These are (1) a combustion chamber where condensed-phase propellants are converted to hot gaseous reaction products, (2) a nozzle to accelerate the gas to high exhaust velocity, (3) propellant containers, (4) a means of feeding the propellants into the combustion chamber, (5) a structure to support and protect the parts, and (6) various guidance and control devices.

Chemical rocket propulsion systems are classified into two general types according to whether they burn solid or liquid propellants. Solid systems are usually called motors, and liquid systems are referred to as engines. Some developmental work has been carried out on so-called hybrid systems, in which the fuel is a solid and the oxidizer is a liquid, or vice versa. The characteristics of such systems differ greatly depending on the requirements of a given mission.

Solid-Rocket Motors

In a solid-rocket motor (SRM), the propellant consists of one or more pieces mounted directly in the motor "case," which serves both as a propellant tank and combustion chamber. The propellant is usually arranged to protect the motor case from heating. Most modern propellant charges are formed by pouring a viscous mix into the motor case with suitable mold fixtures. The propellant solidifies (usually by polymerization) and the mold fixtures are removed, leaving the propellant bonded to the motor case with a suitably shaped perforation down the middle. During operation, the solid burns on the exposed surfaces. These burn away at a predictable rate to give the desired thrust.

The motor case generally consists of a steel or aluminum tube. It has a head-end dome that contains an igniter and an aft-end dome that houses or supports the nozzle. Motor cases ordinarily have insulation on their interior surfaces, especially those not covered by propellant, for protection against thermal degradation. When a mission requires particularly lightweight components, motor cases are often made by filament winding of high-strength fibres on a suitable form. The filaments are held in place by continuous application and curing of plastic during winding. In motor cases, the front and aft domes are wound as integral parts of the case, with suitable openings and fixtures included to permit removal of the (collapsible) motor case form, loading of propellant, and attachment of igniter and nozzle. No matter what type of motor construction is involved, provisions must be made for attaching the structures that connect to the rest of the vehicle and to the launching pad or vehicle. In nearly all applications, the motor case constitutes the main structural component of the rocket and must be designed accordingly.

Propellants for solid-rocket motors are made from a wide variety of substances, selected for low cost, acceptable safety, and high performance. The selection is strongly affected by the specific application. Typical ingredients are ammonium perchlorate (a granular oxidizer), powdered aluminum (a fuel), and polybutadiene-acrylonitrile-acrylic acid (a fuel that is liquid during mixing and that polymerizes to a rubbery binder during curing). This combination is used in major U.S. space boosters (e.g., the Space Shuttle and the Titan). Higher performance is achieved by the use of more energetic oxidizers (e.g., cyclotetramethylene tetranitramine [HMX]) and by energetic plasticizers in the binder or by energetic binders such as a nitrocellulose–nitroglycerin system. In military systems, low visibility of the exhaust plume has sometimes been a requirement, which precludes the use of aluminum powder or very much ammonium perchlorate and makes it necessary to use other materials such as HMX and high-energy binder systems that yield combustion products involving mainly carbon, oxygen, hydrogen, and nitrogen.

Propellant charges must meet a variety of often conflicting requirements. From a performance standpoint, they should burn inward at the burning surface in a consistent and predictable manner that is not unduly sensitive to pressure or bulk temperature at a rate typically in the range of 0.2 to 20 cm per second. They should be as dense as possible—to maximize the amount of propellant in a given motor size—while still producing reaction products of low molecular weight and high temperature. This maximizes exhaust velocity. From a practical standpoint, propellants must be insensitive to accidental ignition stimuli and amenable to safe manufacturing and loading into the motor. Once they have been loaded into the motor, they must achieve and retain the mechanical properties necessary to maintain structural integrity under shipping, storage, and flight conditions. Since the energetic materials used in high-performance propellants are often explosives, manufacturing the propellant to a safe form is a complex technology involving special facilities and strict safety guidelines. To a degree, this is true also of less sensitive propellants (e.g., ammonium perchlorate–aluminum–polymeric binder propellants) used in intermediate-performance systems, such as the Space Shuttle booster motors.

The principal requirement for a nozzle is that it be able to produce an optimum flow of the exhaust gas from combustion chamber pressure to exterior pressure (or thereabouts), a function that is accomplished by proper contouring and sizing of the conduit. The contour is initially convergent to a "throat" section. The velocity of the exhaust gas in this region is equal to the local velocity of sound, and the throat cross-sectional area controls the mass discharge rate (and therefore the operating pressure). Beyond the throat, the channel is divergent and the flow accelerates to high supersonic speeds with a corresponding pressure decrease. Contours are often carefully designed so that shock waves do not form. (Shock waves slow the flow and degrade thrust.)

The details of nozzle design depend strongly on application. Most applications require at least some use of insulation or special high-temperature materials (like graphite) in order to protect the load-carrying structures from thermal degradation. Many applications require that the direction of the exhaust flow be controllable over a few degrees in order to provide for "steering." This is accomplished in a variety of ways that frequently complicate the design considerably and increase nozzle weight.

The igniter in a solid-rocket motor provides a means of heating the surface of the propellant charge to a high enough temperature to induce combustion. At the same time, the igniter is usually designed to produce some initial pressure increase in the motor to assure more reproducible start-up. The igniter consists of a container of material like a metal–oxidizer mixture that is more easily and quickly ignited than the propellant. It is initiated by an electric squib or other externally energized means. The igniter case is designed to be sealed until fired and to disperse hot and burning products when pressurized by its own burning. In large motors the igniter may feed into a miniature motor containing a fast-burning propellant charge, which exhausts into the main motor to produce ignition and pressurization. Most ignition systems include some kind of "arming" feature that prevents ignition by unintended stimuli.

The thrust level of a solid rocket is determined by the rate of burning of the propellant charge (mass rate in equation [2]), which is determined by the surface area (S_c) that is burning and the rate (r) at which the surface burns into the solid. The designer chooses a charge geometry that will vary with time during burning in the manner needed for a particular mission and chooses a propellant formulation that gives the desired burning rate. This means that the thrust-time function is not amenable to much intentional modification after manufacture, and most missions using solid-rocket motors are designed to take advantage of the predictability of the thrust-time function rather than to regulate thrust during flight. The lack of real-time control on thrust is compensated for by the ability to achieve extraordinarily high mass-flow rates without the propellant pumps ordinarily used in liquid-propellant rockets. The thrust levels occurring in practice depend on motor operating pressure, which in turn is shown in internal ballistic theory to depend on motor and propellant properties according to the equation

$$p = \left(\rho_p \frac{C}{C_d} \frac{S_c}{A_t} \right)^{1/(1-n)}, \qquad (5)$$

where A_t is nozzle throat area, C_d is a nozzle discharge coefficient (that depends on the thermochemical properties of the propellant reaction products), ρ_p is the density of the solid propellant, and C and n are constants in an equation that gives the approximate dependence of burning rate of the propellant on pressure,

$$r = Cp^n. \qquad (6)$$

The thrust is then given by an engineering equation,

$$F = C_F A_t p = C_F \left(\rho_p \frac{CS_c}{C_d A_t} \right)^{1/(1-n)} A_t, \qquad (7)$$

where C_F depends on nozzle geometry, thermochemical properties, and to a lesser degree on external pressure.

In most applications, the need to minimize the mass of motor components is a major design consideration. This need is so important that it is often "bought" at the expense of low safety margins and sometimes by the use of exotic construction and structural materials. These considerations are constantly weighed against the cost of mission failures. With the advent of manned flight and payloads sometimes costing $1 billion or more, the thinking on safety margins and acceptable propulsion-system cost is changing.

LIQUID-PROPELLANT ROCKET ENGINES

Liquid-propellant systems carry the propellant in tanks external to the combustion chamber. Most of these engines use a liquid oxidizer and a liquid fuel, which are transferred from their respective tanks by pumps. The pumps raise the pressure well above the operating pressure of the engine, and the propellants are then injected into the engine in a manner that assures atomization and rapid mixing. Liquid-propellant engines have certain features that make them preferable to solid systems in many applications. These features include (1) higher attainable exhaust velocities (v_e), (2) higher mass fractions (propellant mass divided by mass of inert components), and (3) control of operating level in flight (throttleability), sometimes including stop-and-restart capability and emergency shutdown. Also, in some applications it is an advantage that propellant loading is delayed until shortly before launch time, a measure that the use of a liquid propellant allows. These features tend to promote the use of liquid systems in many upper-stage applications where high v_e and high propellant mass fraction are particularly important. Liquid systems also have been used extensively as first-stage launch vehicles for space missions, as, for example, in the Saturn (U.S.), Ariane (European), and Energia (Soviet) launch systems. Many intercontinental ballistic missile (ICBM) systems employ liquid-propellant engines, but solid systems have been widely adopted for these applications in the United States because of their suitability for launch on short notice. The relative merits of solid and liquid propellants in heavy launch vehicles are still under debate and involve not only propulsion performance but also issues related to logistics, capital and operating costs of launch sites, recovery and reuse of flight hardware, and so forth.

The typical components of a liquid-rocket propulsion system are the engine, fuel tanks, and vehicle structure with which to hold these parts in place and connect to payload and launch pad (or vehicle). The fuel and oxidizer tanks are usually of very lightweight construction, as they operate at low pressure. In some applications, the propellants are cryogenic—they are substances like oxygen and hydrogen that are gaseous at ambient temperature and must be tanked at very low temperature to be in the liquid state.

The liquid-propellant engine itself consists of a main chamber for mixing and burning the fuel and oxidizer, with the fore end occupied by fuel and oxidizer manifolds and injectors and the aft end comprised of the nozzle. Integral to the main chamber is a coolant jacket through which liquid propellant (usually fuel) is circulated at rates high enough to allow the engine to operate continuously without an excessive increase of temperature in the chamber. Engine operating pressures are usually in the range of 1,000 to 10,000 kilopascals (10 to 100 atmospheres). The propellants are supplied to the injector manifold at a somewhat higher pressure, usually by high-capacity turbopumps (one for the fuel and another for the oxidizer). From the outside, a liquid-propellant engine often looks like a maze of plumbing, which connects the tanks to the pumps, carries the coolant flow to and from the cooling jackets, and conveys the pumped fluids to the injector. In addition, engines are generally mounted on gimbals so that they can be rotated a few degrees for thrust direction control, and appropriate actuators are connected between the engine (or engines) and the vehicle structure to constrain and rotate the engine.

Each of the main engines of the U.S. Space Shuttle employs liquid oxygen (LO_2) and liquid hydrogen (LH_2) propellants. These engines represent a very complex, high-performance variety of liquid-propellant rocket. Not only does each have a v_e value of 3,630 metres (11,909 feet) per second but is also capable of thrust-magnitude control over a significant range. Moreover, the Shuttle engines are part of the winged orbiter, which is designed to carry both crew and payload for up to 20 missions.

At the opposite extreme of complexity and performance is a hydrazine thrustor used for attitude control of conventional flight vehicles and unmanned spacecraft. This system may employ a valved pressure vessel in place of a pump, and the single propellant flows through a catalyst bed that causes exothermic (heat-releasing) decomposition. The resulting gas is exhausted through a nozzle that is suitably oriented for the required attitude correction. Systems of this kind also are used as gas generators for turbopumps on larger rockets.

Most liquid-propellant rockets use bipropellant systems—those in which an oxidizer and a fuel are tanked separately and mixed in the combustion chamber. Desirable properties for propellant combinations are low molecular weight and high temperature of reaction products (for high exhaust velocity), high density (to minimize tank weight), low hazard factor (like corrosivity and toxicity), and low cost. Choices are based on trade-offs according to the applications. For example, liquid oxygen is widely used because it is a good oxidizer for a number of fuels (giving high flame temperature and low molecular weight) and because it is reasonably dense and relatively inexpensive. It is liquid only below -183° C, which somewhat limits its availability, but it can be loaded into insulated tanks shortly before launch (and replenished or drained in the event of launch delays). Liquid fluorine or ozone are better oxidizers in some respects but involve more hazard and higher cost. The low temperatures of all of these systems require special design of pumps and other components, and the corrosivity, toxicity, and hazardous characteristics of fluorine and ozone have apparently thus far prevented their use in operational systems. Other oxidizers that have seen operational use are nitric acid (HNO_3) and nitrogen tetroxide (N_2O_4), which are liquids under ambient conditions. While they are somewhat noxious chemicals, they are useful in applications where the rocket must be in a near ready-to-fire condition over an extended period of time, as in the case of long-range ballistic missiles.

Liquid hydrogen is usually the best fuel from the standpoint of high exhaust velocity, and it might be used exclusively were it not for the cryogenic requirement and its low density. Such hydrocarbon fuels as alcohol and kerosene are often preferred because they are liquid under ambient conditions and denser than liquid hydrogen. They are also more "concentrated" fuels, meaning they have more fuel atoms in each molecule. The values of exhaust velocity are determined by the relative effects of higher flame (combustion) temperatures and molecular weights of reaction products—as compared to liquid oxygen and liquid hydrogen.

In practice, a variety of choices of propellant systems have been made in major systems, as shown in the table. In flights where cryogenic propellants can be utilized (as in ground-to-earth-orbit propulsion), liquid oxygen is usually used as the oxidizer. In first stages, either a hydrocarbon or liquid hydrogen is employed, while the latter is usually adopted for second stages. In ICBMs and other similar guided missiles that must stand ready for launch on short notice, noncryogenic (or "storable") propellant systems are used, as, for instance, an oxidizer–fuel mixture of nitrogen tetroxide and hydrazine–unsymmetrical dimethyl-hydrazine (also designated UDMH; $[CH_3]_2 NNH_2$). Systems of this sort also find application on longer duration flights such as those involving the Space Shuttle Orbital Maneuvering System and the Apollo Lunar Module. Solid motors have proved useful on long-duration flights, but liquid systems are often preferred because of the need for stop–start capability or thrust control.

OTHER SYSTEMS

As suggested earlier, systems using energy sources independent of the

SIGNIFICANT MILESTONES IN SPACE EXPLORATION			
DATE ACCOMPLISHED	EVENT	DETAILS	COUNTRY OR AGENCY
Oct. 4, 1957	first artificial Earth satellite	Sputnik 1	U.S.S.R.
Nov. 3, 1957	first animal launched into space	dog Laika aboard Sputnik 2	U.S.S.R.
Sept. 14, 1959	first spacecraft to hard-land on another celestial object (the Moon)	Luna 2	U.S.S.R.
Oct. 7, 1959	first pictures of the far side of the Moon	Luna 3	U.S.S.R.
April 1, 1960	first applications satellite launched	TIROS 1 (weather observation)	U.S.
Aug. 11, 1960	first recovery of a payload from Earth orbit	Discoverer 13 (part of Corona reconnaissance satellite program)	U.S.
April 12, 1961	first human to orbit Earth	Yury Gagarin on Vostok 1	U.S.S.R.

DATE ACCOMPLISHED	EVENT	DETAILS	COUNTRY OR AGENCY
Dec. 14, 1962	first data returned from another planet (Venus)	Mariner 2	U.S.
June 16, 1963	first woman in space	Valentina Tereshkova on Vostok 6	U.S.S.R.
July 26, 1963	first satellite to operate in geostationary orbit	Syncom 2 (tele-communications satellite)	U.S.
March 18, 1965	first space walk	Aleksey Leonov on Voskhod 2	U.S.S.R.
July 14, 1965	first spacecraft pictures of Mars	Mariner 4	U.S.
Feb. 3, 1966	first spacecraft to soft-land on the Moon	Luna 9	U.S.S.R.
April 24, 1967	first death during a space mission	Vladimir Komarov on Soyuz 1	U.S.S.R.
Dec. 24, 1968	first humans to orbit the Moon	Frank Borman, James Lovell, and William Anders on Apollo 8	U.S.
July 20, 1969	first human to walk on the Moon	Neil Armstrong on Apollo 11	U.S.
Sept. 24, 1970	first return of lunar samples by an unmanned spacecraft	Luna 16	U.S.S.R.
Dec. 15, 1970	first soft landing on another planet (Venus)	Venera 7	U.S.S.R.
April 19, 1971	first space station launched	Salyut 1	U.S.S.R.

DATE ACCOMPLISHED	EVENT	DETAILS	COUNTRY OR AGENCY
Nov. 13, 1971	first spacecraft to orbit another planet (Mars)	Mariner 9	U.S.
Dec. 2, 1971	first spacecraft to soft-land on Mars	Mars 3	U.S.S.R.
Dec. 3, 1973	first spacecraft to fly by Jupiter	Pioneer 10	U.S.
July 17, 1975	first international docking in space	Apollo and Soyuz spacecraft during Apollo-Soyuz Test Project	U.S., U.S.S.R.
July 20, 1976	first pictures transmitted from the surface of Mars	Viking 1	U.S.
Sept. 1, 1979	first spacecraft to fly by Saturn	Pioneer 11	U.S.
April 12–14, 1981	first reusable spacecraft launched and returned from space	space shuttle *Columbia*	U.S.
Jan. 24, 1986	first spacecraft to fly by Uranus	Voyager 2	U.S.
March 13, 1986	first spacecraft to make a close flyby of a comet nucleus	Giotto at Halley's Comet	European Space Agency
Aug. 24, 1989	first spacecraft to fly by Neptune	Voyager 2	U.S.
April 25, 1990	first large optical space telescope launched	Hubble Space Telescope	U.S., European Space Agency
Dec. 7, 1995	first spacecraft to orbit Jupiter	Galileo	U.S.

DATE ACCOMPLISHED	EVENT	DETAILS	COUNTRY OR AGENCY
Nov. 2, 2000	first resident crew to occupy the International Space Station	William Shepherd, Yury Gidzenko, and Sergey Krikalyov	U.S., Russia
* Feb. 14, 2000 * Feb. 12, 2001	first spacecraft to orbit (2000) and land on (2001) an asteroid	NEAR at the asteroid Eros	U.S.
June 21, 2004	first privately funded manned spacecraft to achieve sub-orbital flight above 100 km (62 miles)	SpaceShipOne	Mojave Aerospace Ventures (commercial joint venture)
July 1, 2004	first spacecraft to orbit Saturn	Cassini-Huygens	U.S., European Space Agency, Italy
Jan. 14, 2005	first spacecraft to land on the moon of a planet other than Earth (Saturn's moon Titan)	Huygens probe of the Cassini-Huygens spacecraft	U.S., European Space Agency, Italy

propellant fluid have been studied, and they offer promise for some future missions. In certain systems, the propellant is heated at elevated pressure by independent means and then accelerated by exhaust through a nozzle. In others, the propellant is accelerated by electromagnetic means, in which case at least part of the fluid must be electrically charged first. In these systems, the energy source may be nuclear, solar, or beamed energy from an independent source. The outlook for most current missions is that on-board energy sources of this kind would be too heavy, especially for high-thrust missions. There are, however, missions—such as manned flights to other planets—where sustained low thrust from on-board energy sources would shorten mission duration greatly, saving both time and consumable materials. Such a mission would very likely originate from Earth orbit, with flight system and on-board materials being transported to Earth orbit by chemical rocket propulsion. Electrically heated fluids would probably be used in missions involving manned space stations, where low-thrust capability is needed to control orbit and station attitude. Consideration is even being given to the use of waste products as propellants. These could be heated electrically from power systems already on board for station operational needs.

Development of Rockets

The technology of rocket propulsion appears to have originated in the period 1200–1300 CE in Asia, where the first "propellant" (a mixture of saltpetre, sulfur, and charcoal called black powder) had been in use for about 1,000 years for other purposes. As is so often the case with the development of technology, the early uses were primarily military. Powered by black powder charges, rockets served as bombardment weapons, culminating in effectiveness with the Congreve rockets (named for William Congreve, a British officer who was instrumental in their development) of the early 1800s. Performance of these early rockets was poor by modern standards because the only available propellant was black powder, which is not ideal for propulsion. Military use of rockets declined from 1815 to 1936 because of the superior performance of guns.

During the period 1880–1930, the idea of using rockets for space travel grew in public interest. Stimulated by the conceptions of such fiction writers as Jules Verne, the Russian scientist Konstantin E. Tsiolkovsky worked on theoretical problems of propulsion-system design and rocket motion. He was the first to recognize the need for rockets to be constructed with separate stages if they were to achieve orbital velocity.

Perhaps more widely recognized are the contributions of Robert H. Goddard, an American scientist and inventor who, from 1908 to 1945, conducted a wide array of rocket experiments. He independently developed ideas similar to those of Tsiolkovsky about spaceflight and propulsion and implemented them, building liquid- and solid-propellant rockets. His developmental work included tests of the world's first liquid-propellant rocket in 1926. It was launched in Auburn, Massachusetts, on March 16, 1926, rose 12.5 metres (41 feet), and traveled 56 metres (184 feet) from its launching place. Goddard's many contributions to the theory and design of rockets earned him the title of "father of modern rocketry."

A third pioneer, Hermann Oberth of Germany, developed much of the modern theory for rocket and spaceflight independent of Tsiolkovsky and Goddard. Oberth's classic 1923 book, *Die Rakete zu den Planetenräumen* ("The Rocket into Interplanetary Space"), explained the mathematical theory of rocketry and applied the theory to rocket design. Oberth's works also led to the creation of a number of rocket clubs in Germany, as enthusiasts tried to turn Oberth's ideas into practical devices. He not only provided inspiration for visionaries of spaceflight but played a pivotal role in advancing the practical application of rocket propulsion that led to the development of rockets in Germany during the 1930s.

Due to the work of these early pioneers and a host of rocket experimenters, the potential of rocket propulsion was at least vaguely perceived prior to World War II, but there were many technical barriers to overcome. Development was accelerated during the late 1930s and particularly during the war years. The most notable achievements in rocket propulsion of this era were the German liquid-propellant V-2 rocket and the Me-163 rocket-powered airplane. (Similar developments were under way in other countries but did not see service during the war.) A myriad of solid-propellant rocket weapons also were produced, and tens of millions were fired during combat operations by German, British, and U.S. forces. The main advances in propulsion that were involved in the wartime technology were the development of pumps, injectors, and cooling systems for liquid-propellant engines and high-energy solid propellants that could be formed into large pieces with reliable burning characteristics.

From 1945 to 1955, propulsion development was still largely determined by military applications. Liquid-propellant engines were refined for use in supersonic research aircraft, ICBMs, and high-altitude research rockets. Similarly, developments in solid-propellant motors were in the areas of military tactical rocket applications and high-altitude research. Bombardment rockets, aircraft interceptors, antitank weapons, and air-launched rockets for air and surface targets were among the primary tactical applications. Technological advances in propulsion included the perfection of methods for casting

Originally used in warfare, the German-engineered V-2 rocket was the precursor of modern space rockets. Camera Press

solid-propellant charges, development of more energetic solid propellants, introduction of new structural and insulation materials in both liquid and solid systems, manufacturing methods for larger motors and engines, and improvements in peripheral hardware (including pumps, valves, engine-cooling systems, and direction controls). By 1955 most missions called for some form of guidance, and larger rockets generally employed two stages. While the potential for spaceflight was present and contemplated at the time, financial resources were directed primarily toward military applications.

The next decade witnessed the development of large solid-propellant rocket motors for use in ICBMs, a choice motivated by the perceived need to have such systems in ready-to-launch condition for long periods of time. This resulted in a major effort to improve manufacturing capabilities for large motors, lightweight cases, energetic propellants, insulation materials that could survive long operational times, and thrust-direction control. Enhancement of these capabilities led to a growing role for

Apollo 15 spacecraft as it lifts off from Cape Kennedy, Florida, U.S., atop a Saturn V three-stage rocket, July 26, 1971. A camera mounted at the mobile launch tower's 110-metre (360-foot) level recorded this photograph. NASA

solid-rocket motors in spaceflight. Between 1955 and 1965, the vision of the early pioneers was realized with the achievement of Earth-orbiting satellites and manned spaceflight. The early missions were accomplished with liquid-propulsion systems adapted from military rockets. The first successful "all-civilian" system was the Saturn launch vehicle for the Apollo Moon-landing program, which used five 680,000-kg (1,499,143-pound) thrust liquid-propellant engines in the first stage. Since then, liquid systems have been employed by most countries for spaceflight applications, though solid boosters have been combined with liquid engines in various first stages of U.S. launch vehicles—those of the Titan 34D, Delta, and Space Shuttle. Solid-rocket motors have been used for several systems for transfer from low Earth orbit to geosynchronous orbit. In such systems, the lower performance of solid-propellant motors is accepted in exchange for the operational simplicity that it provides.

Since 1965, missions have drawn on an ever-expanding technology base, using improved propellants, structural materials, and designs. Present-day missions may involve a combination of several kinds of engines and motors, each chosen according to its function. Because of the performance advantages of energetic propellants and low structural mass, propulsion systems are operated near their safe limits, and one major challenge is to achieve reliability commensurate with the value of the (sometimes human) payload.

LAUNCH VEHICLES

The rockets used to transport a spacecraft beyond Earth's atmosphere, either into orbit around Earth or to some other destination in outer space, are called launch vehicles. Practical launch vehicles have been used to send manned spacecraft, unmanned space probes, and satellites into space since the 1950s. They include the Soyuz and Proton launchers of Russia, the Ariane series of Europe, and the space shuttle and Atlas, Delta, and Titan families of vehicles of the United States.

In order to reach Earth orbit, a launch vehicle must accelerate its spacecraft payload to a minimum velocity of 28,000 km (17,500 miles) per hour, which is roughly 25 times the speed of sound. To overcome Earth's gravity for travel to a destination such as the Moon or Mars, the spacecraft must be accelerated to a velocity of approximately 40,000 km (25,000 miles) per hour. The initial acceleration must also be provided very rapidly in order to minimize both the time that a launch vehicle takes to transit the stressful environment of the atmosphere and the time during which the vehicle's rocket engines and other systems must operate near their performance limits. A launch from Earth's surface or atmosphere usually attains orbital velocity within 8–12 minutes. Such rapid acceleration requires one or more rocket engines burning large quantities of propellant at a high rate, while at the same time the vehicle is controlled so that it follows its planned trajectory. To

Atlas V rocket lifting off from Cape Canaveral Air Force Station, Florida, with the New Horizons spacecraft, on Jan. 19, 2006. NASA/KSC

maximize the mass of the spacecraft that a particular launch vehicle can carry, the vehicle's structural weight is kept as low as possible. Most of the weight of the launch vehicle is actually its propellants—the fuel and the oxidizer needed to burn the fuel. Designing reliable launch vehicles is challenging. The launchers with the best recent records have a reliability rate between 95 and 99 percent.

With the exception of the partially reusable U.S. space shuttle and the Soviet *Buran* vehicle (which was flown only once), all launch vehicles to date have been designed for only a single use. They are thus called expendable launch vehicles. Costs range from more than $10 million each for the smaller launch vehicles used to put lighter payloads into orbit to hundreds of millions of dollars for the launchers needed for the heaviest payloads. Access to space is very expensive, on the order of many thousands of dollars per kilogram taken to orbit. The complexity of the space shuttle has also made it extremely expensive to operate, even though portions of the shuttle system are reusable. Attempts to develop a fully reusable launch vehicle in order to reduce the cost of access to space have so far not been successful, primarily because the propulsion system and materials needed for successful development of such a vehicle have not been available.

Having both its own launch vehicles and a place to launch them are prerequisites if a particular country or group of countries wants to carry out an independent space program. Historically, many launch vehicles have been derived from ballistic missiles, and the link between new countries developing space launch capability and obtaining long-range military missiles is a continuing security concern.

Most launch vehicles have been developed through government funding, although some of those launch vehicles have been turned over to the private sector as a means of providing commercial space transportation services. Particularly in the United States, there have also been a number of entrepreneurial attempts to develop a privately funded launch vehicle. Although none of these attempts has yet been successful, several appear to be potentially viable.

ORIGINS OF LAUNCH VEHICLES

Most space launch vehicles trace their heritage to ballistic missiles developed for military use during the 1950s and early '60s. Those missiles, in turn, were based on the ideas first developed by Konstantin Tsiolkovsky, Robert Goddard, and Hermann Oberth. Each of these pioneers of space exploration recognized the centrality of developing successful launch vehicles if humanity were to gain access to outer space. These launch vehicles began with that terrible weapon of war, the V-2, and culminated with the two most massive rockets ever built, the U.S. Saturn V and the Soviet N-1.

V-2

While Goddard spent the period from 1930 to 1941 in New Mexico working in isolation on increasingly sophisticated rocket experiments, a second generation of German, Soviet, and American rocket pioneers emerged during the 1930s. In particular, a team led by Wernher von Braun, working for the German army during the Nazi era, began development of what eventually became known as the V-2 rocket. Although built as a weapon of war, the V-2 later served as the predecessor of some of the launch vehicles used in the early space programs of the United States and, to a lesser extent, the Soviet Union.

Early U.S. Launch Vehicles

With the end of World War II and the beginning of the Cold War, rocket research in the United States and the Soviet Union focused on the development of missiles for military use, including intermediate-range ballistic missiles (IRBMs) capable of carrying nuclear warheads over distances of approximately 2,400 km (1,500 miles) and intercontinental ballistic missiles (ICBMs) with transoceanic range. Braun and his team had been transported to the United States after the war, together with a number of captured V-2 rockets. These rockets were launched under army auspices to gain operational and technological experience. During the 1950s, Braun's team developed the Jupiter IRBM, which was in many ways a derivative of the V-2 rocket. A version of the Jupiter was the launch vehicle for the first U.S. artificial satellite, Explorer 1, launched on Jan. 31, 1958. Another V-2

Robert H. Goddard and a liquid oxygen–gasoline rocket in its frame; the rocket was first fired on March 16, 1926, at Auburn, Mass. NASA

derivative, called Redstone, was used to launch the first U.S. astronaut, Alan Shepard, on his May 5, 1961, suborbital flight.

Another line of development within the U.S. industry led, in the early 1950s, to the Navaho cruise missile. (A cruise missile flies like an unpiloted airplane to its target, rather than following the ballistic trajectory of an IRBM.) This program was short-lived, but the rocket engine developed for Navaho, which itself was derived from the V-2 engine, was in turn adapted for use in a number of first-generation ballistic missiles, including Thor, another IRBM, and Atlas and Titan, the first two U.S. ICBMs. A version of Atlas was used to launch John Glenn on the first U.S. orbital flight on Feb. 20, 1962, and Titan was adapted to be the launch vehicle for

WERNHER VON BRAUN

Wernher von Braun was born in Wirsitz, Germany, on March 23, 1912. Braun was born into a prosperous aristocratic family. His mother encouraged young Wernher's curiosity by giving him a telescope upon his confirmation in the Lutheran church. Braun's early interest in astronomy and the realm of space never left him thereafter. In 1920, his family moved to the seat of government in Berlin. He did not do well in school, particularly in physics and mathematics. A turning point in his life occurred in 1925 when he acquired a copy of Oberth's Die Rakete zu den Planetenräumen ("The Rocket into Interplanetary Space"). Frustrated by his inability to understand the mathematics, he applied himself at school until he led his class. In the spring of 1930, while enrolled in the Berlin Institute of Technology, Braun joined the German Society for Space Travel. In his spare time, he assisted Oberth in liquid-fueled rocket motor tests.

By the fall of 1932, the rocket society was experiencing grave financial difficulties. At that time Capt. Walter R. Dornberger was in charge of military solid-fuel rocket research. Dornberger recognized the military potential of liquid-fueled rockets, and he arranged a research grant for Braun at a small development station near Dornberger's existing facility near Berlin. Two years later, Braun received a Ph.D. in physics from the University of Berlin. His thesis, which for reasons of military security bore the nondescript title "About Combustion Tests," contained the theoretical investigation and developmental experiments on 136- and 299-kilogram (300- and 660-pound) thrust rocket engines. By December 1934, Braun's group had successfully launched two rockets that rose vertically to more than 2.4 km (1.5 miles). But by this time there was no longer a German rocket society. Rocket tests had been forbidden by decree, and the only way open to such research was through the military forces.

Since the test grounds near Berlin had become too small, a large military development facility was erected at the village of Peenemünde in northeastern Germany on the Baltic Sea, with Dornberger as the military commander and Braun as the technical director. Liquid-fueled rocket aircraft and jet-assisted takeoffs were successfully demonstrated, and the long-range ballistic missile A-4 and the supersonic antiaircraft missile Wasserfall were developed. The A-4 was designated by the Propaganda Ministry as the V-2, meaning Vengeance Weapon 2. By 1944, the level of technology of the rockets and missiles being tested at Peenemünde was many years ahead of that of any other country.

At the end of World War II, Braun, his younger brother Magnus, Dornberger, and the entire German rocket development team surrendered to U.S. troops. Within a few months, Braun and about 100 members of his group were at a test site at White Sands, New Mexico, where they launched captured V-2s for high-altitude research purposes. Developmental studies were made of advanced ramjet and rocket missiles. The technical competence of Braun's group was outstanding. "After all," he said, "if we are good, it's because we've had 15 more years of experience in making mistakes and learning from them!"

Moving to Huntsville, Alabama, in 1952, Braun became technical director of the U.S. Army ballistic-weapon program. Under his leadership, the Redstone, Jupiter-C, Juno, and Pershing missiles were developed. During the 1950s Braun became a national and international focal point for the promotion of space flight. He was the author or coauthor of popular articles and books and gave lectures and speeches on the subject.

In 1954, a secret army-navy project to launch an Earth satellite, Project Orbiter, was thwarted by the launching of Sputnik 1 by the Soviet Union on Oct. 4, 1957. This was followed by Sputnik 2 on November 3. Given leave to proceed, Braun and his army group launched the first U.S. satellite, Explorer 1, on Jan. 31, 1958.

After the National Aeronautics and Space Administration (NASA) was formed to carry out the U.S. space program, Braun and his organization were transferred to that agency. As director of NASA's George C. Marshall Space Flight Center in Huntsville, Braun led the development of the large space launch vehicles, Saturn I, IB, and V. The engineering success of each of the Saturn class of space boosters, which contained millions of individual parts, remains unparalleled in rocket history.

In attempting to justify his involvement in the development of the German V-2 rocket, Braun stated that patriotic motives outweighed whatever qualms he had about the moral implications of his nation's policies under Hitler. He also emphasized the innate impartiality of scientific research, which in itself has no moral dimensions until its products are put to use by the larger society. During his later career Braun received numerous high awards from U.S. government agencies and from professional societies in the United States and other countries. He died on June 16, 1977, in Alexandria, Virginia.

the two-person Gemini program in the mid-1960s.

Another significant launch vehicle was derived from the Thor missile, which was initially developed by the U.S. Air Force as an intermediate-range ballistic missile. Thor was subsequently modified to serve as the first stage of launch vehicles for several spacecraft. The Thor missile force was withdrawn in 1963. Propelled by liquid oxygen and kerosene, the basic rocket was 19.8 metres (65 feet) in length, with a body diameter of 2.4 metres (8 feet), a weight at firing of 49,900 kg (110,000 pounds), and a speed at burnout of 7,670 to 12,300 to 18,500 km (11,505 miles) per hour.

For space launching, three additional small auxiliary motors were strapped to a Thor rocket used as a first stage, resulting in the Thrust-Augmented Thor (TAT)—nearly twice as powerful as the

Launch of the Mercury spacecraft Friendship 7 carrying U.S. astronaut John H. Glenn, Jr., on Feb. 20, 1962. Riding into space atop a modified Atlas intercontinental ballistic missile, Glenn became the first American to orbit Earth. **NASA**

appeared in the summer of 1966. It was capable of placing military payloads into space that were 20 percent heavier than what TAT could place. It had an overall length of 21.5 metres (70.5 feet) and a body diameter of 2 metres (8 feet).

Thor became known as Thor-Delta and then simply as Delta. The Delta, which began development in 1959, was a three-stage space-launch vehicle. The first version was capable of placing a 220-kg (480-pound) payload into a 480-km (300-mile) orbit. In the early 1960s Delta launched the TIROS weather satellites, Echo 1, and the Telstar, Relay, and Syncom communication satellites. An improved Delta, which had a more powerful first stage and was capable of placing 450 kg (1,000 pounds) into a 800-km (500-mile) orbit, put the Syncom 3 communication satellite into orbit on Aug. 19, 1964. Several Long Tank Deltas were also built.

After Pres. John F. Kennedy's announcement in 1961 that sending Americans to the Moon would be a national goal, Braun and others in and outside of the National Aeronautics and Space Administration (NASA) set about developing a launch vehicle that would enable a lunar mission based on rendezvous either in Earth or Moon orbit. The Braun team

original Thor. Total thrust at liftoff was 150,000 kilograms (330,000 pounds). Adding an Agena rocket as a second stage resulted in the two-stage Thor-Agena rocket, used to launch the U.S. Air Force's Discoverer space satellites.

Long Tank Thor, an advanced version of the Thor space launch vehicle, first

already had a less powerful rocket called Saturn I in development. Their advanced design, intended for lunar missions, was configured to use five F-1 engines, and on that basis was named Saturn V.

The Saturn V with the Apollo spacecraft on top stood 110.6 metres (363 feet) tall. Its weight at the time of liftoff was over 3,000,000 kg (6,600,000 pounds). Its first stage provided 33,000 kilonewtons (7,500,000 pounds) of lifting power at takeoff. The second stage accelerated the rocket to 24,600 km (15,300 miles) per hour, or nearly orbital velocity. The third stage accelerated the spacecraft to a velocity of 39,400 km (24,500 miles) per hour, or over 10 km (6 miles) per second, sending the three Apollo crewmen toward the Moon. The Saturn V was used from 1968 to 1972 during the Apollo program and launched the Skylab space station in 1973.

The Saturn family of launch vehicles, which also included the Saturn IB, was the first American launch vehicle family developed specifically for space use. The less powerful Saturn IB was used to launch Apollo spacecraft on Earth-orbiting missions and during the U.S.-Soviet Apollo-Soyuz Test Project in 1975. After Apollo-Soyuz, the Saturn family was retired from service as the United States decided to use the space shuttle as the sole launch vehicle for future government payloads.

Early Soviet Launch Vehicles

A similar pattern was followed in the Soviet Union. Under the direction of the rocket pioneer Sergey Korolyov, during the 1950s, the Soviet Union developed an ICBM that was capable of delivering a heavy nuclear warhead to American targets. That ICBM, called the R-7 or Semyorka ("Number 7"), was first successfully tested on Aug. 21, 1957. Because Soviet nuclear warheads were based on a heavy design, the R-7 had significantly greater weight-lifting capability than did initial U.S. ICBMs. When used as a space launch vehicle, this gave the Soviet Union a significant early advantage in the weight that could be placed in orbit or sent to the Moon or nearby planets. There have been a number of variants of the R-7 with an upper stage, each with a different name, usually matching that of the payload, and each optimized to carry out specific missions. An unmodified R-7 was used to launch the first Soviet satellite, Sputnik 1, on Oct. 4, 1957. An R-7 variant, the Vostok, launched the first Soviet cosmonauts in a series of six launches over a two-year period of 1961–1963. The first of these launches, on April 12, 1961, sent into orbit Yury Gagarin, the first human in space. Other variants include the Voshkod, used to launch reconnaissance satellites, and the Molniya, used to launch communication satellites. A multipurpose variant, the Soyuz, was first used in 1966 and, with many subsequent variants and improvements, is still in service. This family of launch vehicles has carried out more space launches than the rest of the world's launch vehicles combined.

In the early 1960s, Soviet designers began work on the N-1, which was originally designed to undertake journeys that would require true heavy-lift capability—that is, the ability to lift more than 80,000 kg (176,000 pounds) to low Earth orbit. When the Soviet Union decided in 1964 to race the United States to a first lunar landing, that became the sole mission for the N-1. The N-1 was a five-stage vehicle. The N-1 vehicle and the L3 lunar landing spacecraft mounted atop it stood 105 metres (344 feet) tall and weighed 2,735,000 kg (6,000,000 pounds) fully fueled. To provide the 44,000 kilonewtons (10,000,000 pounds) of thrust needed to lift the vehicle off of its launchpad, 30 small rocket engines, firing in unison, were required.

There were four N-1 launch attempts between February 1969 and November 1972. All failed, and on the second test launch, on July 3, 1969, the vehicle exploded on the launchpad, destroying it and causing a two-year delay in the program. In 1974 the N-1 program was canceled.

In 1976 approval was given for development of the Energia heavy-lift launch vehicle (named for the design bureau that developed it) and its primary mission, the space shuttle *Buran*. Energia could lift 100,000 kg (220,000 pounds) to low Earth orbit, slightly more than the Saturn V. Takeoff thrust was 29,000 kilonewtons (6,600,000 pounds). The Energia was 60 metres (197 feet) high. Its spacecraft payload was attached to the side of its core stage, not placed on top as with almost all other launch vehicles.

Energia's first launch was in 1987 and had Polyus, an experimental military space platform, as its payload. In 1988, its second and final launch carried *Buran* to orbit on its only mission, without a crew aboard. Energia was deemed too expensive for the Soviet Union to continue to operate, and no other uses for the vehicle emerged.

Sounding Rockets

Another contributor to the development of space launch capability in the post-World War II period was work on sounding rockets, which are used to carry scientific instruments and other devices to heights above those that can be reached by high-altitude balloons but which do not have the power to accelerate their payloads to orbital velocities. Rather, sounding rockets provide several minutes of data-gathering time above the atmosphere for the instruments they carry. Those instruments then fall back to Earth. A sounding rocket usually has a vertical trajectory as it travels through the upper atmosphere. Sounding rockets range in size, performance, and cost from simple, single-stage solid-propellant rockets that can lift a 5.4-kg (12-pound) meteorologic payload 60 km (35 miles) to two-stage solid-propellant vehicles capable of lifting a 22-kg (49-pound) payload 3,000 km (1,900 miles). Most countries that have developed space launch capability have first developed sounding rockets as, among other factors, a way of gaining experience with the technologies needed for launch vehicle development. Sounding rockets remain in use for some areas of scientific investigations that do not require the more expensive and technically demanding access to Earth orbit.

The sounding rocket program of the International Geophysical Year (1957–58) brought a number of results: the detection of X-rays and auroral particles high above Earth; photographs of the solar ultraviolet spectrum from above the masking layers of Earth's lower atmosphere; and records of atmospheric pressure, temperature, composition, and density to altitudes of nearly 320 km (199 miles). Sounding rockets have also determined regions of intense turbulence below 96 km (60 miles) altitude.

LAUNCH VEHICLES OF THE WORLD

There are many different expendable launch vehicles in use around the world today. As the two countries most active in space, the United States and Russia have developed a variety of launch vehicles, with each vehicle being best suited to a particular use. The ESA, China, India, and Japan have fewer types of launch vehicles; Israel and Iran have only one type.

United States

Most U.S. launch vehicles in use since the late 1950s have been based on the Thor IRBM or the Atlas and Titan ICBMs. The last launch of a vehicle based on the Titan ICBM was on Oct. 19, 2005. The two other families of launch vehicles, Delta and Atlas, have undergone a series of modifications and improvements since they were developed in the 1950s. The Delta II is used to launch small to medium payloads. Its lifting power can be adjusted by varying the number of solid rocket motors attached as "strap-ons" to its first stage. The Delta IV and Atlas V vehicles, which both entered service in 2002, have little in common with the original ballistic missiles or early space launchers of the same names. The Delta IV uses the first new rocket engine developed in the United States since the 1970s space shuttle main engine. That engine, the RS-68, burns cryogenic propellant (liquefied gas kept at very low temperatures). The Delta IV has several configurations, depending on the weight and type of payload to be launched. Several configurations use solid rocket motors attached to the vehicle's core first stage; the Delta IV model used to launch heavy spacecraft consists of three core stages strapped together. The Atlas V uses in its first stage a Russian-produced rocket engine, the RD-180, the design of which is based on the RD-170 developed for the Soviet Energia and Zenit launch vehicles. Like the Delta IV, the Atlas V offers several configurations. These two so-called evolved expendable launch vehicles are intended to be the workhorses for U.S. government launches for years to come.

These launch vehicles are used to carry medium-weight spacecraft into orbit or beyond. The Delta IV Heavy vehicle can launch payloads weighing from 6,275 kg (13,805 pounds) to geo-stationary orbit and can lift more than 23,000 kg (50,600 pounds) to low Earth orbit. Atlas V vehicles can launch pay-loads weighing up to 20,500 kg (45,100 pounds) to low Earth orbit and up to 3,750 kg (8,250 pounds) to geostationary orbit; a heavier lift version of the Atlas V is also possible. In addition, a number of smaller launch vehicles have been devel-oped to launch lighter spacecraft at a lower overall cost (although not necessarily a lower cost per kilogram), though they have not found a wide mar-ket for their use. These include the solid-fueled Pegasus launch vehicle, which had its first flight in 1990 and is launched from under the fuselage of a carrier aircraft. First launched in 1994, a version of Pegasus known as Taurus lifts off from the ground, using a converted ICBM as a first stage and Pegasus as a second stage. A new small launch vehicle called Falcon was first tested in 2006. It was developed on the basis of private investment rather than being funded by

Launch of the U.S. space shuttle Discovery, July 2006. Gianni Woods/NASA

government contracts and is intended to be the first in a new, lower-cost family of liquid-fueled expendable launch vehicles.

The U.S. space shuttle is unique in that it combines the functions of launch vehicle and spacecraft. The first partially reusable launch vehicle, it is one of the most complex machines ever developed, with more than 2.5 million parts. Its main elements are an orbiter, which houses a cockpit, a crew compartment, and a large payload bay and has three high-performance reusable rocket engines. It also includes a large external tank that contains the cryogenic liquid hydrogen fuel and the liquid oxygen oxidizer for those engines and two large solid rocket motors, called boosters, attached to the external tank. These solid rocket motors provide 85 percent of the thrust needed for liftoff.

With the promise of partial reusability and routine operation, the shuttle was promoted when it was approved for development in 1972 as a means of providing regular access to space at a much lower cost than was possible with the use of expendable launch vehicles. The intent was to use the space shuttle as the only launch vehicle for all U.S. government spacecraft and to attract commercial spacecraft launch business in competition with other countries' launchers. The promise of low cost and routine operations has not been realized. Preparing the shuttle for each launch has proven to be an intensive and expensive process, and many of the shuttle orbiter's elements have had to be replaced or refurbished more often than anticipated. Each shuttle launch has cost hundreds of millions of dollars.

The three space shuttle main engines and the two solid rocket motors are ignited at the time of liftoff. Combined, they provide 31,000 kilonewtons (7,000,000 pounds) of thrust. The solid rocket motors burn for just over two minutes. They are then detached from the external tank and parachuted into the ocean, where their now empty casings are recovered for reuse. The three space shuttle main engines continue to fire for an additional six and a half minutes, at which point they shut down and the external tank is detached, falling into the atmosphere and disintegrating over the Indian Ocean. A final small firing of the space shuttle's Orbital Maneuvering System engines, which use hypergolic propellant (fuel that ignites when it comes into contact with its oxidizer), places the orbiter into the desired orbit.

The height of the shuttle stack on the launchpad is 56.1 metres (184.2 feet), and the shuttle orbiter itself is 37.2 metres (122.2 feet) long. The shuttle's fueled weight at liftoff is 2,000,000 kg (4,500,000 pounds). Unlike other launch vehicles that detach themselves from their spacecraft payload when orbital speed is achieved, the shuttle orbiter—which weighs approximately 104,000 kg (229,000 pounds) when empty—is carried into orbit along with whatever payload it is carrying, two to seven crew members and their supplies, and fuel for orbital maneuvering and reentry. It is thus the heaviest spacecraft ever launched. Maximum weight for cargo in the shuttle's payload bay was planned to be 28,803 kg (63,367 pounds), but the vehicle has never carried such heavy payloads. The heaviest payload carried into space by the space shuttle was the Chandra X-ray Observatory and its upper stage, which weighed 22,753 kg (50,162 pounds) when the satellite was launched on the STS-93 mission on July 23, 1999.

A new privately developed family is Falcon, which consists of two launch vehicles, Falcon 1 and Falcon 9, built by the U.S. corporation SpaceX with funding from South African-born American entrepreneur Elon Musk. Falcon 1 was designed to place a 420-kg (925-pound) payload into orbit at a lower cost than that of other launch vehicles, in part by using a recoverable first stage. Falcon 9 was designed to compete with the Delta family of launchers in that it was planned to lift payloads of 4,640 kg (10,200 pounds) to geostationary orbit. One of the payloads it is expected to launch to low Earth orbit is Dragon, a spacecraft designed to carry crew and cargo to the International Space Station. A heavy-lift version of the Falcon 9 was designed to carry payloads of 15,000 kg (33,000 pounds) to geostationary orbit.

The first test flight of the Falcon 1 took place on March 24, 2006, on Kwajalein Atoll in the Pacific Ocean but failed just 25 seconds after liftoff. Corrosion between a nut and a fuel line had allowed the line to leak, which caused an engine fire. Later in 2006, Space Exploration Technologies (SpaceX) won a $278 million contract from NASA for three demonstration launches of the company's Dragon spacecraft and Falcon 9 launcher in 2009–10. Two subsequent tests of Falcon 1 ended in failure, but on Sept. 28, 2008, Falcon 1 successfully entered Earth orbit.

Russia and Ukraine

Russia has the most diverse set of launch vehicles of any spacefaring country. Most were developed while under the rule of the Soviet Union, which included both Russia and Ukraine, and both countries continue to produce launch vehicles. Like the United States, the Soviet Union used various ballistic missiles as the basis for several of its space launch vehicles. The approach taken was to use a version of the ballistic missile as a first stage and then add a variety of upper stages to modify the vehicle for different missions. The most famous of these ballistic missiles was the aforementioned R-7, developed in the 1950s under the direction of Sergey Korolyov. Other Soviet launchers based on ICBM first stages include the Kosmos and Tsyklon (which is built in the Ukraine).

Proton was originally designated the UR-500 and was designed as an intercontinental ballistic missile for the most powerful Soviet thermonuclear weapons by the design bureau headed by Vladimir Chelomey. Its purpose was changed during development, and since its first launch—of the Proton-1 satellite in July 1965—it has been used only as a space launch vehicle. The name of the launcher was changed to Proton after its initial payload, the Proton satellite, which studied high-energy particles in space. With various upper stages, the Proton has been used to launch spacecraft to geostationary orbit—an orbit with a 24-hour period that keeps a satellite above a specific point on Earth—and to destinations beyond Earth orbit. It is also used to launch elements of the Salyut and Mir space stations and of the International Space Station. The launcher has been produced in two-, three-, and four-stage versions and has undergone continuous improvements since it entered service. Its first three stages are fueled by a combination of nitrous oxide and unsymmetrical dimethylhydrazine (UDMH) liquid fuels. Earlier versions of the fourth stage were fueled by a combination of liquid oxygen and kerosene, but the current fourth stage uses the nitrous tetroxide-UDMH combination.

Launchpads for the Proton are located at the Baikonur Cosmodrome in Kazakhstan. Proton's reliability has been greater than 90 percent over its many years of service. The prime contractor for the vehicle is now the Khrunichev State Research and Production Space Centre, located near Moscow. Commercial launches on Proton are marketed globally by International Launch Services—a joint venture of Khrunichev and the Russian firm RSC Energia.

First launched in 1985, the Zenit launch vehicle was developed in Ukraine. It was not derived from an existing ICBM. The Zenit uses an RD-170 first-stage engine, considered to be one of the most efficient and reliable rocket engines ever made. It was used by the Soviet Union and is now used by Russia to launch both military payloads to low Earth orbit and communication satellites to geostationary orbit. It was also used as a strap-on booster for the two flights of the heavy-lift Energia launcher.

Several other Russian launch vehicles are derived from decommissioned ballistic missiles. These include Start, Rokot, Dnepr, and the submarine-launched Shtil.

Europe

Several European countries, with France playing a leading role, decided in 1973 that it was essential for Europe to have its own access to space, independent of the United States and the Soviet Union. To develop a new launcher, these countries formed a new space organization, the ESA, which in turn delegated lead responsibility of what was named the Ariane launch vehicle to the French space agency. The French space agency, Centre National d'Études Spatiales (CNES), has managed Ariane development and upgrades with the support of the ESA, with a number of European countries contributing to the program's budget and carrying out a share of development and production work. Ariane is named after Ariadne (Ariane in French), the mythical Cretan princess who helped Theseus escape from the Labyrinth.

The first launch of the Ariane 1 vehicle took place in December 1979.

Ariane 1 was 50 metres (164 feet) tall and had a thrust at liftoff of 2,400 kilonewtons (550,000 pounds), which allowed it to launch an 1,850-kg (4,070-pound) satellite into geostationary orbit. Ariane 1 was liquid-fueled, originally using a mixture of unsymmetrical dimethylhydrazine (UMDH) and nitrogen tetroxide. However, after a launcher exploded in May 1980, the fuel mixture was changed to the more stable mixture of UMDH and hydrazine.

Improved versions of Ariane were developed during the 1980s. The first Ariane 3 vehicle was launched in August 1984, but the first Ariane 2—which had the same launch vehicle design as the Ariane 3 but without the two solid-fuel strap-on boosters—debuted in May 1986. Ariane 3, the more powerful of the two new models, had a thrust of 4,000 kilonewtons (900,000 pounds), which could carry a 2,700-kg (5,900-pound) satellite to geostationary orbit.

The first Ariane 4 vehicle was launched in June 1988. Ariane 4 was even more powerful than Ariane 3. With a thrust of 5,700 kilonewtons (1.3 million pounds), it could place a 4,800-kg (11,000-pound) satellite in geostationary orbit. The first two stages of Ariane 2–4 were fueled by a mixture of UMDH and hydrazine, with nitrogen peroxide as an oxidizer. The third stage used cryogenic fuel. The first four generations of Ariane shared the same basic design but achieved increased performance and flexibility through modifications of that design. By the end of its 15-year-long career, Ariane 4 had achieved over 97 percent reliability.

In 1985, the ESA decided to develop the more powerful Ariane 5 launcher with a totally new design based on a cryogenically fueled first stage, flanked by two large solid-fuel boosters, and having a second stage fueled by monomethylhydrazine with nitrogen peroxide as the oxidizer. A strong impetus for developing the more powerful Ariane 5 was the ESA's ambition to launch a manned space glider named Hermes. However, the Hermes project was canceled in 1992. Since then, Ariane 5 has launched only unmanned satellites.

With a much more powerful upper stage than previous Ariane models, the Ariane 5 is capable of carrying a 10,500-kg (23,100-pound) satellite to geostationary orbit. The first test launch of the Ariane 5, in June 1996, was a spectacular failure, but in subsequent years, the vehicle operated reliably. Since the Ariane 4 was retired from service in 2003, all ESA launches have used Ariane 5, and there has been a continuing effort to lower its costs and improve its reliability and performance—particularly its ability to launch two communications satellites to geostationary orbit. The Ariane 5 ECA version can launch two satellites with a combined weight of 9,600 kg (21,000 pounds) to that orbit. The Ariane 5 has achieved 89 percent reliability.

In January 1980, the ESA decided to entrust Arianespace—an organization owned by both public- and private-sector entities—with the management of Ariane production and launch for government use. It was also given the task of marketing of the vehicle to commercial customers. Arianespace succeeded in establishing the Ariane family as the single largest provider of commercial launch services in the world. Among the many European satellites launched by Ariane have been Giotto, the probe to Halley's Comet; Hipparcos, the stellar distance-measuring satellite; Rosetta, a comet rendezvous mission; and Envisat, a large Earth-observing satellite.

In order to complement Ariane 5, the ESA decided in 2000 to develop a small launch vehicle called Vega. The first launch for this vehicle was set for late 2009. In 2003, the ESA also decided to build a launch facility for the Russian Soyuz launcher at the European launch site in French Guiana. This would give Europe a medium-lift launch vehicle capability and could also provide Europe with the capability to launch humans into space, since that is one of the roles that the Soyuz launcher plays for Russia.

China

Like the United States and the Soviet Union, China's first launch vehicles were also based on ballistic missiles. The Chang Zheng 1 (CZ-1, or Long March 1) vehicle, which put China's first satellite into orbit in 1970, was based on the Dong Feng 3 IRBM. The Chang Zheng 2 family of launch vehicles, which has been used for roughly half of Chinese launches, was based on the Dong Feng 5 ICBM. There are several models of the CZ-2 vehicle, with different first stages and solid strap-ons. A CZ-2F vehicle was used to launch the first Chinese astronaut into space in October 2003. There are also CZ-3 and CZ-4 launchers. The CZ-3 is optimized for launches to geostationary orbits, and the CZ-4, first launched in 1988, uses hypergolic propellants rather than the conventional kerosene–liquid oxygen combination used in previous Chang Zheng variants. China has begun development of a second-generation family of launchers, identified as CZ-5, or Long March 5, that are not based on an ICBM design. These vehicles can launch payloads to geostationary orbit that are more than five times heavier than those carried by the CZ-4.

Japan

Until 2003, Japan had three separate space agencies, two of which developed their own line of launch vehicles. Japan did not have a previous ballistic missile program.

Japan's Institute of Space and Astronautical Science based its launch vehicles on the use of solid propellants. Its Lambda L-4S vehicle sent the first Japanese satellite, Osumi, into orbit in 1970. Each subsequent launcher in the Mu series gave the institute greater lifting power for its scientific satellites, with the M-5 vehicle—first launched in 1997—capable of sending spacecraft beyond Earth orbit.

During the 1970s, the National Space Development Agency developed the N-I and N-II launchers based on licensed U.S. Delta technology. As an interim step to its own launch vehicle, in the 1980s, the agency next developed the H-I, which had a Delta-derived first stage but a Japanese-designed cryogenically fueled upper stage. In 1984, Japan decided to develop an all-Japanese launch vehicle, the H-II, using cryogenic propellants in both stages and a very advanced first-stage rocket engine. The H-II was first launched in 1994. It proved a very expensive vehicle because of its total dependence on Japanese-manufactured components. Thus, Japan decided in 1996 to develop an H-IIA vehicle that would use some foreign components and simplified manufacturing techniques to reduce the vehicle's costs. There are several models of the H-IIA, with both solid rocket motors and liquid-fueled strap-ons possible. The first H-IIA launch took place in August 2001.

India

India launched its first satellite in 1980 using the four-stage solid-fueled Satellite Launch Vehicle 3 (SLV-3), which was developed from the U.S. Scout launch vehicle first used in the 1960s. India did not have a prior ballistic missile program, but parts of the SLV-3 were later incorporated into India's first IRBM, Agni. The four-stage Polar Satellite Launch Vehicle (PSLV) was then developed. It used a mixture of solid- and

An H-IIA launch vehicle lifting off on Dec. 18, 2006, from the Tanegashima Space Center in Japan. JAXA

liquid-fueled stages. The first PSLV launch took place in 1993. During the 1990s, India developed the liquid-fueled Geostationary Space Launch Vehicle (GSLV), which used cryogenic fuel in its upper stage. The GSLV was first launched in 2001. Both the PSLV and GSLV remain in service.

Israel

Israel's Shavit launch vehicle is a small three-stage solid-fueled vehicle, first launched in 1988. It was based on the Jericho 2 ballistic missile. Because of its geographic location and hostile relations with surrounding countries, Israel must launch its vehicles to the west, over the Mediterranean Sea, in order to avoid flying over those countries. This necessity imposes a penalty of 30 percent on the Shavit's lifting capability, since the Shavit is unable to take advantage of the velocity imparted by Earth's rotation.

Iran

Iran's launch vehicle is the Safīr (Farsi for "messenger"). It has two liquid-fueled stages and is based on the North Korean Taepodong-1 missile. It was 22 metres (72 feet) long and 1.4 metres (4.6 feet) across. Its estimated payload was less than 100 kg (220 pounds). On Feb. 2, 2009, a Safīr rocket launched Omīd, the first satellite put into orbit by Iran.

HOW A LAUNCH VEHICLE WORKS

The primary goal of launch vehicle designers is to maximize the vehicle's weight-lifting capability while at the same time providing an adequate level of reliability at an acceptable cost. Achieving a balance among these three factors is challenging. In order for the launch vehicle to lift off of Earth, its upward thrust must be greater than the combined weight of its spacecraft payload, the vehicle's propellants, and its structure. This puts a premium on making the vehicle's mechanical structure, fuel tanks, and rocket engines as light as possible—but strong enough to withstand the forces and stresses associated with rapid acceleration through a resistant atmosphere. Most often, propellant makes up 80 percent or more of the total weight of a launch vehicle–spacecraft combination prior to launch.

Stages

A basic approach to launch vehicle design, first suggested by Konstantin Tsiolkovsky, is to divide the vehicle into "stages." The first stage is the heaviest part of the vehicle and has the largest rocket engines, the largest fuel and oxidizer tanks, and the highest thrust. Its task is to impart the initial thrust needed to overcome Earth's gravity and lift the total weight of the vehicle and its payload off of Earth. When the first-stage propellants are used up, that stage is detached from the remaining parts of the launch vehicle and falls back to Earth, either into the ocean or onto sparsely populated territory. With the weight of the first stage gone, a second stage, with its own rocket engines and propellants, continues to accelerate the vehicle. Most expendable launch vehicles in use today have only two or three stages, but in the past, up to five stages, each lighter than its predecessor, were needed to attain orbital velocity. When an upper stage has completed its mission, it either falls back to Earth's surface, enters orbit itself, or, most frequently, disintegrates and evaporates as it encounters atmospheric heating on its fall back toward Earth.

A particular launch vehicle can be configured in several different ways, depending on its mission and the weight of the spacecraft to be launched. This reconfiguration can be done by adding a varying number of strap-on boosters, usually solid rocket motors, to the vehicle's first stage or by using different upper stages.

In principle, a space launcher could reach Earth orbit using only one stage, and in fact there have been several attempts to develop a reusable "single stage to orbit" vehicle. However, all attempts have failed. The propulsion and materials needed to make a single-stage vehicle light and powerful enough to achieve orbital velocity, while carrying a meaningful payload, have not been developed.

Upper Stages

All launch vehicles employ more than one stage to accelerate spacecraft to orbital velocity. Since the first orbital launch (Sputnik), in 1957, there have been many different upper stages. Most are used as part of only one type of launch vehicle. The evolution of these upper stages is driven by a desire to introduce more modern technology that will increase the overall lift capability of the launch vehicle, lower its costs, and increase its reliability—or a combination of these factors. Small improvements in upper stages can produce significant gains in launch vehicle performance, since these stages operate only after the first stage has accelerated the vehicle to a high speed through the thickest parts of the atmosphere.

Several upper stages have been used with more than one family of launch vehicle. For example, the Agena upper stage was first developed in the United States as part of its initial reconnaissance satellite program. The Agena upper stage of a Thor-Agena launch vehicle propelled the Corona spacecraft into orbit, stayed attached to it, and provided power and pointing for the spacecraft's operation. Agena used hypergolic propellant. It was also combined with the Atlas and Titan first stages on a number of subsequent missions. Later versions of Agena were able to restart their engine in orbit, carried other national security payloads, sent Ranger and Lunar Orbiter spacecraft to the Moon and Mariner spacecraft to Venus and Mars, and served as the target vehicle for rendezvous by the Gemini two-man spacecraft. Use of the Agena upper stage extended through the mid-1980s.

Another U.S. upper stage, used with the Atlas and Titan launch vehicles, is Centaur. This was the first U.S. rocket

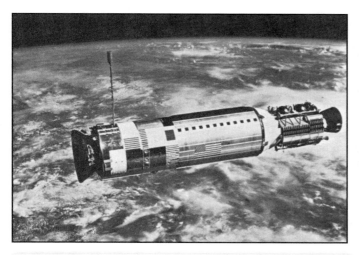

Upper stage Agena, the target vehicle for the Gemini 12 rendezvous and docking, launched two hours before the Gemini spacecraft, on Nov. 11, 1966. NASA

have also been used with the Delta and Titan launch vehicles.

Soviet and Russian launch vehicles have used a variety of upper stages. Most have used conventional kerosene as fuel. More recently two upper stages, the Block DM using cryogenic propellant and the more popular Briz M using hypergolic propellant, have been developed for the Proton launcher. There has been a constant evolution of upper stages used with the Soyuz launcher. In 1999, upper stages with restartable rocket engines entered service.

The ESA used a cryogenic upper stage for its Ariane 1–4 launchers. Initial versions of the Ariane 5 used hypergolic propellant in its upper stage, though a new cryogenic upper stage was introduced in 2006. Japan and India use cryogenic propellants in the upper stages of their most powerful launch vehicles, the H-IIA and the GSLV, respectively.

Payload Protection

The spacecraft that a launch vehicle carries into space is almost always attached to the top of the vehicle. During the transit of the atmosphere, the payload is protected by some sort of fairing, often made of lightweight composite material. Once the launch vehicle is beyond the densest part of the atmosphere, this

stage to employ cryogenic propellant. The first use of the Atlas-Centaur launch vehicle was to send Surveyor spacecraft to the Moon in 1966 and 1967. It flew many subsequent missions atop an Atlas first stage. When combined with powerful versions of the Titan launch vehicle, Centaur also has been used to send various spacecraft to Mars and the outer planets and to launch various heavy national security payloads.

Various upper stages using solid propellants were used to carry payloads from the space shuttle's low Earth orbit to higher orbits. There were plans to carry the liquid-fueled Centaur on the shuttle to launch planetary spacecraft, but those plans were canceled after the 1986 *Challenger* accident because of safety concerns. Solid-propellant upper stages

fairing is shed. After the spacecraft reaches initial orbital velocity, it may be detached from the launch vehicle's final upper stage to begin its mission. Alternatively, if the spacecraft is intended to be placed in other than a low Earth orbit, the upper-stage rocket engine may be shut down for a period of time as the spacecraft payload coasts in orbit. The engine is then restarted to impart the additional velocity needed to move the payload to a higher Earth orbit or to inject it into a trajectory that will carry it deeper into space.

Navigation, Guidance, and Control

In order for a launch vehicle to place a spacecraft in the intended orbit, it must have navigation, guidance, and control capabilities. Navigation is needed to determine the vehicle's position, velocity, and orientation at any point in its trajectory. As these variables are measured, the vehicle's guidance system determines what course corrections are needed to steer the vehicle to its desired target. Control systems are used to implement the guidance commands through movements of the vehicle's rocket engines or changes in the direction of the vehicle's thrust. Navigation, guidance, and control for most launch vehicles are achieved by a combination of complex software, computers, and other hardware devices.

Reliability

A launch vehicle comprises one or more rocket engines; fuel for those engines

carried in fuel tanks; guidance, navigation, and control systems; a payload; and a structure housing all of these elements, to which extra engines may be attached for added lift. There are also various attachments between the launch vehicle and its launchpad and associated structures. An expendable launch vehicle has only one opportunity to perform its mission successfully, so all of its elements must be designed and manufactured precisely and for very high operational reliability. Also, as noted, launch vehicles are designed to be as light as possible, in order to maximize their payload lifting capability. As a result, every part in a launch vehicle operates close to its breaking point during a launch, as the vehicle undergoes the stresses associated with accelerating past the speed of sound and transiting the atmosphere. Its rocket engines operate under extremes of pressure, temperature, shock, and vibration.

The end result is that launching a spacecraft into outer space remains an extremely difficult undertaking. Launch failures are a fact of life for those seeking access to space. Many space launches, particularly those carrying commercial spacecraft, are insured against failure, since they often represent an investment of more than $100 million.

Launch vehicles that carry people into space are "human rated." This means that they use components of the highest possible reliability, have redundancy in critical systems, undergo more testing prior to launch than does a launch vehicle carrying an automated spacecraft, and contain systems that warn of impending problems so that a crew might be able to escape an accident. There has been only one failure of a launch vehicle at liftoff that resulted in crew fatalities. This was the explosion of the *Challenger*, on Jan. 28, 1986, which killed all seven astronauts aboard.

Launching into Outer Space

Although they differ in many details for various vehicles and at different launch bases, the steps needed to prepare a launch vehicle and its spacecraft payload for launch are, in general, similar.

Most often, the different stages and other elements of a launch vehicle are manufactured separately and transported to the launch base for assembly. That assembly can take place either in a facility away from the launchpad or on the launchpad itself. The advantage of a separate assembly building is that many of the steps needed to prepare the vehicle for launch, including assembly and then checkout of the integrated vehicle, can be performed in a closed environment. This also means that the launchpad is available for other uses during the assembly and checkout period.

Launch vehicle assembly and check-out are carried out either vertically or horizontally. Vertical assembly requires a facility tall enough to shelter the whole vehicle and spacecraft. The various components are "stacked," starting with the first stage and often ending with the attachment of the spacecraft to the launch vehicle. (Sometimes the spacecraft and the launch vehicle are mated only at the launchpad.) Strap-on solid rocket engines, if they are to be used, are attached to the core first stage.

Horizontal assembly is carried out on an end-to-end basis and does not require a high building with vehicle access at multiple levels. After assembly, as much testing as possible is conducted on the integrated vehicle to check its readiness for launch before it is transported to the launchpad.

Once it reaches the launchpad, the vehicle is attached to a launch tower, which contains the various umbilical connections and access points needed to complete the checkout process and to monitor the vehicle's final readiness for launch. If the vehicle has been assembled horizontally, it must be raised into a vertical position as it reaches the launchpad. Often, the launchpad includes some sort of shelter to protect the launch vehicle and spacecraft from the elements until close to the time for launch and to allow technicians to continue the checkout process. The launch vehicle is held on the pad by some form of attachment device.

If the launch vehicle is assembled on the launch pad, all of the above steps are conducted there. Assembly and checkout can take several months, and during this period, the launchpad cannot be used for other purposes.

As the time for launch approaches, a countdown is initiated. Countdown time can range from hours to days. During the countdown, various final steps are carried out at specific times to make the vehicle ready for launch. If the vehicle uses liquid propellants, they are loaded in the hours before launch, after being stored in tanks near the launchpad. Cryogenic propellants are difficult to maintain in a liquid state. They tend to become gaseous and "boil off" of the vehicle. Therefore, they are loaded into the vehicle's fuel tanks as close to the time of launch as possible and must be constantly topped off to ensure that the fuel and oxidizer tanks are full. Some hours before a scheduled launch, the structure that has been protecting the vehicle is rotated away from it and the launch tower.

Launch bases must have access to up-to-date weather information. There are usually pre-set rules with respect to what weather conditions are acceptable for a space launch, including winds at the launch site and aloft, visibility (for monitoring the vehicle during the first few minutes of flight), and temperature. These conditions vary among launch sites and for different launch vehicles. For example, manned spacecraft can be launched from Russian sites during much more severe weather conditions than those deemed acceptable for the launch of a U.S. space shuttle from its Florida launch base.

In the last few minutes of the countdown, a final check is made to ensure that the vehicle and spacecraft are ready for launch and that all other conditions are in a "go" status. All umbilical connections between the launch tower and the vehicle are detached. Liquid-fueled rocket engines are usually allowed to fire for a few seconds before the vehicle is committed to launch. A rapid computer check is performed, and the engines can be shut down if there are any indications of a problem. Once solid rocket engines are ignited, the vehicle is committed to launch. When the moment of launch arrives, the devices holding the vehicle to the launchpad are explosively detached, and the vehicle begins its liftoff.

Launchpads have trenches for channeling exhaust flames away from the vehicle, and frequently large volumes of water are injected into the flames. This is done to minimize damage to vehicle and launchpad from the heat and sonic vibrations associated with liftoff.

Associated with each launch base is a launch range with facilities for tracking and closely monitoring the launch vehicle through all stages of its mission. A range safety officer makes sure that no aspects of the vehicle's performance could pose a threat to public safety or destroy property. If such a condition arose, the officer would be able to command the launch vehicle to destroy itself.

LAUNCH BASES

Most launch vehicles take off from sites on land, although a few are air- or sea-launched. To function as a launch base, a particular location has to have facilities for assembling the launch vehicle, handling its fuel, preparing a spacecraft for launch, mating the spacecraft and launch vehicle, and checking them out for launch readiness. In addition, it must have launchpads and the capability to monitor the launch after liftoff and ensure safety in the launch range. This usually requires a significant amount of land located away from heavily populated areas but with good air, sea, rail, or land access for transport of various components. Other desirable characteristics include a location that allows the early stages of launch—when first stages are separated and most launch accidents happen—to take place over water or sparsely populated land areas.

Another desirable characteristic is a location as near as possible to the Equator. Many launches take place in an eastward direction to take advantage of the velocity imparted by the rotation of Earth in that direction. This velocity is greatest at the equator and decreases with increased latitude. For example, the additional velocity provided by Earth's rotation is 463 metres per second (1,037 miles per hour) at the European launch base in French Guiana, which is located very close to the Equator at latitude 5.2° N. It is 410 metres per second (918 miles per hour) at the U.S. launch site at Cape

An Ariane 5G launch vehicle at the European Space Agency's launch base in Kourou, Fr.Guia., on Feb. 25, 2004. ESA/CNES/ARIANESPACE-S. Corvaja

Canaveral, Florida, located at latitude 28° N, and it is only 328 metres per second (735 miles per hour) at the Russian Baikonur Cosmodrome in Kazakhstan, which is located at latitude 46° N. Earth's naturally imparted velocity, though small in comparison with the velocity provided by the rocket engines, lessens the demands on the launch vehicle.

Many satellites are intended to be placed in a geostationary orbit. Geostationary orbit is located 35,785 km (22,236 miles) above the Equator. Spacecraft launched from a base near the equator require less maneuvering, and therefore use less fuel, to reach this orbit than do spacecraft launched from higher latitudes. Fuel saving translates into either a lighter spacecraft or additional fuel that can be used to extend the operating life of the satellite.

The benefits of an equatorial location do not apply to launches into a polar or near-polar orbit, since there is no added velocity from Earth's rotation for launches in a northward or southward direction. Launch bases used for polar orbits do need to have a clear path over water or empty land for the early stages of a launch.

Space launches have taken place at more than 25 different land-based locations around the globe, though not all of these bases are in operation at any one time. Most are government-operated facilities. There have been a number of proposals to build commercially operated launch bases at various locations around

the globe, and several such bases in the United States have begun operation.

Not all space launches lift off from land. The U.S.-Russian-Norwegian-Ukrainian commercial launch firm Sea Launch uses the innovative approach of a mobile launch platform, based on a converted offshore oil-drilling rig. The rig is towed by a command ship from its home base in Long Beach, California, to a near-equatorial location in the Pacific Ocean. Once the platform reaches the desired location, the firm's Ukrainian Zenit launch vehicle is transferred along with its communications satellite payload from the command ship to the launch platform, checked out, and launched to geostationary orbit. This approach gives Sea Launch the advantages associated with an equatorial launch site without the need for a permanent installation in an equatorial country.

Other spacecraft have been launched with the Shtil launch vehicle from a converted Russian submarine and with Pegasus from under the wings of an airplane owned by the U.S. firm Orbital Sciences Corporation. The advantages of an air-based launch are the flexibility in the launch location and the use of a carrier aircraft to lift the launch vehicle above Earth, thus reducing the propulsion requirements needed to reach orbit. Typically, the vehicle—a small-winged, multistage rocket—is carried aloft under the fuselage of a modified commercial jetliner to an altitude of about 12 km (40,000 feet) over open ocean, where it is dropped. After the vehicle free-falls briefly in a horizontal position, its first-stage rocket motor ignites, and it pulls away from the aircraft and begins to ascend. The wing, which provides aerodynamic lift for the first part of the flight, is shed with the expended first stage. Such a system is capable of delivering only lightweight satellites—as heavy as 500 kg (1,100 pounds)—into a low Earth orbit.

COMMERCIAL LAUNCH INDUSTRY

Until the early 1980s, all launches into space were carried out under government auspices, even those launches intended to place commercially owned and operated communications satellites into geostationary orbit. With the growth of the commercial communications satellite industry around the world, there was a market opportunity to provide launch services on a commercial basis, since those wanting to launch communications satellites were willing to pay many millions of dollars to do so.

First to take advantage of this opportunity was Europe, which formed the Arianespace Corporation to market Ariane launches to commercial customers.

The second stage (right) of the Orbital Sciences Pegasus XL rocket ready to be mated to the first stage (left) for the launch of NASA's Aeronomy of Ice in the Mesosphere (AIM) spacecraft. NASA

Arianespace was a mixed public-private corporation with close ties to the French government. The French space agency was a major shareholder.

Once the space shuttle had been declared operational in 1982 after its first four flights, the United States pursued a contradictory policy. The U.S. government offered to turn over ownership and operation of existing expendable launch vehicles such as Delta, Atlas, and Titan to the private sector for commercial use. At the same time, it pursued an aggressive policy of marketing the space shuttle as a commercial launcher. The private sector could not compete with this government activity. After the 1986 *Challenger* accident, the space shuttle was prohibited from launching commercial spacecraft. This provided a renewed opportunity for the manufacturers of the Delta, Atlas, and Titan vehicles to seek commercial customers in competition with Arianespace, and they took advantage of that opportunity. After a few years, the Titan was removed from this competition because it had failed to attract many commercial users. Evolved versions of Atlas and Delta continue in commercial service.

In 1983, the Soviet Union began to seek commercial customers through a marketing organization called Glavkosmos. China followed in 1985; its Chang Zheng family of launchers was marketed by the China Great Wall Industry Corporation. Soviet and Chinese entry into the commercial launch market was slowed by quotas imposed by the United States, which argued that Russian and Chinese launchers had an unfair price advantage because of the nonmarket nature of their countries' economies. Japan also planned to market its H-II launch vehicle on a commercial basis but was hindered by the H-II being much more expensive than competing launch vehicles. However, the H-IIA was more successful and less expensive, and Japan has marketed it as a commercial launcher. India had its first commercial launch in April 2007.

In addition to commercial launch services marketed by entities in a particular country, several transnational launch service providers have emerged. International Launch Services is jointly owned by the British Virgin Islands firm Space Transport, the Russian Khrunichev State Research and Production Space Centre, and the Russian firm RSC Energia and markets both the Atlas and Proton launch vehicles. Starsem is a joint venture of European and Russian companies and the Russian Federal Space Agency to market the Soyuz launcher. Sea Launch is an alliance of U.S., Ukrainian, and Russian aerospace companies and a Norwegian offshore oil drilling and shipbuilding company to market the Zenit launch vehicle.

In the mid-1990s, the rapid growth in the geostationary communications satellite industry and plans to launch several multisatellite constellations in low Earth orbit created a sense of optimism that the commercial space launch market would grow rapidly. However, none of the satellite constellations was an economic success, and the demand for communications via satellite leveled off by the turn of the century. This led to an oversupply of launch services. In 1997, there were 23 commercial launches worldwide, but by 2003, the number of launches had declined to 12. That same year, the commercial space launch industry had the capacity to carry out almost 60 launches. Although the launch industry rebounded somewhat afterward—with 21 launches in 2006—demand still lags behind supply.

THE QUEST FOR REUSABILITY

One important limiting factor in the use of space is the high cost of launching spacecraft. In particular, using an expendable launch vehicle involves the single use of a vehicle that costs approximately as much as a jet transport. Since the start of spaceflight, there has been a hope that it might be possible to avoid such high costs by making space launch vehicles reusable for multiple launches. The original plans for the space shuttle called for it to be a two-stage, fully reusable vehicle. Unfortunately, both technological barriers and financial constraints made it impossible to pursue those plans, and the space shuttle is in fact only partially reusable. Indeed, a space shuttle launch is even more expensive than the launch of an expendable vehicle. The United States has made several subsequent attempts to develop a fully reusable single-stage-to-orbit launch vehicle (that is, one that can fly directly to orbit without shedding any of its parts). Among these attempts were the National Aerospace Plane project (1986–93) and the X-33 project (1995–2001). Both programs were canceled before any flights were attempted. In both cases, neither the materials needed to construct the vehicle nor a rocket engine to propel it proved to be at a stage of adequate technological maturity.

In the United States, a number of entrepreneurial firms have also investigated various approaches to lower the cost of space access, with an emphasis on reusability. These approaches have included using a variation of the rocket engine used on the Soviet N-1 lunar launch vehicle and parachuting spent rocket stages and their engines back to Earth for reuse and using technologically advanced rocket engines and materials to construct a totally new vehicle design. None of these efforts have been technically successful, and all have struggled to attract the investments needed for them to proceed. In 2002, the American firm Space Exploration Technologies (SpaceX) began efforts to develop a low-cost expendable launch vehicle, Falcon, using primarily proven technology.

BEYOND ROCKETS

It is difficult to find alternatives to chemically fueled rocket propulsion for lifting mass out of Earth's gravity well. One concept, originally advanced by Konstantin Tsiolkovsky in 1895, is a "space elevator"—an extremely strong cable extending from Earth's surface to the height of geostationary orbit or beyond. The competing forces of gravity at the lower end and outward centripetal acceleration at the farther end would keep the cable under tension and stationary over a single position on Earth. It would then be possible to attach a payload to this cable on Earth and lift it by mechanical means to an orbital height. When released at that point, it would have the velocity to remain in orbit or to use an additional in-space propulsion system to send it to deep-space destinations. This concept, far-fetched as it may seem, has been the subject of serious preliminary research.

Another Earth-to-space transportation concept is called a mass driver. A mass driver is an electromagnetic accelerator, probably miles in length, that would use pulsed magnetic fields to accelerate payloads to orbital or near-orbital velocity. The advantage of a mass driver is that the accelerating device and its source of energy remain on Earth for reuse, rather than accompanying a spacecraft into space. The mass driver concept was given the most attention during the 1970s and '80s by American physicist Gerard O'Neill and his colleagues as part of his proposal to build large orbital space colonies. Mass drivers have also been considered as a means of launching material from the lunar surface.

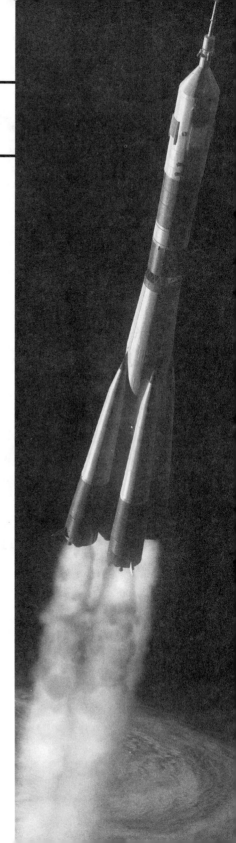

CHAPTER 2

TRAVELING IN SPACE

Once a launch vehicle has lifted the satellite from Earth on its pillar of fire, the satellite follows a precise path and travels at a specific speed necessary for it to fulfill its purpose. Many times the satellite enters orbit around Earth. For probes to other planets, the satellite must escape Earth's gravity and take a course that strikes a balance between using too much fuel and dawdling in interplanetary space. Satellites must also know where they are; they must navigate. Sometimes they must dock with other objects in space, and other times they must return to Earth. The following section deals with the basic concepts associated with the launch and return of unmanned and manned spacecraft and their travel, navigation, and rendezvous and docking in space.

LAUNCHING INTO SPACE: GRAVITY

Earth's gravitational attraction was one of the major obstacles to spaceflight. Because of the observations and calculations of earlier scientists, rocket pioneers understood Newton's laws of motion and other principles of spaceflight, but the application of those principles had to await the development of rocket power to launch a spacecraft to the altitude and velocity required for its mission.

Earth's gravitational pull on the rising spacecraft subsides gradually. At an altitude of 160 km (100 miles), it is still 95 percent of that at Earth's surface. At 2,700 km (1,680 miles), it is 50 percent (4.9 metres, or 16 feet, per second per second). For the purpose of spaceflight, the gravitational pull of Earth becomes negligible only at distances of several million kilometres, except when a spacecraft approaches the Moon and lunar gravity (one-sixth that of Earth) becomes predominant.

FLIGHT TRAJECTORIES

The path a launch vehicle and its payload take is also called the trajectory. There are four general types of trajectories: sounding rocket, Earth orbit, Earth escape, and planetary. A satellite's purpose determines which type it will use.

SOUNDING ROCKET

Sounding rockets provide the only means of making scientific measurements at altitudes of 45–160 km (28–100 miles), between the maximum altitude of balloons and the minimum altitude of orbiting satellites. They can be single-stage or multistage vehicles and are launched nearly vertically. After all the rocket stages have expended their fuel and have dropped away, the payload section continues to coast upward, slowly losing speed because of gravity. Upward velocity drops to zero at peak altitude, and the payload then begins to fall. Typically, the payload is retrieved by parachute and flown again. Prior to parachute deployment, the flight path follows a parabolic trajectory, and flight time is less than 30 minutes.

EARTH ORBIT

Flight into Earth orbit usually is achieved by launching a rocket vertically from Earth's surface and then tilting its trajectory so that its flight is parallel to the surface at the time that the space-faring portion of the vehicle reaches orbital velocity at the desired altitude. Orbital velocity is the speed that provides the centrifugal acceleration, or pull, needed to balance exactly the pull of Earth's gravity on the vehicle at that altitude. The surface of Earth may be thought of as curving away from the projectile, or satellite, as fast as the latter falls toward it.

When a launch vehicle reaches orbital velocity, the rocket engine is shut down. At an altitude of 200 km (125 miles), the velocity required to orbit Earth is about 29,000 km (18,000 miles) per hour. Because this altitude is above most of the atmosphere, aerodynamic drag is not great, and the spacecraft will continue to orbit for an extended time.

The time required for an orbiting spacecraft to make one complete revolution is called the orbital period. At 200 km (124 miles), this is about 90 minutes. The orbital period increases with altitude for two reasons. First, as the altitude increases, Earth's gravity decreases, so the orbital velocity needed to balance it decreases. Second, the spacecraft has to travel farther to circle Earth. For example, at an altitude of 1,730 km (1,075 miles), the orbital velocity is 25,400 km (15,780 miles) per hour, and the period is two hours.

At about 35,800 km (22,250 miles), a spacecraft's velocity is 11,100 km (6,900 miles) per hour, and its orbital period has a special value. It is equal to a sidereal day, the rotational period of Earth measured against the fixed stars—about four minutes shorter than the conventional 24-hour solar day. A spacecraft in this orbit has properties desirable for certain applications. For example, if the orbit lies in the plane of Earth's equator, the spacecraft appears to an observer on Earth to be stationary in the sky. This particular orbit, called a geostationary orbit, is used for communications and meteorological satellites.

All these figures assume a circular orbit, which for a spacecraft is often ideal but difficult to achieve. Usually a spacecraft's orbit is an ellipse with a perigee altitude (nearest distance to Earth) and an apogee altitude (farthest distance from Earth). If thrust is available, a spacecraft's orbit may be made more nearly circular by reducing the velocity at perigee, lowering the apogee, or by increasing the velocity at apogee, raising the perigee. Thrust in such instances is applied against or in the direction of flight, respectively.

EARTH ESCAPE

In order to escape completely from Earth's gravity, a spacecraft requires a launch velocity of about 40,000 km (25,000 miles) per hour. If it subsequently does not come under the gravitational influence of another celestial body, it will go into an orbit around the sun like a tiny planetoid. Escape velocity decreases with altitude and is equal to the square root of 2 (or about 1.414) times the velocity necessary to maintain a circular orbit at the same altitude. With precise timing, a spacecraft can be sent on a trajectory that will carry it near the Moon. In the case of the Apollo lunar landing flights, the spacecraft was placed on a trajectory calculated to pass ahead of the Moon and, under the influence of lunar gravity, to swing around the far side. If no velocity-changing maneuver had been made, then spacecraft would have looped around the Moon and returned on a trajectory toward Earth. By reducing flight speed on the Moon's far side, Apollo astronauts placed their craft in a lunar orbit held by lunar gravity. Similar maneuvers were used to orbit quite a number of spacecraft around Mars, the Magellan spacecraft around Venus, the Galileo spacecraft around Jupiter, the Near Earth Asteroid Rendezvous Shoemaker (NEAR Shoemaker) spacecraft around the asteroid Eros, and the Cassini spacecraft around Saturn.

The so-called three-body problem of celestial mechanics (in the case of the Apollo missions, the relative motions of Earth, the spacecraft, and the Moon under their mutual gravitational influence) is extremely complex and has no general solution. Although equations expressing the relative motions can be written for specific cases, no expedient approximate solutions were possible before the development of high-speed digital computers for calculating trajectories of long-range missiles. Computers integrate the complicated equations of motion numerically, show the spacecraft's complete trajectory at successive positions through space, and compare the actual flight path to the preplanned path at any point in time.

PLANETARY TRAJECTORY

Because of the elliptical nature of planetary orbits, distances vary between Earth and the other planets. In the case of Earth's nearest neighbours, Venus and Mars, a so-called favourable launch opportunity occurs about every two years. Flights can be made at other times, but the velocity required is greater and the length of time longer or, for a given launch vehicle, the payload must be lighter in weight.

The trajectory from Earth to Venus or Mars can be planned to take advantage of the changing orbital relationships of the planets for the most economical flight in terms of fuel and energy. Such advantageous paths, called Hohmann orbits or transfer orbits, were described in the 1920s. The German engineer Walter Hohmann showed in 1925 that elliptical orbits tangent to the orbits of both the planet of departure and the target planet require the least fuel and energy. Although these trajectories require the least velocity, they are of long duration—as long as 260 days to Mars, for example. About two years and eight months would be needed for a round-trip, allowing for a waiting period of 455 days on Mars while the planets realigned themselves properly

so that Earth would be present at the time the returning craft was crossing Earth's orbit. To reach Venus, 146 days would be required. Including waiting time, a round-trip would take two years and one month. Thus, a compromise trajectory is often used, as in the case of Mariners 6 and 7 in 1969. Launched on Feb. 24, 1969, Mariner 6 passed within 3,430 km (2,130 miles) of Mars 157 days later, when the planet was 92.8 million km (57.7 million miles) from Earth.

Some trajectories use the fall into a planet's gravitational field to transfer momentum from the planet to the spacecraft, thereby increasing its velocity and altering its direction. This gravity-assist, or slingshot, technique has been used numerous times to send planetary probes to their destinations. For example, the Galileo probe, during its six-year voyage to Jupiter, swung by Venus once and Earth twice in order to reach its ultimate target in 1995.

The same considerations for planetary trajectories apply to spacecraft destined for other objects in deep space, such as asteroids and comets. For instance, the flight path of NEAR Shoemaker incorporated a trajectory-reshaping flyby of Earth.

Placing a spacecraft into orbit around a planet (or comet or asteroid) requires sufficient reduction of the spacecraft's velocity to allow the planet's gravity to capture it. Until 1997, such maneuvers were implemented by using the spacecraft's onboard propulsion system to impart the necessary impulse, as was done for Apollo. A new process called

Earth as photographed by the Galileo space probe during its December 1990 gravity-assist flyby of the planet. Earlier, in February, Galileo had skirted Venus, and it passed near Earth again in December 1992 before heading out of the inner solar system to an encounter with Jupiter in December 1995. NASA/JPL

aerobraking, first tested on the Magellan radar-mapping spacecraft at Venus in 1993, was used in 1997–98 to reduce the velocity of the Mars Global Surveyor. This saved a considerable amount of propellant and allowed a larger payload to be flown. In this process, the spacecraft uses a short burn of its onboard propulsion system to place the spacecraft into a highly eccentric elliptical orbit with a perigee that dips just below the outer fringes of the planet's atmosphere. During each pass through that fringe, the atmosphere's drag slows the spacecraft down slightly, reducing the orbit's apogee. After a number of passes, the orbit becomes circular, and the orbital mission can be conducted. The same process was used again successfully on Mars Odyssey in 2001–02 and has since become standard practice for orbiting spacecraft around planets with atmospheres.

NAVIGATION, DOCKING, AND RECOVERY

Once a satellite is launched, it does not just passively follow one of the four types of trajectory. To ensure that it remains in its correct course, it must be able to navigate. Navigation is also useful when one satellite must rendezvous and dock with another. Sometimes a satellite must leave its trajectory and return to Earth, but it must return in such a way that it can be safely recovered and will not burn up when reentering Earth's atmosphere.

NAVIGATION

Traveling from point A to point B in space is almost never in a straight line or at constant velocity because of the many influences on the body in motion. The basis for space navigation is inertial guidance—guidance based on the inertia of a spinning gyroscope, irrespective of external forces and without reference to the Sun or stars. By the use of three gyroscopes and accelerometers, a spacecraft's navigation system can make precise measurements of any change in velocity, either positive or negative, along any or all of the three principal axes. By changing attitude (conducting rotation about one or more axes) and firing one or more thrust motors, a spacecraft can make corrections to its trajectory.

Inertial guidance systems, no matter how accurate, are subject to tiny errors that can accumulate over long voyages to significant departures from the required trajectory. Therefore, many planetary-exploration spacecraft employ a star tracker with a small telescope that tracks several preprogrammed stars, providing an accurate continuous celestial "fix" on the spacecraft's position. This also directs the spacecraft's computer to correct the inertial guidance system. When sufficient funding is available, some deep-space probes are monitored on Earth by human flight controllers, who send commands to the spacecraft's computer from time to time to correct the spacecraft's course.

During the launch phase, corrections to deviations in the planned flight path are usually made at once by small thrust motors on the launch vehicle, by deflection of the rocket exhaust jet, or by swinging one or more of the rocket engines in a gimbal mount. In the case of a rendezvous and docking between two spacecraft, radar data inform a crew—or, in the case of automated maneuvers, a computer—of the corrections required

KONSTANTIN TSIOLKOVSKY

Another pioneer of space exploration, Konstantin Eduardovich Tsiolkovsky, was born on Sept. 5, 1857, in Izhevskoye, Russia. He was from a family of modest means. His father, Eduard Ignatyevich Tsiolkovsky, a provincial forestry official, was a Polish noble by birth. His mother, Mariya Ivanovna Yumasheva, was Russian and Tatar. As a boy, Tsiolkovsky lost his hearing at age nine because of scarlet fever. Four years later, his mother died. These two events had an important bearing on his early life in that, being obliged to study at home, he became withdrawn and lonely, yet self-reliant. Books became his friends. He developed an interest in mathematics and physics and, while still a teenager, began to speculate on space travel.

At the age of 16, Tsiolkovsky went to Moscow, where for three years he attended lectures on chemistry, mathematics, astronomy, and mechanics—aided by an ear trumpet, thus expanding his grasp of the problems of flight. But the elder Tsiolkovsky wanted his deaf son, notwithstanding his growing ability to deal with abstruse questions in physics, to achieve financial independence. After discovering that the youth was going hungry and overworking himself in Moscow, his father called him home to Vyatka (now Kirov) in 1876.

The future scientist soon passed the teachers examination and was assigned to a school in Borovsk, about 100 km (60 miles) from Moscow, where he began his teaching career. He then married Varvara Yevgrafovna Sokolovaya and renewed his deep interest in science. Isolated from scientific centres, Tsiolkovsky made discoveries on his own. He worked out equations on the kinetic theory of gases. He then sent the manuscript of this work to the Russian Physico-Chemical Society in St. Petersburg but was informed by the chemist Dmitry Ivanovich Mendeleyev that it already had been done a quarter century before. Undaunted and encouraged by Mendeleyev, he continued his research. The Russian Physico-Chemical Society, impressed by the intellectual independence of this young provincial schoolteacher, invited him to become a member.

In 1892, Tsiolkovsky was transferred to another teaching post in Kaluga, where he continued his research in astronautics and aeronautics. At that time, he took up the problem that occupied almost all his life: the construction of an all-metal dirigible with an adjustable envelope. In order to demonstrate the validity of his experiment, he built a wind tunnel—the first in Russia—incorporating into it features that would permit testing of the aerodynamic merits of various aircraft designs. Since he did not receive any financial support from the Russian Physico-Chemical Society, Tsiolkovsky was obliged to dip into his family's household budget in order to build the tunnel. He investigated about 100 models of quite diverse designs.

Tsiolkovsky's experiments were subtle and extremely clever. He studied the effects of air friction and surface area on the speed of the air current over a streamlined body. The Academy of Sciences learned of his work and granted him the modest financial aid of 470 rubles, with which he built a larger wind tunnel. Tsiolkovsky then compared the feasibility of dirigibles and airplanes, which led him to develop advanced aircraft designs.

While investigating aerodynamics, Tsiolkovsky began to devote more attention to space problems. In 1895, his book Gryozy o zemle i nebe *(Dreams of Earth and Sky) was published, and in 1896, he published an article on communication with inhabitants of other planets. That same year, he began to write his largest and most serious work on astronautics, "Exploration of Cosmic Space by Means of Reaction Devices," which dealt with theoretical problems of using rocket engines in space, including heat transfer, a navigating mechanism, heating resulting from air friction, and maintenance of fuel supply.*

The first 15 years of the 20th century undoubtedly were the saddest time of Tsiolkovsky's life. In 1902, his son Ignaty committed suicide. In 1908, a flood of the Oka River inundated his home and destroyed many of his accumulated scientific materials. The Academy of Sciences did not recognize the value of his aerodynamic experiments, and, in 1914, at the Aeronautics Congress in St. Petersburg, his models of an all-metal dirigible were met with complete indifference.

In the final 18 years of his life, Tsiolkovsky continued his research, with the support of the Soviet state, on a wide variety of scientific problems. His contributions on stratospheric exploration and interplanetary flight were particularly noteworthy and played a significant role in contemporary astronautics. In 1919, Tsiolkovsky was elected to the Socialist Academy (later the Academy of Sciences of the U.S.S.R.). On Nov. 9, 1921, the council of the People's Commissars granted him a pension for life in recognition of his services in education and aviation. He died on Sept. 19, 1935, in Kaluga.

along each axis. With the implementation of the satellite-based Navstar Global Positioning System (GPS) in the 1980s, it became possible for spacecraft in Earth orbit to verify their locations within a few centimetres and their speeds within a few centimetres per second.

RENDEZVOUS AND DOCKING

Rendezvous is the process of bringing two spacecraft together, whereas docking is their subsequent meeting and physical joining. The essential elements of a rendezvous are the matching of orbital trajectories and the movement of one spacecraft within close proximity of the other, typically within 100 metres (330

feet). Ideally, the two spacecraft also should lie in the same orbital plane.

Ordinarily for a rendezvous mission, one spacecraft is already in orbit, and the second spacecraft is launched to meet it. To achieve rendezvous, the launch of the second craft is timed within a fraction of a second. Because the orbiting spacecraft already has a high velocity relative to the second spacecraft on the ground, the second craft is launched well before the first passes overhead. The aim is to establish a coplanar orbit just below the first spacecraft. In this configuration the second craft, being at a lower orbit, is traveling at a faster speed and will overtake the first. When it is slightly ahead of the first spacecraft, it fires thrusters in a way that causes it to rise in orbit and thus to slow down until it matches the first craft's orbital altitude and velocity. Radar systems and onboard computers are necessary for such operations.

In 1965, Gemini 6 and 7 were the first spacecraft to perform a rendezvous. While the United States has relied on human crews for close rendezvous and docking, Russian spacecraft can perform these maneuvers automatically using technology developed and refined in the Soviet space program.

Because of payload limitations, spacecraft beyond a certain size and complexity cannot be launched into Earth orbit at one time. Building a large structure such as the International Space Station—or a future spacecraft for a human trip to Mars or a large solar-power space station—requires reliable rendezvous and docking techniques that can be used to assemble component parts taken to orbit on separate launches.

REENTRY AND RECOVERY

Reentry refers to the return of a spacecraft into Earth's atmosphere. The blanket of relatively dense gas surrounding Earth is useful as a braking, or retarding, force resulting from aerodynamic drag. One concomitant effect, however, is the severe heating caused by the compression of

Shuttle orbiter Discovery making a landing on the runway at the John F. Kennedy Space Center at Cape Canaveral, Fla., on Jan. 27, 1985. NASA

atmospheric air in front of the rapidly moving spacecraft. Initially, heat shields were made of ablative materials that carried away the heat of reentry as they were shed, but the space shuttle introduced refractory materials—silica tiles and a reinforced carbon-carbon material—that withstood the heat directly. Newer vehicle designs use active cooling and refractory metallic alloys.

Inherent in the safe reentry of a spacecraft is precise control of the angle of reentry. If the reentry angle is too shallow, the spacecraft will skip or bounce off the atmosphere and back into space. If the angle is too great, the heat shield will not survive the extreme heating rates nor the spacecraft the high forces of deceleration.

During the final phases of descent, some spacecraft—especially capsule-type manned craft—deploy parachutes, which lower the vehicle to a soft landing. Small unmanned spacecraft, or objects (such as photographic film capsules) ejected from satellites, have been recovered in midair by aircraft while still descending to Earth by parachute.

CHAPTER 3

NOTABLE SATELLITES

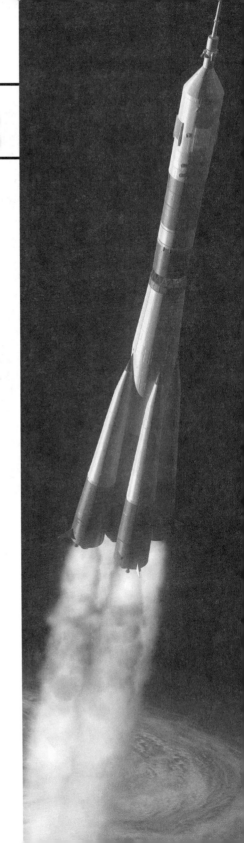

Satellites differ greatly in size, shape, complexity, and purpose. Those that share similarities in design, function, or both are often grouped into program families. Lightness of weight and functional reliability are primary features of satellite design. Depending on their mission, satellites may spend minutes, days, months, or years in the environment of space. Mission functions must be performed while exposed to high vacuum, microgravity, extreme variations in temperature, and strong radiation.

A general differentiation of satellites is by function—scientific or applications. A scientific satellite or probe carries instruments to obtain data on magnetic fields, space radiation, Earth and its atmosphere, the sun or other stars, planets and their moons, and other astronomical objects and phenomena. Applications satellites have utilitarian tasks, such as telecommunications, Earth observation, military reconnaissance, navigation and position-location, power transmission, and space manufacturing.

Although the designs of the various satellite families and special-purpose spacecraft vary widely, there are nine general categories of subsystems found on most satellites. They are (1) the power supply, (2) onboard propulsion, (3) communications, (4) attitude control (maintaining a satellite's orientation toward a specific direction and pointing its instruments precisely at selected targets), (5) environmental control (mainly regulation of the satellite components'

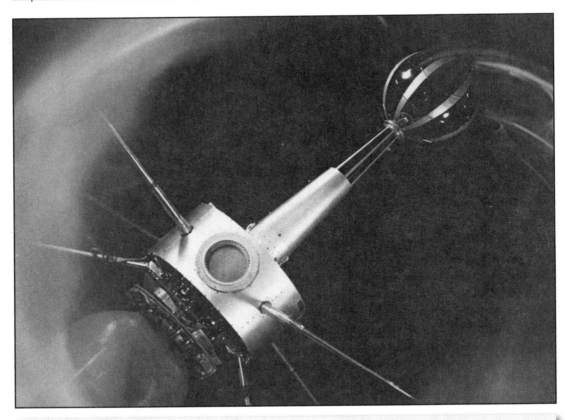

U.S. Explorer 10 satellite shown undergoing testing in a National Aeronautics and Space Administration laboratory. Explorer 10 was launched March 25, 1961, and relayed magnetic field data from a high Earth orbit. The satellite was one of more than 50 scientific spacecraft launched as part of the Explorer program between 1958 and 1975. NASA

temperatures), (6) guidance, navigation, and flight control, (7) computer and data processing, (8) structure (the skeleton framework of the satellite that physically supports all other subsystems), and (9) a "health-monitoring" system that monitors the status of the satellite and its payload.

Several notable unmanned satellites have been developed and launched over the years. All of them, from Sputnik to the technological marvel of the Hubble Space Telescope, have played an important role in history and the vast field of space exploration.

THE 1950S

At the beginning of the space age, the first satellite, Sputnik 1, was an elementary device that contained only a radio transmitter. Subsequent satellites, such as Explorer 1, studied Earth's magnetosphere. Others, such as those in the Luna and Pioneer series, began the exploration of interplanetary space.

SPUTNIK

Sputnik was a series of 10 artificial Earth satellites whose launching by the Soviet Union beginning on Oct. 4, 1957, inaugurated the space age. Sputnik 1, the first satellite launched by man, was a 83.6-kg

Sputnik 3, the first multipurpose space-science satellite placed in orbit. Launched May 15, 1958, by the Soviet Union, it made and transmitted measurements of the pressure and composition of Earth's upper atmosphere, the concentration of charged particles, and the influx of primary cosmic rays. Tass/Sovfoto

(184-pound) capsule. It achieved an Earth orbit with an apogee (farthest point from Earth) of 940 km (584 miles) and a perigee (nearest point) of 230 km (143 miles). It circled Earth every 96 minutes and remained in orbit until early 1958, when it fell back and burned in Earth's atmosphere. Launched on Nov. 3, 1957, Sputnik 2 carried the dog Laika, the first living creature to be shot into space and orbit Earth. Eight more Sputnik missions with similar satellites carried out experiments on a variety of animals to test spacecraft life-support systems. They also tested reentry procedures and furnished data on space temperatures, pressures, particles, radiation, and magnetic fields.

EXPLORER

Explorer was the largest series of unmanned U.S. spacecraft, consisting of 55 scientific satellites launched between 1958 and 1975. Explorer 1 (launched Jan. 31, 1958) was the first space satellite orbited by the United States. It discovered the innermost of the Van Allen radiation belts, two zones of charged particles that surround Earth. Explorer 1's discovery of the Van Allen belts was the first scientific discovery made by an artificial satellite. Explorer 6 (launched

Aug. 7, 1959) took the first pictures of Earth from orbit. Other notable craft in the series included Explorer 38 (a.k.a. Radio Astronomy Explorer, launched July 4, 1968), which measured galactic radio sources and studied low frequencies in space, and Explorer 53 (a.k.a. Small Astronomy Satellite-C, launched May 7, 1975), which was sent out to explore X-ray sources both inside and outside the Milky Way galaxy.

VANGUARD

The second artificial satellite placed in orbit around Earth by the U.S., Vanguard, was a series of three unmanned U.S. experimental test satellites. Vanguard 1, launched March 17, 1958, consisted of a tiny 1.47-kg (3.25-pound) sphere equipped with two radio transmitters. By monitoring Vanguard's flight path, scientists found that Earth was almost imperceptibly pear-shaped, in confirmation of earlier theories. (As of 2009, Vanguard 1 was the oldest satellite in orbit.) Vanguard 2, orbited on Feb. 17, 1959, carried light-sensitive photocells that were designed to provide information about Earth's cloud cover, but the tumbling motion of the satellite rendered the data unreadable. Vanguard 3, the last in the series, was launched several months later. It was used to map Earth's magnetic field.

PIONEER

The first series of unmanned U.S. space probes designed chiefly for interplanetary study was Pioneer. Whereas the first five Pioneers (0–4, launched from 1958 to 1959) were intended to explore the vicinity of the Moon, all other probes in the series were sent to investigate planetary bodies or to measure various interplanetary-particle and magnetic-field effects. Pioneer 6 (launched Dec. 16, 1965), for example, was injected into solar orbit to determine space conditions between Earth and Venus. It transmitted much data on the solar wind and solar cosmic rays in addition to measuring the Sun's corona and the tail of Comet Kohoutek. As of 2009, Pioneer 6 was the oldest functioning spacecraft. Pioneer 10, which was launched March 3, 1972, flew by Jupiter in December 1973. It was the first space

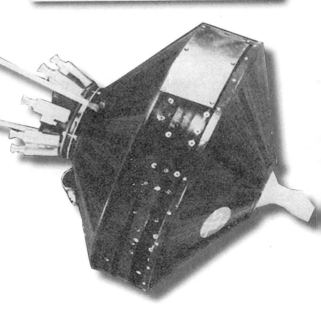

Pioneer 1, 1958. NASA

probe to do so, and, in the process, discovered Jupiter's huge magnetic tail, an extension of the planet's magnetosphere. Pioneer 11 (launched April 6, 1973), also called Pioneer Saturn, passed by Jupiter in December 1974 and flew within about 20,900 km (13,000 miles) of Saturn in September 1979. It transmitted data and photographs that enabled scientists on Earth to identify two additional rings around the planet and the presence of radiation belts within its magnetosphere. Pioneers 10 and 11 each carried a gold plaque inscribed with a pictorial message in the event that extraterrestrial beings ever found the spacecraft. Two complementary Pioneer Venus spacecraft (Pioneer 12 and 13) reached their destination at the end of 1978. The first, called the Orbiter, studied Venus's clouds and atmosphere and mapped more than 90 percent of its surface by radar. The second spacecraft, the Multiprobe, dropped one large and three small instrument packages into the planet's atmosphere at different locations to measure various physical and chemical properties.

DISCOVERER

Discoverer was a series of 38 unmanned experimental satellites launched by the U.S. Air Force. Although the Discoverer satellites had several apparent applications—such as testing orbital maneuvering and reentry techniques—the program was actually a cover story for Corona, a joint Air Force–Central Intelligence Agency project to develop a military reconnaissance satellite. *Discoverer 1* (launched Feb. 28, 1959) was equipped with a camera and an ejectable capsule capable of carrying exposed film back to Earth. Like later reconnaissance satellites, it was placed in a low polar orbit. By orbiting almost directly over the poles, *Discoverer* was in position to photograph the entire surface of Earth every 24 hours. All other satellites in the series were launched into a similar fixed orbit. The capsule ejection system was repeatedly tested, but in-air payload recovery was achieved only once during the early years of the program. The capsule released by *Discoverer 14* was retrieved on Aug. 18, 1960. *Discoverer 38* (launched Feb. 27, 1962) was the last Discoverer model to be officially announced.

LUNA

Luna was a series of 24 unmanned Soviet lunar probes launched between 1959 and 1976. Luna 1 (launched Jan. 2, 1959) was the first spacecraft to escape Earth's gravity. It failed to impact the Moon as planned and became the first man-made object to go into orbit around the Sun. Luna 2 (Sept. 12, 1959) was the first spacecraft to strike the Moon, and Luna 3 (Oct. 4, 1959) made the first circumnavigation of the Moon and returned the first photographs of its far side. Luna 9 (Jan. 31, 1966) made the first successful lunar soft landing. Luna 16 (Sept. 12, 1970) was the first unmanned spacecraft to carry lunar soil samples back to Earth. Luna 17 (Nov. 10, 1970) soft-landed a robot

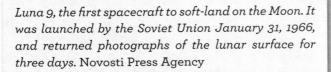

Luna 9, the first spacecraft to soft-land on the Moon. It was launched by the Soviet Union January 31, 1966, and returned photographs of the lunar surface for three days. Novosti Press Agency

vehicle, Lunokhod 1, for exploration. It also contained television equipment, by means of which it transmitted live pictures of several kilometres of the Moon's surface. Luna 22 (May 29, 1974) orbited the Moon 2,842 times while conducting space research in its vicinity. Luna 24 (Aug. 9, 1976) returned with lunar soil samples taken from a depth of about two metres (seven feet) below the surface.

THE 1960S

In the 1960s, unmanned spacecraft took on many roles, from military (Midas and Transit) to meteorological (TIROS) to scientific (Orbiting Astronomical Observatory). The race between the U.S. and the Soviet Union to put a man on the Moon also led to such programs as Lunar Orbiter, Surveyor, and Zond.

MIDAS

The Midas program was a series of 12 unmanned U.S. military satellites developed to provide warning against surprise attacks by Soviet ICBMs. Midas (an abbreviation of Missile Defense Alarm System) was the first such warning system in the world. Launched during the early 1960s, the reconnaissance satellites were equipped with infrared sensors capable of detecting the heat of a ballistic missile's rocket exhaust shortly after firing. To provide global coverage, the Midas satellites were placed into polar orbits. Midas 1 and 2, launched Feb. 25 and May 24, 1960, respectively, suffered mechanical failures. The first successful satellite was Midas 3, launched on July 12, 1961. The last Midas satellite, Midas 12, was launched on Oct. 5, 1966. Because of launch and mechanical failures, the Midas satellites were unable to provide the desired continuous coverage of the Soviet Union. The infrared sensors could not distinguish between missile launches and sunlight reflected off of clouds in the upper atmosphere. The subsequent satellite early warning system, the Defense Support Program, succeeded where Midas had failed.

TIROS

The TIROS (Television and Infrared Observation Satellite) Program constituted the first worldwide weather observation system. The first TIROS satellite was launched on April 1, 1960. Equipped with specially designed miniature television cameras, infrared detectors, and videotape recorders, the satellites were able to provide global weather coverage at 24-hour intervals. The cloud-cover pictures transmitted by the TIROS craft enabled meteorologists to track, forecast, and analyze storms. There were 10 TIROS satellites; the last of which, TIROS 10, was launched on July 2, 1965. From 1969, a series of advanced weather satellites known as Nimbus largely supplanted TIROS.

TRANSIT

The first U.S. navigation satellites were those of the Transit program. Launched by the U.S. Navy from 1960 to 1988, the Transit satellites were developed to provide an accurate, all-weather navigational aid for seagoing vessels (particularly submarines) and aircraft. The system was so designed that any such craft could pinpoint its position by using a computer specially programmed to translate coded radio signals beamed from the satellites into latitude and longitude.

Transit 1-B, the first in the series, was placed in a north-south polar orbit on April 13, 1960. However, it had only a 40-month life-span. Three advanced Transit models equipped with nuclear-power generators were launched from June 22, 1960, to Nov. 15, 1961. In 1997, Transit was replaced as a means of navigation by the Global Positioning System (GPS). The satellites then became the Navy Ionospheric Monitoring System and studied Earth's upper atmosphere.

VENERA

The Venera probes were a series of unmanned Soviet planetary probes that were sent to Venus. Radio contact was lost with the first probe, Venera 1 (launched Feb. 12, 1961), before it flew by Venus. Venera 2 (launched Nov. 12, 1965)

Descent capsule of the Soviet Venera 4 spacecraft prior to its launch to Venus on June 12, 1967. Equipped with a parachute and several instruments for measuring atmospheric temperature, pressure, and density, it reached its destination on October 18, becoming the first human-made object to travel through the atmosphere of another planet and return data to Earth. Tass/Sovfoto

ceased operation before it flew to within 24,000 km (15,000 miles) of Venus in February 1966. Venera 3 (launched Nov. 16, 1965) crash-landed on the surface of Venus on March 1, 1966, becoming the first spacecraft to strike another planet. Venera 4 (launched June 12, 1967), an atmospheric probe that descended toward the surface by parachute, analyzed the chemical composition of Venus's upper atmosphere and provided scientists with the first direct measurements for a model of the planet's atmospheric makeup. Veneras 5 and 6 (launched Jan. 5 and 10, 1969, respectively) were also atmospheric probes. Like Venera 4, they succumbed to Venus's extreme heat and pressure and ceased transmitting data before reaching the surface.

Venera 7 (launched Aug. 17, 1970), a lander, made the first successful soft touchdown on another planet and transmitted for 23 minutes. The Venera 8 lander (launched March 27, 1972) measured concentrations of certain long-lived radioactive isotopes that hinted at a rock composition similar to granite or other igneous rocks on Earth. The Venera 9 and 10 landers (launched June 8 and 14, 1975, respectively) sent back the first close-up photographs (in black and white) of the surface of another planet. Veneras 11 and 12 (launched Sept. 9 and 14, 1978, respectively) conducted detailed chemical measurements of the Venusian atmosphere on their way to soft landings. The Venera 13 and 14 landers (launched Oct. 30 and Nov. 4, 1981, respectively) analyzed a number of nonradioactive elements in the surface rocks, finding them similar to earthly basalts. The landers also returned colour images of rocky landscapes bathed in yellow-orange sunlight that filtered through the clouds. Veneras 15 and 16 (launched June 2 and 7, 1983, respectively) were orbiters equipped with the first high-resolution imaging radar systems flown to another planet. They mapped about a quarter of Venus's surface, primarily around the north pole. Two related Soviet spacecraft, Vega (a Russian acronym for Venus-Halley) 1 and Vega 2 (launched Dec. 15 and 21, 1984, respectively), flew past Venus en route to successful flybys of Halley's Comet in 1986. Each released a Venera-style lander and an atmospheric balloon to investigate the Venusian middle cloud layer.

RANGER

NASA's earliest attempt at lunar exploration was Project Ranger, a series of nine unmanned probes launched from 1961 to 1965. Ranger 1 and 2 (launched Aug. 23 and Nov. 18, 1961, respectively) failed to leave Earth orbit. Ranger 3 (launched Jan. 26, 1962) missed the Moon and went into orbit around the Sun. Ranger 4 (launched April 23, 1962) became the first U.S. spacecraft to hit the moon, crash-landing on its surface as designed. Ranger 5 (launched Oct. 18, 1962) suffered the same fate as Ranger 3. The last three probes in the series, Ranger 7, 8, and 9 (1964–65), transmitted more than 17,000 high-resolution photographs of the Moon, including many from as close as 300 metres (1,000 feet) above the lunar surface, before crashing.

COSMOS

Cosmos is a series of unmanned Soviet and then Russian satellites launched from the early 1960s to the present day. As of 2009, there were 2,450 satellites in the series. The first satellite in the series was launched on March 16, 1962. Cosmos satellites have been used for a wide variety of purposes, including scientific research, navigation, and military reconnaissance. In the Soviet years, failures of probes in other programs were given a Cosmos number. Cosmos 26 and 49 (both launched in 1964), for example, were equipped to measure Earth's magnetic field. Others were employed to study certain technical aspects of spaceflight as well as physical phenomena in Earth's upper atmosphere and in deep space. A number of them, such as Cosmos 597, 600, and 602, were apparently used to collect intelligence information on the Yom Kippur War between the Arab states and Israel in October 1973. Some Cosmos spacecraft had the ability to intercept satellites launched by other nations. Some other Cosmos satellites have proved much more notable for how their missions ended. Cosmos 954, a Soviet Navy satellite powered by a nuclear reactor, crashed in the Northwest Territories of Canada on Jan. 24, 1978, scattering radioactive debris.

ARIEL

Ariel was the first international cooperative Earth satellite. It was launched on

April 26, 1962, as a joint project of agencies of the United States and the United Kingdom. Design, construction, telemetry, and launching of the 14.5-kg (32-pound) satellite. It was handled in the United States by NASA. The United Kingdom was responsible for designing the equipment and the experiments to measure electron density and temperature and composition of positive ions, intensity of solar radiation in ultraviolet Lyman-alpha line, and cosmic rays.

MARINER

The probes in the U.S. Mariner series were sent to the vicinities of Venus, Mars, and Mercury. Mariner 1 (launched July 22, 1962) was intended to fly by Venus, but it was destroyed shortly after liftoff when it veered off course. Mariners 2 (launched Aug. 27, 1962) and 5 (launched June 14, 1967) passed Venus within 35,000 and 4,000 km (22,000 and 2,500 miles), respectively, and made measurements of temperature and atmospheric density. Mariner 3 (launched Nov. 5, 1964) was supposed to fly by Mars, but contact was lost shortly after liftoff. Mariners 4 (launched Nov. 28, 1964), 6 and 7 (launched Feb. 24 and March 27, 1969, respectively), and 9 (launched May 30, 1971) obtained striking photographs of the Martian surface and made significant analyses of the atmosphere of that planet. Mariner 8 (launched May 8, 1971) was intended to study Mars with Mariner 9, but its upper stage malfunctioned shortly after launch. Mariner 10 (launched Nov. 3, 1973), which flew by Venus once and Mercury three times, came within 330 km (200 miles) of the latter planet on its third pass. It transmitted back to Earth the first close-up pictures of Mercury's surface, as well as analyses of its atmosphere and magnetic field.

VELA

The 12 U.S. Velas were reconnaissance satellites developed to detect radiation from nuclear explosions in Earth's atmosphere. Launched from 1963 to 1970, the Vela satellites were supposed to make certain that no countries violated the 1963 international treaty banning the testing of nuclear weapons on the ground or in the atmosphere. Although their primary function was military reconnaissance, the Velas made several significant astronomical discoveries, including the discovery of gamma-ray bursts.

Each Vela spacecraft carried radiation detectors sensitive to X-ray and gamma-ray emissions. The satellites were always launched in pairs to an orbit of more than 60,000 miles (96,000 km) above Earth. The first twin craft were orbited on Oct. 17, 1963. By 1967, an advanced version of the satellite had been developed. The new model was equipped with more sophisticated detection instruments and was designed to continually point toward Earth, unlike the earlier version, which viewed the heavens as well. The first pair of advanced Vela satellites was orbited on April 28, 1967. The last two pairs in the series were launched in 1969 and 1970.

ZOND

Zond was a series of eight unmanned Soviet lunar and interplanetary probes. Zond 1 (launched April 2, 1964) and Zond 2 (Nov. 30, 1964) were aimed at Venus and Mars, respectively, but failed to send back data on the planets. Zond 3 (launched July 18, 1965) transmitted close-up photographs of 7,800,000 square km (3,000,000 square miles) of the lunar surface, including the hidden side, before going into solar orbit. The remaining flights in the Zond program were tests of Soyuz spacecraft modified for flights around the Moon. Zond 4 (launched March 2, 1968) was placed into an orbit away from the Moon that carried it 330,000 km (205,000 miles) from Earth. When a landing in the Soviet Union became impossible, Zond 4 was ordered to explode in Earth's atmosphere. Zond 5 (launched Sept. 14, 1968) became the first spacecraft to orbit the Moon and return to a splashdown on Earth. It too carried living specimens. Zond 6, 7, and 8 (launched Nov. 10, 1968, Aug. 7, 1969, and Oct. 20, 1970, respectively) also made circumlunar flights. They carried biological specimens and transmitted photography of the Moon's surface.

ORBITING GEOPHYSICAL OBSERVATORY

The Orbiting Geophysical Observatories (OGO) were six unmanned scientific satellites launched by the United States from 1964 to 1969. Equipped with a complex of magnetometers, these orbiting satellites were designed to study Earth's magnetosphere (the zone of strong magnetic forces around the planet) and its effect on high-energy particles emitted by the sun. These studies included investigations of auroral displays, magnetic storms, and other related phenomena.

OGO-1, the first in the series, was launched on Sept. 4, 1964. It weighed about 113 kg (250 pounds) and carried instrumentation for 20 to 25 experiments. The other OGO satellites were identical in size and equipment. OGO-6, the last in the series, was launched on June 5, 1969.

PEGASUS

Three U.S. scientific satellites called Pegasus were launched in 1965. These spacecraft were named for the winged horse in Greek mythology because of their prominent wing-like structure. This "wing," which spanned 29 metres (96 feet), was specially designed to record the depth and frequency with which it was pierced by micrometeoroids. The information was used to design the outer shell of the manned Apollo spacecraft to prevent penetration of such high-speed particles of space dust. The data also enabled engineers to develop space suits that would shield astronauts from micrometeoroids when working outside their craft. At the time of their launch, the Pegasus satellites were among the largest U.S. spacecraft ever built, with their centre section extending 21.6 metres (71 feet) in length.

ORBITING ASTRONOMICAL OBSERVATORY

The four Orbiting Astronomical Observatories (OAO) were U.S. scientific satellites developed to observe cosmic objects from above Earth's atmosphere. OAO-1 was launched on April 8, 1966, but its power supply failed shortly after liftoff. OAO-2, launched Dec. 7, 1968, carried two large telescopes and a complement of spectrometers and other auxiliary devices. It weighed more than 1,900 kg (4,200 pounds), the heaviest satellite orbited up to that time. OAO-2 was able to photograph young stars that emit mostly ultraviolet light. Astronomers had detected very few such stars with ground-based telescopes because ultraviolet radiation is absorbed by Earth's atmosphere. OAO-2 remained in operation until January 1973. OAO-B failed to reach orbit after its launch on Nov. 30, 1970. Copernicus (OAO-3) was equipped with more powerful instruments, including a reflecting telescope with a 81-cm (32-inch) mirror. Launched on Aug. 21, 1972, this satellite was primarily used to study ultraviolet emissions from interstellar gas and stars in the far reaches of the Milky Way. Copernicus also carried four X-ray detectors that discovered several pulsars. Copernicus continued observing until February 1981.

SURVEYOR

The seven Surveyor U.S. space probes were sent to the Moon between 1966 and 1968 to photograph and study the lunar surface. Surveyor 1 (launched May 30, 1966), carrying a scanning television camera and special sensors, landed on the Moon on June 2, 1966, and transmitted 11,150 photographs as well as

Surveyor 1. NASA

information about environmental conditions on the Moon. Surveyor 2 crashed on the Moon (Sept. 23, 1966). Surveyor 3 (April 17, 1967) included additional equipment such as a surface-sampling device and two small mirrors to expand the camera vision. It returned 6,315 photographs. (More than two years later, the Apollo 12 astronauts landed about 200 metres [650 feet] from Surveyor 3 and removed some of Surveyor 3's instruments to study how they were affected by exposure to the lunar environment.) Surveyor 4 crashed or soft-landed on the Moon (July 16, 1967). Surveyor 5 (Sept. 8, 1967) measured the proportions of chemical elements in lunar soil and studied other surface properties. It returned 18,000 photographs.

After taking photographs of one area of the Moon's surface, Surveyor 6 (Nov. 7, 1967) was lifted, moved 2.4 metres (8 feet), and repositioned to continue photographing another area. This marked the first liftoff from an extraterrestrial body. Altogether, 27,000 photographs were obtained. Surveyor 7 (Jan. 7, 1968) was the only probe in the series that was soft-landed in the highland region of the Moon. Data transmitted by the craft revealed that the chemical composition and landscape of this region was quite different from those of sites at lower elevations. This craft obtained 21,000 photographs.

LUNAR ORBITER

Five unmanned U.S. spacecraft called Lunar Orbiters were placed in orbit around the Moon. Lunar Orbiter 1 was launched on Aug. 10, 1966. The last in the series, Lunar Orbiter 5, was launched on Aug. 1, 1967. The orbiters obtained 1,950 wide-angle and high-resolution photographs of much of the Moon's surface, including the polar regions and the far side, some from as close as 45.6 km (28.5 miles) above the surface. These pictures enabled the selection of five primary landing sites for the manned Apollo missions and also made possible the construction of lunar maps with as much as 100 times the detail available from Earth-based telescopic observations.

BIOSATELLITE

Biosatellite was a series of three U.S. Earth-orbiting scientific satellites designed to study the biological effects of weightlessness, cosmic radiation, and the absence of Earth's 24-hour day-night rhythm on several plants and animals, ranging from a variety of microorganisms to a primate. Such space laboratories were equipped with telemetering equipment with which to monitor the condition of the specimens. Biosatellite 1 (launched Dec. 14, 1966) was not recovered because it failed to reenter Earth's atmosphere. Biosatellite 2 (launched Sept. 7, 1967) was a complete success. It involved an assortment of biological experiments, including one concerned with mutations induced in the offspring of insects exposed to ionizing radiation in space. The flight of Biosatellite 3 (launched June 29, 1969), scheduled to last 31 days, had to be cut short after 9 days when the trained pigtail monkey that was aboard became ill.

THE 1970S

In the 1970s, several nations launched their first satellites. These have included Japan's Ōsumi, China's China 1, and Great Britain's Prospero. Space science also advanced with the two Viking Mars landers and the International Ultraviolet Explorer.

ŌSUMI

Ōsumi was the first Earth satellite orbited by Japan. It was launched on Feb. 11, 1970, from Kagoshima Space Center on Kyushu and was named for the peninsula on which the centre is located. Ōsumi consisted of the fourth stage of the U.S.-built Lambda-4S launch rocket that was used to place it into an elliptic orbit 400 km (250 miles) above Earth. It was equipped with several sounding devices and weighed 18 kg (40 pounds). Its purpose was to practice using a rocket to put a satellite into orbit. Ōsumi was destroyed upon reentry into Earth's atmosphere in 2003.

CHINA 1

The first Earth satellite orbited by the People's Republic of China was China 1 (also known as Chicom 1 or PRC 1). It was launched on April 24, 1970, from the rocket facility at Shuang Cheng Tsu, and it made China the fifth nation to place a satellite into Earth orbit. Little is known about China 1. It weighed approximately 173 kg (381 pounds) and carried a radio transmitter that broadcast a patriotic anthem.

SHINSEI

The first Japanese scientific satellite was Shinsei, launched on Sept. 28, 1971. Shinsei observed solar radio emissions, cosmic rays, and plasmas in Earth's ionosphere. The 66-kg (145-pound) satellite was launched under the auspices of the Institute of Space and Astronautical

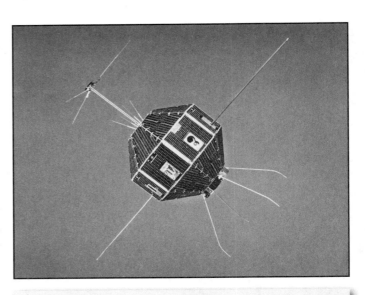

Shinsei, the first Japanese scientific satellite, which was active from 1971 to 1973. It observed solar radio waves, cosmic rays, and ionospheric plasma. Courtesy of JAXA

Science, which was then part of the University of Tokyo. The launch vehicle was a solid-fueled M-4S rocket. *Shinsei* is the Japanese word for "new star." The satellite ceased operations in 1973, but it still remained in orbit.

PROSPERO

The first and only Earth satellite launched by Great Britain was Prospero. It was launched with a British Black Arrow missile on Oct. 28, 1971, from the rocket-testing facility at Woomera, Australia. Prospero weighed 66 kg (145 pounds) and was primarily designed to test the efficiency of various technical innovations, such as a new system of telemetry and solar cell assemblies. It also carried detectors to measure the density of high-speed micrometeoroid particles of space dust in Earth's upper atmosphere.

HELIOS

Helios was a series of two unmanned solar probes developed by West Germany in cooperation with NASA. Helios 1 and Helios 2 were launched by NASA from the John F. Kennedy Space Center in Cape Canaveral, Florida, on Dec. 10, 1974, and Jan. 15, 1976, respectively. Both traveled closer to the sun than any other spacecraft. Helios 1 passed within 45,000,000 km (28,000,000 miles) and Helios 2 within 43,400,000 km. Equipped with special heat-dispersal systems, the probes were able to withstand extremely high temperatures, which reached an estimated 700°F (370°C). Both returned useful data about the sun's magnetic field, the solar wind, the relative strength of cosmic rays, and measurements of meteoroid loss from the solar system.

ARYABHATA

The first Earth satellite built by India was Aryabhata. It was named for a prominent Indian astronomer and mathematician of the 5th century CE. The satellite was assembled at Peenya, near Bangalore, but was launched from within the Soviet Union by a Russian-made rocket on April 19, 1975. Aryabhata weighed 360 kg (794 pounds) and was instrumented to explore conditions in Earth's ionosphere, measure neutrons and gamma rays from the sun, and perform investigations in X-ray astronomy. The scientific instruments had to be switched off during the fifth day in orbit because of a failure in the satellite's electrical power system. Useful information, nevertheless, was collected during the five days of operation.

VIKING

The two U.S. Viking spacecraft were launched by NASA for extended study of the planet Mars. The Viking project was the first planetary exploration mission to transmit pictures from the Martian surface.

Viking 1 and Viking 2, which lifted off on Aug. 20 and Sept. 9, 1975, respectively, each comprised an instrumented orbiter and lander. After completing nearly

A Viking lander, photographed on Earth in its deployed configuration. Beneath the high-gain communication dish antenna (at top) can be seen the lander's two cameras (large domed canisters) and, between them, the partially extended sampling arm (projecting from upper right to lower left). The boom supporting the meteorology sensors extends from the right landing leg. NASA

yearlong journeys, the two spacecraft entered orbits around Mars and spent about a month surveying landing sites. They then released their landers, which touched down on flat lowland sites in the northern hemisphere about 6,500 km (4,000 miles) apart. Viking 1 landed in Chryse Planitia (22.48° N, 47.97° W) on July 20, 1976. Viking 2 landed in Utopia Planitia (47.97° N, 225.74° W) seven weeks later, on September 3.

The Viking orbiters mapped and analyzed large expanses of the Martian surface, observed weather patterns, photographed the planet's two tiny moons—Deimos and Phobos—and relayed signals from the two landers to Earth. The landers measured various properties of the atmosphere and soil of Mars and made colour images of its yellow-brown rocky surface and dusty pinkish sky. Onboard experiments designed to detect evidence of living organisms in soil samples ultimately provided no convincing signs of life on the surface of the planet. Each orbiter and lander functioned long

Viking 1 lander sampling arm (lower centre) *and several trenches that it dug in the sandy soil of Mars's Chryse Planitia, in a photograph made by the lander. The digging and collection tool on the end of the arm was designed to scoop samples of material and deposit them into a chamber in the lander for distribution to the appropriate experiments. The larger jointed boom at the left holds the meteorology sensors.* NASA

past its design lifetime of 90 days after touchdown. The final Viking data was transmitted from Mars (from the Viking 1 lander) in November 1982, and the overall mission ended the following year.

International Ultraviolet Explorer

The International Ultraviolet Explorer (IUE) was an astronomical research satellite built in the 1970s as a cooperative project of NASA, the Science and Engineering Research Council of the United Kingdom, and the European Space Agency (ESA). Launched on Jan. 26, 1978, the IUE functioned until it was shut down on Sept. 30, 1996, and was one of the most productive astronomical instruments in history.

The cylindrical satellite measured 4.2 metres (13.8 feet) in length and weighed 644 kg (1,420 pounds) on launch. In addition to telemetry units, a computer, batteries, and a pair of solar panels for power, the IUE carried a 45-cm (17.7-inch) reflecting telescope equipped with two spectrographs linked to television cameras. The spectrographs covered a range of ultraviolet wavelengths that are prevented from reaching the ground by Earth's atmosphere.

The IUE observed space from geosynchronous orbit and was operated from ground stations at ESA's Villafranca del Castillo Satellite Tracking Station near Madrid (8 hours per day) and NASA's Goddard Space Flight Center in Maryland (16 hours per day). A primary goal in designing the IUE was to provide a satellite observatory that astronomers could use in the same manner as they might use a modern ground-based telescope—by directing observations in real time and inspecting data as it was collected. Among its strengths was the ability to respond quickly to transient targets such as comets and supernovas. Astronomers accessed the satellite through a competitive peer-review process that encouraged collaboration and time-sharing. Over its operational lifetime, thousands of astronomers used the IUE, publishing more than 2,500 scientific papers and collecting more than 100,000 spectroscopic images.

IUE observations contributed to knowledge of planetary atmospheres, the composition of comets, magnetic fields surrounding stars, stellar winds and other aspects of the stellar environment, the composition of planetary nebulae, the existence of hot galactic halos, physical conditions in the nuclei of active galaxies, and the nature of supernovas—most notably the rapidly changing ultraviolet spectrum of Super-

nova 1987A, which became the focus of the IUE's attention only hours after its discovery in the Large Magellanic Cloud in February 1987.

The IUE operated for almost 19 years, far beyond its expected three-year lifetime. Although it suffered minor mechanical and optical problems, it remained fully operational because project engineers were able to adapt its control systems to function under reduced capabilities. By the time it ceased scientific operations, an entire generation of astronomers had enjoyed access to the ultraviolet sky. All of the data collected by the IUE is preserved for use through archives established by the participating agencies.

Seasat

Seasat was an experimental U.S. ocean surveillance satellite launched June 27, 1978. During its 99 days of operation, Seasat orbited Earth 14 times daily and monitored nearly 96 percent of its oceanic surface every 36 hours. Instruments of the unmanned spacecraft, engineered to penetrate cloud cover, provided data on a wide array of oceanographic conditions and features, including wave height, water temperature, currents, winds, icebergs, and coastal characteristics. Although Seasat ceased data transmission on Oct. 9, 1978, as a result of a power failure, it achieved its primary purpose—to demonstrate that much useful information about oceanographic phenomena could be obtained by means of satellite surveillance. Data transmitted by Seasat was made available to scientists representing 23 government and academic organizations. The information was also used to aid the crews of transoceanic vessels and aircraft.

THE 1980S

The satellites of the 1980s were built upon the knowledge gained in previous decades. Venus and Jupiter were explored in greater detail with the Magellan and Galileo probes, respectively. Other satellites, such as the Infrared Astronomical Satellite and the Cosmic Background Explorer, made significant discoveries about our universe.

INFRARED ASTRONOMICAL SATELLITE

The U.S.-British-Netherlands satellite Infrared Astronomical Satellite (IRAS) was the first space observatory to map the entire sky at infrared wavelengths.

After a series of brief studies by infrared instruments carried on sounding rockets had detected about 4,000 celestial sources of infrared radiation, the

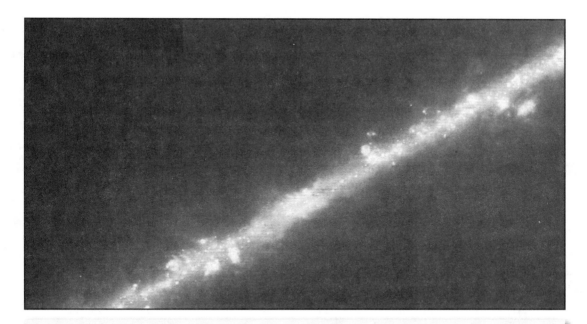

Image of the centre of the Milky Way Galaxy, produced from the observations made by IRAS. The bulge in the band is the centre of the galaxy. The yellow spots and blobs are giant clouds of interstellar gas and dust. The warmest material appears blue and the colder material red. NASA

United States, the United Kingdom, and The Netherlands built IRAS to map the sky at infrared wavelengths of 12, 25, 60, and 100 micrometres (0.004 inches). It was launched on Jan. 25, 1983, on a Delta rocket from Vandenberg Air Force Base in California into a polar orbit at an altitude of 900 km (550 miles).

Its 60-cm- (24-inch-) diameter telescope was cooled by superfluid helium that chilled the structure down to 10 K (-263°C, or -442°F) and the detector to 2 K (-271°C, or -456°F). This was necessary because if the telescope were not cooled down, its own thermal radiation at infrared wavelengths would swamp the much fainter radiation from astronomical objects. During each orbit, IRAS scanned a strip of sky 30 arc minutes wide, and successive strips overlapped by 15 arc minutes to ensure that nothing was missed. On its first day of observations (Feb. 10, 1983), it doubled the number of known infrared sources. Its operational life was defined by the rate at which it consumed its coolant, and it had to be shut down on Nov. 21, 1983, by which time it had noted over a quarter of a million sources. Various preliminary data sets were released between 1984 and 1986, and these were then refined several times to produce the final IRAS Sky Survey Atlas, which was published in 1993.

IRAS proved adept at discovering comets—it is credited as "discoverer" of six of them. It revealed that some young stars have disks of minute, solid dust particles, suggesting that such stars are in the process of forming planetary systems.

IRAS also discovered many previously unknown galaxies that emit most of their energy in the infrared portion of the electromagnetic spectrum (these are known as ultraluminous infrared galaxies), apparently owing to a massive burst of star formation during the merger of two galaxies.

GIOTTO

The European space probe Giotto came within 596 km (370 miles) of the nucleus of Halley's Comet on March 13, 1986.

Giotto was named after the 14th-century Italian painter Giotto di Bondone, whose 1305–06 fresco *The Adoration of the Magi* includes a realistic depiction of a comet as the Star of Bethlehem in the Nativity scene. This image is believed to have been inspired by the artist's observation of the passage of Halley's Comet in 1301.

Giotto was the first solar system exploration mission carried out by the ESA. Its objective was to image and analyze the nucleus of Halley's Comet and to study other characteristics of the comet during its next periodic swing through the inner solar system in 1986. The spacecraft was launched by an Ariane rocket on July 2, 1985. Data from the Soviet Vega spacecraft, which also investigated Halley's Comet, enabled Giotto's controllers to home in on the comet's nucleus. In its approach to the nucleus, Giotto returned a wealth of scientifically valuable data, including vivid images. It determined that the comet was 80 percent

Composite image of the nucleus of Halley's Comet produced from 68 photographs taken on March 13–14, 1986, by the Halley Multicolour Camera onboard the Giotto spacecraft. Courtesy of H.U. Keller; copyright Max-Planck-Institut für Aeronomie, Lindau, Ger., 1986

six years, to carry out a July 10, 1992, close encounter with the nucleus of Comet Grigg-Skjellerup. Giotto, no longer returning data, remained in orbit around the sun.

BURAN

Buran was a Soviet orbiter similar in design and function to the U.S. space shuttle. Designed by the Energia aerospace bureau, it made a single unmanned, fully automated flight in 1988—only to be grounded shortly thereafter due to cost overruns and the collapse of the Soviet Union.

Approval was given in 1976 for the joint development of the Buran and its companion launch vehicle, the heavy-lift Energia booster rocket. Energia could lift 100,000 kg (220,000 pounds) to low Earth orbit, slightly more than the U.S. Saturn V, and it was seen as a dramatic improvement over the previous generation of Soviet launch vehicles. The Energia-Buran system was envisioned as a counter to the U.S. space shuttle program, but its role within the Soviet aerospace industry was never clear. While both scientific and military applications were proposed, delays in its development forced existing missions—such as maintenance and expansion of the Mir space station—to be prolonged, modified, or scrapped entirely.

water, with a dust-covered, uneven surface that was darker than coal. It was also discovered that the comet was composed of primitive material dating from the formation of the solar system.

Fourteen seconds before closest approach, Giotto was hit by a large particle ejected from the comet nucleus. This caused loss of data from the spacecraft and damaged some of its instruments, but others survived with little or no damage. The surviving instruments allowed Giotto, after "hibernating" for more than

Energia's first launch was in 1987, with Polyus, an experimental military space platform, as its payload. On Nov. 15, 1988, the joint Energia-Buran system lifted off from the Baikonur Cosmodrome, without a crew aboard. Buran performed flawlessly, completing two orbits before returning to Earth under remote control. In the 12 years since the project was first proposed, however, political realities had changed, and the costly Energia-Buran program was quietly retired, with funding trickling to a halt in 1993. While the Buran orbiter had a brief operational life, much of the research and technology that went into it would prove useful in the Russian-designed elements of the International Space Station.

MAGELLAN

Magellan was a U.S. spacecraft that, from 1990 to 1994, used radar to create a high-resolution map of the surface of Venus.

The Magellan spacecraft with its attached Inertial Upper Stage booster, in the space shuttle orbiter Atlantis payload bay on April 25, 1989. NASA

The Magellan spacecraft was launched by NASA from the space shuttle on May 4, 1989. The primary spacecraft instrument was a synthetic aperture radar that could obtain images of the Venusian surface through the clouds that permanently surround the planet. Magellan arrived at Venus on Aug. 10, 1990. It was placed in an orbit over the planet's poles so that, as the planet rotated, the spacecraft could obtain images of almost all of its surface. There were three eight-month mapping cycles between 1990 and 1992. Magellan mapped 98 percent of the planet's surface with a resolution of 100

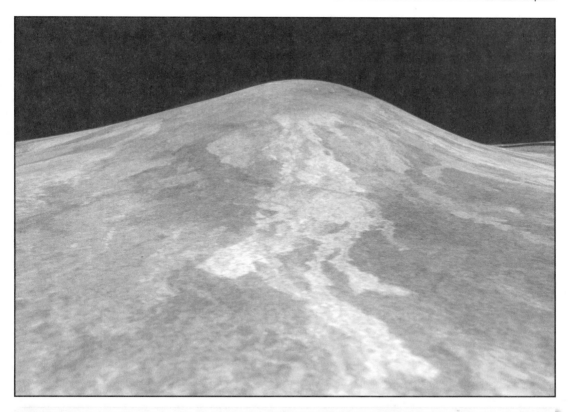

Sif Mons, a shield volcano on Venus, in a low-angle computer-generated view based on radar data from the Magellan spacecraft. Located at the western end of the elevated region Eistla Regio, south of Ishtar Terra, the volcano is about 2 km (1.2 miles) high and has a base 300 km (200 miles) in diameter. In this radar image, lava flows having rougher surfaces appear brighter than smoother flows and are therefore presumably more recent. The length of the flows suggests that the lava was very fluid. The image is somewhat exaggerated in the vertical direction to accentuate the relief. Its simulated colour is based on photos recorded by Soviet Venera landers. NASA/JPL

metres (330 feet) or better. The radar images showed that most of the surface was covered by volcanic materials, that there were few impact craters (suggesting that the surface is relatively young geologically), and that there was no evidence of plate tectonic activity or water erosion—although there was some evidence of wind erosion. The Magellan mission also determined the topography of the Venusian surface, measured the Venusian gravity field, and provided suggestive evidence that the planet's interior differs in major ways from Earth's interior. On Oct. 12, 1994, Magellan was sent to a crash landing on Venus.

HIPPARCOS

Hipparcos (or the High Precision Parallax Collecting Satellite) was launched by the ESA on Aug. 8, 1989. Over the next four years, it measured the distances to more than 100,000 stars by direct triangulation using observations of parallax from either side of Earth's orbit around the sun. It was named after the ancient Greek astronomer Hipparchus, who drew up an accurate star catalog in the 2nd century BCE.

Hipparcos got off to a rocky start when a rocket engine failed to insert the satellite into a circular geostationary orbit, leaving the satellite in a highly elliptical orbit that passed in and out of Earth's radiation belts. It was nevertheless able to operate, and the computer analysis was modified to take the noncircularity of the orbit into account.

As Hipparcos slowly rotated, a "split" Schmidt telescope continuously scanned the sky along two lines of sight 58° apart. The manner in which the light from pairs of point sources impinged upon 2,688 very narrow parallel slits on the focal plane enabled angular separations to be precisely determined. By integrating observations, individual positions were computed to within 0.001 arc second—an improvement of 20 times over terrestrial estimates. The positions of 118,000 selected stars brighter than about 12th magnitude (roughly the observable limit for a 10-cm [4-inch] telescope) were thereby measured. Furthermore, observations taken years apart enabled the proper

motions of these stars across the sky to be estimated.

About 12,000 of the sampled stars proved to have variable brightness. Three-quarters of these stars had not previously been suspected of being variable. Of particular interest were the Cepheid variables, whose period of variation is longer or shorter in direct proportion to their luminosity. Cepheid variables had been used as "standard candles" to measure the distances of nearby galaxies as the first step toward measuring the scale of the universe. Hipparcos refined the basis of this distance scale. For example, observations from Hipparcos showed that M31 (the Andromeda Galaxy)—the dominant member of the Local Group, to which the Milky Way Galaxy belongs—is actually 24 percent farther away from the Milky Way than had been previously believed. The recalibration of the Cepheid period-luminosity relationship also helped to refine the value of Hubble's constant, which measures the rate at which the universe is expanding.

GALILEO

Galileo was a U.S. spacecraft launched to Jupiter for extended orbital study of the planet, its magnetic field, and its moons. Galileo was a follow-up to the much briefer flyby visits of Pioneers 10 and 11 and Voyagers 1 and 2.

Galileo was placed into Earth orbit on Oct. 18, 1989, by the space shuttle *Atlantis*. It then was boosted into a roundabout trajectory toward Jupiter.

Along the way, it benefited from a series of gravity-assist, or slingshot, procedures during flybys of Venus (Feb. 10, 1990) and Earth (Dec. 8, 1990 and Dec. 8, 1992). In addition to sensors to monitor the particles and fields of the solar wind throughout the interplanetary cruise and then within Jupiter's magnetosphere, Galileo was equipped with a scan platform that carried four optical instruments. A high-resolution camera was complemented by a near-infrared mapping spectrometer. This was used for studying the thermal, chemical, and structural nature of Jupiter's moons and the composition of the planet's atmosphere. There was also an ultraviolet spectrometer for measuring gases and aerosols and detecting complex molecules. Lastly, there was an integrated photopolarimeter and radiometer for studying atmospheric composition and thermal energy distribution.

During two passes into the asteroid belt, Galileo flew past the asteroids Gaspra (Oct. 29, 1991) and Ida (Aug. 28, 1993), providing the first close-up views of such bodies. In the process, it discovered a tiny satellite (Dactyl) orbiting Ida. This is the first proof that some asteroids have natural satellites. Galileo also

Asteroid Ida and its satellite, Dactyl, photographed by the Galileo spacecraft on August 28, 1993, from a distance of about 10,870 km (6,750 miles). Ida is about 56 km (35 miles) long and shows the irregular shape and impact craters characteristic of many asteroids. Photo NASA/ JPL/Caltech

furnished a unique perspective of the collision of Comet Shoemaker-Levy 9 with Jupiter as it closed on the planet in July 1994.

On July 13, 1995, Galileo released a 339-kg (747-pound) atmospheric probe on a collision course with Jupiter. Nearly five months later, the probe penetrated the Jovian cloud tops slightly north of the equator. As it slowly descended by parachute through 165 km (about 100 miles) of atmosphere, its instruments reported on ambient temperature, pressure, density, net energy flows, electrical discharges, cloud structure, and chemical composition. After almost 58 minutes, having achieved its mission, the probe's transmitter failed because of the rising temperature. A few hours later, completing a journey of six years and 3.7 billion km (2.3 billion miles), the main Galileo craft entered orbit around Jupiter.

Over the next five years, Galileo flew a series of orbits that produced close encounters with Jupiter's four largest moons—in order of distance from the planet, Io, Europa, Ganymede, and Callisto. Despite the fouling of its high-gain main antenna early in the mission, which frustrated transmission of the lavish imaging coverage that originally had been planned, Galileo yielded revealing close-up portraits of selected features on the moons and dramatic images of Jupiter's cloud layers, auroras, and storm systems, including the long-lived Great Red Spot. One particular highlight was its detailed views of the shattered icy surface of Europa, which showed evidence of a possible subsurface ocean of liquid water. Following completion of Galileo's two-year primary mission, its orbit was adjusted to send it into the intense, potentially damaging radiation near the planet to make a very close pass of Io and scrutinize its active volcanoes in unprecedented detail. After undertaking coordinated studies of Jupiter's magnetic environment with the Cassini spacecraft (launched Oct. 15, 1997) as that craft flew through the Jovian system in December 2000 en route to Saturn, Galileo's activity was curtailed. In September 2003 it was sent plunging into Jupiter's atmosphere to destroy itself in order to prevent its possible contamination of a Jovian moon.

COSMIC BACKGROUND EXPLORER

The U.S. satellite Cosmic Background Explorer (COBE) was placed in Earth orbit in 1989 to map the "smoothness" of the cosmic background radiation field and, by extension, to confirm the validity of the Big Bang theory of the origin of the universe.

In 1964 Arno Penzias and Robert Wilson—working together at Bell Laboratories in New Jersey to calibrate a large microwave antenna prior to using it to monitor radio-frequency emissions from space—discovered the presence of microwave radiation that seemed to permeate the cosmos uniformly. Now known as the cosmic background radiation, this uniform field provided spectacular support for the Big Bang model, which held that the early universe was very hot and the subsequent expansion of the universe would redshift the thermal radiation of the early universe to much longer wavelengths corresponding to much cooler thermal radiation. Penzias and Wilson shared a Nobel Prize for Physics in 1978 for their discovery, but, in order to test the theory of the early history of the universe, cosmologists needed to know whether the radiation field was isotropic (the same in every direction) or anisotropic (having spatial variation).

The 2,200-kg (4,900-pound) COBE satellite was launched by NASA on a Delta rocket on Nov. 18, 1989, to make these fundamental observations. COBE's Far Infrared Absolute Spectrophotometer (FIRAS) was able to measure the spectrum of the radiation field 100 times more accurately than had previously been possible using balloon-borne detectors in Earth's atmosphere. In doing so, it confirmed that the spectrum of the radiation precisely matched what had been predicted by the theory. The Differential Microwave Radiometer (DMR) produced an all-sky survey that showed "wrinkles" indicating that the field was isotropic to 1 part in 100,000. Although this may seem minor, the fact that the Big Bang gave rise to a universe that was slightly denser in some places than in others would have stimulated gravitational separation and, ultimately, the formation of galaxies. COBE's Diffuse Infrared Background

Experiment measured radiation from the formation of the earliest galaxies. After four years of observations, the COBE mission was ended, but the satellite remained in orbit.

In 2006, John Mather, COBE project scientist and FIRAS team leader, and George Smoot, DMR principal investigator, won the Nobel Prize for Physics for the FIRAS and DMR results.

THE 1990S

Large observatories in space, such as the Chandra X-ray Observatory and the Compton Gamma Ray Observatory, were a highlight of the 1990s. There were also notable triumphs in the exploration of the solar system, particularly the first landing on another planet's moon when Huygens landed on Titan.

GREAT OBSERVATORIES

The Great Observatories was a semiformal grouping of four U.S. satellite observatories that had separate origins: the Hubble Space Telescope, the Compton Gamma Ray Observatory, the Chandra X-ray Observatory, and the Spitzer Space Telescope. The grouping came about because the four would provide unprecedented spatial and temporal coverage across much of the electromagnetic spectrum from gamma rays (Compton) through X-rays (Chandra) and visible light (Hubble) to the infrared (Spitzer).

Hubble Space Telescope, photographed by the space shuttle Discovery. NASA

The Compton Gamma Ray Observatory as seen through the space shuttle window during deployment in 1990. NASA

The Great Observatories concept was developed in the mid-1980s by American engineer Charles Pellerin—then Director of Astrophysics at NASA—as a way of providing an umbrella for four large, expensive astrophysics missions that otherwise might be viewed as funding competitors. The idea was that, by spanning the electromagnetic spectrum, the four would offer a comprehensive view of the universe that would help unify previous diverse perceptions. The magnitude of this was compared to hearing an entire symphony rather than just a solo instrument. In 1985, NASA introduced the program to the public in a full-colour booklet, *The Great Observatories for Space Astrophysics*, which was written by American astronomer Martin Harwit and American science writer Valerie Neal.

While linked conceptually, the four missions had vastly different origins and histories and shared little in the way of technology. Although they often joined in coordinated observing campaigns, no effort was made to consolidate their observing programs. Indeed, Spitzer was launched three years after

Mars, with the dark feature Syrtis Major visible near the planet's centre and its north polar cap at the top, imaged by the Hubble Space Telescope, 1997. NASA/JPL/David Crisp and the WFPC2 Science Team

Compton's mission ended. Furthermore, the four were not identical in their ability to observe the heavens. Spitzer's 0.85-metre (2.79-foot) primary mirror is about one-third the size of Hubble's 2.4-metre (7.9-foot) primary and observes at much longer wavelengths than Hubble. Spitzer's angular resolution is thus much coarser than Hubble's. Because gamma rays have the shortest wavelength of all,

NASA's Chandra X-ray Observatory being prepared for testing in a large thermal/vacuum chamber. NASA/CXC/SAO

Workers at the Kennedy Space Center at Cape Canaveral, Fla., inspecting the Spitzer Space Telescope on May 2, 2003. NASA

they cannot be focused by mirrors or lenses in the same way as longer wavelength light. Therefore, Compton's instruments used collimators and other techniques that narrowed the field of view and therefore produced images coarser than those of the other three Great Observatories. Nevertheless, the four provided much sharper views of

the universe than had been available previously. (Radio was not included in the Great Observatories. The long wavelength of radio waves required much larger satellites than were possible at that time, and most radio wavelengths can be detected from the ground.)

As befitted the "Great" aspect of the program, the four spacecraft (listed here in order of launch) were named for American astrophysicists who made landmark contributions in their fields:

- Hubble Space Telescope, named for Edwin Hubble, who discovered the expansion of the universe. It was launched on April 24, 1990, and is planned to operate until 2013.
- Compton Gamma Ray Observatory, named for Arthur H. Compton, a pioneer in gamma-ray studies. It was launched on April 5, 1991, and was deorbited on June 4, 2000.
- Chandra X-ray Observatory, named for Subrahmanyan Chandrasekhar, who defined the upper mass limit for a white dwarf star. It was launched on July 23, 1999.
- Spitzer Space Telescope, named for Lyman Spitzer, who proposed the concept of orbiting observatories in 1946 and campaigned for such a mission from the 1950s through the '70s. It was launched on Aug. 25, 2003, and is planned to operate until 2014.

The success of the Great Observatories has led NASA to outline a pair of Physics of the Cosmos space missions: the International X-ray Observatory, designed to observe X-rays in finer detail than Chandra, and the Laser Interferometer Space Antenna (LISA), designed to seek gravity waves. These two observatories will be complemented by three smaller missions that will study dark energy, cosmic inflation, and black holes.

LASER INTERFEROMETER SPACE ANTENNA (LISA)

LISA, a Beyond Einstein Great Observatory, is scheduled for launch in 2015. Jointly funded by NASA and the European Space Agency (ESA), LISA will consist of three identical spacecraft that will trail the Earth in its orbit by about 50 million km (30 million miles). The spacecraft will contain thrusters for maneuvering them into an equilateral triangle, with sides of approximately 5 million km (3 million miles), putting the triangle's centre along the Earth's orbit. By measuring the transmission of laser signals between the spacecraft (essentially a giant Michelson interferometer in space), scientists hope to detect and accurately measure gravity waves.

ULYSSES

The joint European-U.S. space probe Ulysses was the first spacecraft to fly over the poles of the sun and return data on the solar wind, the sun's magnetic field, and other activity in the sun's atmosphere at high solar latitudes. Understanding such solar activity is important, not only because the sun is an average star that is available for close scrutiny, but also because its activity has important consequences for Earth and its inhabitants. Dependence is increasing on space-based systems that can be affected by what has come to be called "space weather," which is largely driven by solar phenomena.

The Ulysses spacecraft was launched on Oct. 6, 1990, on the space shuttle. It flew by Jupiter in February 1992, and that planet's strong gravity field was used to send the spacecraft out of the ecliptic of the solar system so that it could enter a polar orbit around the sun. Ulysses flew past the south pole of the sun on Sept. 13, 1994, and over the sun's north pole in 1995, at a time of minimum solar activity. It once again flew over the poles in 2000–01, this time during maximum solar activity, and again in 2006–08, during another solar minimum, but with the polarity of the sun's magnetic field reversed from that of the previous minimum.

Among Ulysses's discoveries was that the solar wind speed did not increase continuously toward the poles, but rather at high latitudes leveled off at 750 km (450 miles) per second. The elemental composition of the solar wind was found to differ between fast and slow solar wind streams. In the polar regions, the cosmic-ray flux was not enhanced as much as was expected because the sun's magnetic waves, themselves discovered by Ulysses, scattered the cosmic rays.

COMPTON GAMMA RAY OBSERVATORY

The U.S. Compton Gamma Ray Observatory (CGRO) was one of NASA's "Great Observatories" satellites and was designed to identify the sources of celestial gamma rays. In operation from 1991 to 1999, it was named in honour of Arthur Holly Compton, one of the pioneers of high-energy physics.

In the late 1960s and early 1970s, satellites built to detect nuclear explosions by emitted gamma rays yielded many false reports. It was realized that momentary random "bursts" of gamma radiation wash across the solar system from sources beyond. The primary objective of CGRO was to determine whether these gamma-ray bursts are within the Milky Way Galaxy and of modest energy or are in remote galaxies and of extreme energy.

The 15-metric-ton (16-ton) satellite was deployed by the space shuttle on April 11, 1991. Four instruments spanned the energy range from 20 keV (kiloelectron volts, or thousand electron volts) to the observable limit of 30 GeV (gigaelectron volts, or billion electron volts). A spectrometer measured the gamma rays in the range 0.5–10 MeV (megaelectron volts, or million electron volts) by the optical flash produced by their passage through a scintillation detector. The spectrometer had poor spatial resolution, but, by measuring spectral lines from radioactive decay, it could identify the chemical composition of the gamma-ray sources.

Two planar arrays of scintillation detectors set 1.5 metres (5 feet) apart provided sky images with an angular resolution of 2°, which was excellent for a telescope at this energy. Eight other scintillation detectors (one at each corner of the satellite) that were sensitive from 10 keV to 2 MeV had sufficient temporal resolution to trace the "light curve" of a gamma-ray flash lasting only a few milliseconds. In addition, a telescope incorporating a spark chamber that was an order of magnitude larger and more sensitive than any previously flown mapped the sky at energies of 1–30 MeV.

Through CGRO's instruments, the gamma-ray bursts were seen to be scattered evenly throughout the sky. This proved that the bursts were at cosmological distances, because, if they were from events in the Milky Way Galaxy, they would have appeared predominantly in the galactic plane. This result (when integrated with data from later satellites such as the Italian-Dutch BeppoSAX and with post-burst observations at optical wavelengths) proved that the bursts result from exceedingly violent events in galaxies, some of which are extremely distant.

In addition, CGRO also made significant observations

of supermassive black holes in active galaxies; quasars; blazars (a class of newly discovered quasars that shine brightest in the gamma-ray range); stellar-mass black holes and neutron stars produced when stars destroy themselves in supernova explosions; and supernova remnants.

After one of CGRO's gyroscopes failed in November 1999, NASA decided

Artist's conception of the Yohkoh satellite. Yohkoh was a Japanese solar mission that was launched into Earth orbit in August 1991. **NASA**

to deorbit the satellite, and it reentered the atmosphere on June 4, 2000.

YOHKOH

Yohkoh was a Japanese satellite that provided continuous monitoring of the sun from 1991 to 2001.

Originally designated Solar-A, Yohkoh ("Sunlight") was launched on Aug. 30, 1991, from the Kagoshima Space Center by Japan's Institute of Space and Astronautical Science. It had an international payload of two whole-disk cameras. One was for soft X-rays in the range of 0.25–3 kiloelectron volts (or thousand electron volts; keV). The other for hard X-rays (in the range of 10–100 keV).

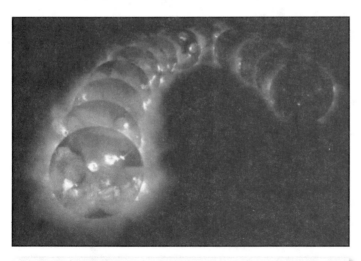

Twelve solar X-ray images obtained by Yohkoh between 1991 and 1995. The solar coronal brightness decreases by a factor of about 100 during a solar cycle as the sun goes from an "active" state (left) to a less active state (right). G.L. Slater and G.A. Linford; S.L. Freeland; the Yohkoh Project

Also included were two spectrometers to study flares and other energetic events during the period of maximum sunspot activity. It lasted far beyond its three-year baseline mission and continued to make observations through the solar minimum and the following renewal of activity, becoming the first spacecraft to observe the sun continuously in X-rays over an entire 11-year solar cycle. Yohkoh's long-term monitoring of how the sun ejects material provided a basis for predicting "space weather" in the vicinity of Earth.

Ironically, Yohkoh's sun-centring system lost its reference during a solar eclipse on Dec. 14, 2001. Because this occurred at a time when Yohkoh was out of communication, the Kagoshima Space Center was unable to intervene before the spacecraft had spun out of control and was lost. Yohkoh burned up during reentry into Earth's atmosphere on Sept. 12, 2005.

CLEMENTINE

The U.S. spacecraft Clementine orbited and observed all regions of the Moon over a two-month period in 1994 for purposes of scientific research and in-space testing of equipment developed primarily for national defense. It carried out geologic mapping in greater detail than any previous lunar mission. Some of its data hinted at the possibility that

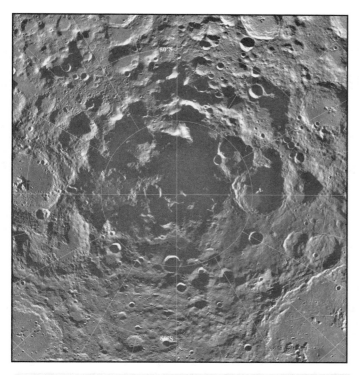

The Moon's south polar region in a mosaic of images made by the U.S. Clementine spacecraft from lunar orbit in 1994. The mosaic, which is centred on the south pole and combines the illumination received over more than two of the Moon's solar days (each about 29 Earth days), reveals the existence of appreciable permanently shadowed areas where water ice could exist. Ice deposits, if they could be mined economically, would constitute an important resource for a future manned lunar outpost. NASA/Goddard Space Flight Center

various sensors and space-craft components intended for ballistic-missile-defense applications. In the process, it returned a vast amount of scientific data. Its suite of remote-sensing instruments allowed imaging at various visible, ultraviolet, and infrared wavelengths (multispectral imaging); detailed topographic mapping by laser altimetry; and charged-particle measurements. Clementine's multispectral imagery was used to create global and regional maps of iron and titanium concentrations in lunar soil, and radar studies employing its radio transmitting equipment suggested that water might be present in the form of ice deposits in permanently shadowed craters near the lunar south pole. Measurements of perturbations in the motion of the spacecraft were used to map the lunar gravity field and its anomalies, called mascons. Clementine was originally intended to observe a near-Earth asteroid, Geographos, after leaving lunar orbit, but a spacecraft malfunction canceled that portion of the mission.

INFRARED SPACE OBSERVATORY

The Infrared Space Observatory (ISO) was a satellite of the ESA that observed

water exists as ice in craters at the Moon's south pole.

Clementine, launched on Jan. 25, 1994, was a joint project of the Department of Defense's Strategic Defense Initiative and NASA. The ingenious mission design used the Moon as a "target" for testing

Infrared Space Observatory. European Space Agency

The Eagle Nebula as seen by the Infrared Space Observatory. ESA/ISO, CAM & The ISOGAL Team

astronomical sources of infrared radiation from 1995 to 1998.

After the spectacular success in 1983 of the short-lived IRAS, which produced the first infrared all-sky survey, the ESA developed ISO to undertake detailed infrared studies of individual objects. ISO was launched by an Ariane 4 rocket on Nov. 17, 1995, and was placed into a highly elliptical 24-hour orbit with a 70,000-km (43,400-mile) apogee. This enabled it to spend most of its time both far from terrestrial thermal interference and in communication with the control centre at Villafranca, Spain. The 60-cm (24-inch) telescope had a camera sensitive to infrared radiation at wavelengths in the range of 2.5–17 micrometres and a photometer and a pair of spectrometers that, between them, extended the range out to 200 micrometres. The container of superfluid helium coolant was designed for a baseline mission of 18 months but survived for 28 months. Observations ceased on April 8, 1998, when the temperature of the telescope's detectors rose above 4 K (-269°C, or -452°F), which made detecting sky sources impractical.

ISO's program included both solar-system and deep-sky objects. The satellite was able to see through the dust that prevents optical astronomers from viewing the centre of the Milky Way Galaxy and found a large number of red giant stars expelling vast quantities of dust. It made significant observations of protoplanetary disks of dust and gas around young stars, suggesting that individual planets can form over periods as brief as 20 million years. It was also discovered that these disks are rich in silicates, the minerals that form the basis of many common types of rock. The satellite also found a large number of brown dwarfs—objects in interstellar space that are too small to become stars but too massive to be considered planets. In its "deep field" survey, ISO found that stars were being formed at a rate several times greater than that inferred from optical observations of the relatively dust-free regions of starburst galaxies in the early universe.

The Near Earth Asteroid Rendezvous (NEAR) Shoemaker spacecraft being assembled. NASA

NEAR EARTH ASTEROID RENDEZVOUS SHOEMAKER

The Near Earth Asteroid Rendezvous (NEAR) Shoemaker was the first spacecraft to orbit and then land on an asteroid (Eros, on Feb. 12, 2001).

The NEAR spacecraft was launched by NASA on Feb. 17, 1996. Its destination, Eros, was the second largest known

A close-up of the asteroid Eros shows dust and fragments of rocky debris inside a large crater. The NEAR Shoemaker spacecraft took the image from about 50 km (30 miles) above the asteroid's surface. NASA/The Johns Hopkins University Applied Physics Laboratory

NEAR flew within 1,200 km (740 miles) of Mathilde, an asteroid in the main belt between Mars and Jupiter. Rendezvous with Eros was originally scheduled for January 1999, but a spacecraft problem delayed the rendezvous for more than a year until Feb. 14, 2000—Valentine's Day, a date chosen because the asteroid was named for the Greek god of love. At the time of rendezvous, the spacecraft was renamed NEAR Shoemaker in honour of geologist Eugene Shoemaker, a pioneer in the study of asteroid impacts, who had died in an automobile accident in 1997.

During a year spent in close orbit (5–56 km [3–35 miles]) around Eros, NEAR Shoemaker studied the object's mass, structure, geology, composition, gravity, and magnetic field. The surface of Eros had both very smooth, flat areas and regions covered with large boulders. NEAR found that Eros, unlike the planets of the solar system, had not undergone extensive melting and differentiation into distinct layers. On Feb. 12, 2001, the spacecraft survived a landing on the surface of Eros, returning images of objects as small as 1 cm (0.4 inch) across during its final descent and sending back scientific data

asteroid in an Earth-crossing orbit. The asteroid is roughly the size of the Caribbean island country of Barbados. The spacecraft's trajectory took it as far from Earth as 330 million km (205 million miles). It then returned to Earth for a gravity assist, passing as close to the planet as 540 km (335 miles). On June 27, 1997,

from the asteroid's surface for a few more days after landing. Communication with NEAR was ended on Feb. 28, 2001. On Dec. 10, 2002, an attempt to reestablish communication with NEAR failed.

MARS GLOBAL SURVEYOR

The U.S. Mars Global Surveyor spacecraft launched to the planet Mars to carry out long-term study from orbit of the entire surface, the atmosphere, and aspects of the interior. High-resolution images returned from the spacecraft indicated that liquid water may have existed on or near the planet's surface in geologically recent times and may still exist in protected areas.

Mars Global Surveyor was launched on Nov. 7, 1996. Weighing just over a ton, it carried a high-resolution camera to make both wide-angle and detailed images of the Martian surface, a thermal emission spectrometer to measure heat emission related to atmospheric phenomena and surface mineral composition, a laser altimeter to map the height of the planet's surface features, and instruments to examine Mars's magnetic properties and help determine its precise shape. It also carried equipment for use in relaying signals to Earth from future Mars lander craft.

After a 10-month journey, Mars Global Surveyor took up a highly elliptical orbit above Mars on Sept. 12, 1997. It employed a technique known as aerobraking—using the drag of the Martian upper atmosphere on the spacecraft to slow it down gradually—to achieve a final 400-km (250-mile) circular polar orbit in which it circled Mars 12 times a day. This orbital configuration allowed the spacecraft to collect data from the entire Martian surface once about every seven days as Mars rotated beneath it. Problems with one of the spacecraft's solar panels prolonged the aerobraking process, delaying the start of its primary mapping mission by more than a year, to March 1999. The spacecraft completed the primary mission in January 2001, after having observed Mars during an entire Martian year (687 Earth days), but it continued in an extended mission phase.

In its first three years of operation, Mars Global Surveyor returned more data about Mars than all prior Mars missions combined. Close-up images of erosional features on cliffs and crater walls that resembled fresh-appearing gullies suggested the possibility of recent water seepage from levels near the surface. In addition, the mission yielded new information about the global magnetic field and interior of early Mars, allowed real-time observation of the changing weather over the Martian seasonal cycle, and revealed that Mars's moon Phobos is covered with a dust layer at least 1 metre (about 3 feet) thick—caused by millions of years of meteoroid impacts. The mission produced many spectacular images and detailed topographic maps of various features on the Martian surface. A high-resolution image of the "face on Mars," an anthropomorphic rock

Mars Global Surveyor in orbit over the Martian volcano Olympus Mons, in an artist's conception. The spacecraft's two long solar-panel wings supply its electrical power. Tipped with drag-flap extensions, the wings also provide most of the surface area used for aerobraking the craft into its circular mapping orbit around Mars. Other prominent features are the orbiter's Earth-directed high-gain dish antenna (at top) and its Mars-facing suite of instruments, which includes a high-resolution camera and a laser altimeter. NASA/JPL/Illustration by Corby Waste

formation photographed from orbit by Viking 1 in 1976, showed it to be clearly of natural origin and not an artifact of an ancient civilization, as had been purported by some.

Contact was lost with Mars Global Surveyor in November 2006. A subsequent investigation determined that the most likely cause was the failure of the spacecraft's batteries.

MARS PATHFINDER

The U.S. spacecraft Mars Pathfinder was launched to Mars to demonstrate a new way to land a spacecraft on the planet's surface and the operation of an independent robotic rover. Developed by NASA as part of a low-cost approach to planetary exploration, Pathfinder successfully completed both demonstrations, gathered scientific data, and returned striking images from Mars. Its observations added to evidence that, at some time in its history, Mars was much more Earth-like than it is today, with a warmer, thicker atmosphere and much more water.

Mars Pathfinder was launched on Dec. 4, 1996, and landed on Mars seven months later, on July 4, 1997. As it descended through the Martian atmosphere, it was slowed successively by a heat shield, a parachute, and rockets. Its impact on the surface was cushioned by an enveloping cluster of air bags, on which it bounced to rest—the first time such a landing technique had been tried. Its landing site in Chryse Planitia (19° N, 33° W), about 850 km (530 miles) southeast of the location of the Viking 1 lander, was at the mouth of a large flood channel.

The spacecraft consisted of two small elements, a 370-kg (816-pound) lander and a 10.6-kg (23-pound) rover. Once on the surface, the lander was formally named the Carl Sagan Memorial Station after the 20th-century American astronomer. The rover was named Sojourner in honour of the 19th-century African American civil rights advocate Sojourner Truth.

The six-wheeled Sojourner carried two black-and-white cameras used for navigating the surface, one colour camera, and an alpha proton X-ray spectrometer for determining the composition of rocks and soil. Its maximum speed was 1 cm per second (2 feet per minute). It rolled down a ramp from the lander on July 5, and over the next 2½ months, explored the vicinity of the landing site, collecting data on soil and several individual rocks. Sojourner relayed 550 images to Earth through the lander.

In addition to communication equipment, the lander carried a stereo camera system that sent back more than 16,500 images. The images portrayed Sojourner at work and provided a vivid view of the Martian surface. They were also used to help direct the rover, to investigate the Martian atmosphere, and to measure wind direction and speed. Pathfinder transmitted its last data on Sept. 27, 1997.

CASSINI-HUYGENS

The U.S.-European space mission to Saturn, Cassini-Huygens, was launched

Artist's conception of the Huygens probe separating from the Cassini orbiter and beginning its descent into the atmosphere of Titan. NASA/JPL

on Oct. 15, 1997. The mission consisted of NASA's Cassini orbiter, which was the first space probe to orbit Saturn, and the ESA's Huygens probe, which landed on Titan, Saturn's largest moon. Cassini was named for French astronomer Gian Domenico Cassini, who discovered four of Saturn's moons and the Cassini division, a large gap in Saturn's rings. Huygens was named for the Dutch scientist Christiaan Huygens, who discovered Saturn's rings and Titan.

Cassini-Huygens was one of the largest interplanetary spacecraft. The Cassini orbiter weighs 2,125 kg (4,685

Jupiter as seen by NASA's Cassini spacecraft on Dec. 7, 2000. NASA/JPL/University of Arizona

pounds) and is 6.7 metres (22 feet) long and 4 metres (13 feet) wide. The instruments on board Cassini include radar to map the cloud-covered surface of Titan and a magnetometer to study Saturn's magnetic field. The disk-shaped Huygens probe was mounted on the side of Cassini. It weighed 349 kg (769 pounds), was 2.7 metres (8.9 feet) across, and carried six instruments designed to study the atmosphere and surface of Titan.

Cassini draws its electric power from the heat generated by the decay of 33 kg (73 pounds) of plutonium, the largest amount of a radioactive element ever launched into space. Protesters at the time claimed that an accident during launch or Cassini's flyby of Earth could expose Earth's population to harmful

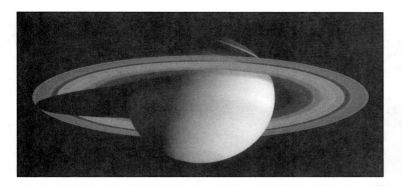

Saturn and its spectacular rings, in a natural-colour composite of 126 images taken by the Cassini spacecraft on October 6, 2004. The view is directed toward Saturn's southern hemisphere, which is tipped toward the sun. Shadows cast by the rings are visible against the bluish northern hemisphere, while the planet's shadow is projected on the rings to the left. NASA/JPL/Space Science Institute

Geysers of ice towering over the south polar region of Enceladus in an image taken by the Cassini spacecraft in 2005. Enceladus is backlit by the sun. NASA/JPL/Space Science Institute

View from the Huygens probe of Titan's surface on Jan. 14, 2005. ESA/NASA/JPL/University of Arizona

plutonium dust and tried to block the launch with a flurry of demonstrations and lawsuits. However, NASA countered that the casks encasing the plutonium were robust enough to survive any mishap. Cassini-Huygens flew past Venus for a gravity assist in April 1998 and did the same with Earth and Jupiter in August 1999 and December 2000, respectively.

Cassini-Huygens entered Saturn orbit on July 1, 2004. Huygens was released on Dec. 25, 2004, and landed on Titan on Jan. 14, 2005—the first landing on any celestial body beyond Mars. Data that Huygens transmitted during its final descent and for 72 minutes from the surface included 350 pictures that showed a shoreline with erosion features and a river delta. In error, one radio channel on the satellite was not turned on, and data were lost concerning the winds Huygens encountered during its descent.

As of 2009, Cassini continued to orbit Saturn and complete many flybys of Saturn's moons. One particularly exciting discovery during its continuing mission was that of geysers of water ice and organic molecules at the south pole of Enceladus, which may indicate an underground ocean and a possible environment for life. Cassini's radar mapped much of

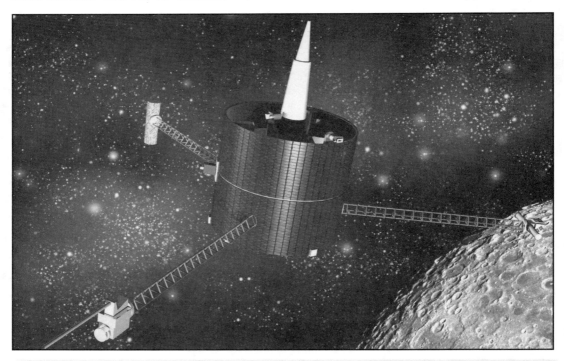

Artist's rendering of the Lunar Prospector spacecraft. NASA/JPL

Titan's surface and found large lakes of liquid methane. Cassini also discovered six new moons and two new rings of Saturn. In July 2008, Cassini's mission was extended to 2010.

LUNAR PROSPECTOR

The U.S. space probe Lunar Prospector studied the chemistry of the Moon's surface. Lunar Prospector was launched on Jan. 6, 1998, by an Athena II rocket from Cape Canaveral, Florida. It entered lunar orbit on January 11 and achieved its final mapping orbit, 100 km (60 miles) high, four days later.

Lunar Prospector carried a neutron spectrometer with which to investigate the composition of the topmost layer of lunar soil, the regolith, within about 1 metre (3 feet) of the surface. Neutrons originating underground because of radioactivity and cosmic ray bombardment interact with the nuclei of elements in the regolith en route to space, where they can be detected from orbit. A neutron loses more energy in an interaction with a light nucleus than with a heavy one, so the observed neutron spectrum can reveal whether light elements—particularly hydrogen—are present in the regolith. Lunar Prospector gave clear indications of hydrogen concentrations at both poles in craters protected from sunlight. This was interpreted as proof of excess hydrogen atoms bound in water ice. Such water would represent a major resource for future interplanetary missions. The water could be electrolyzed into oxygen (valuable as a rocket oxidizer and for crew air) and hydrogen (valuable as a rocket fuel).

Lunar Prospector also mapped the Moon's gravitational field. It discovered three mascons on the near side of the Moon and showed that the Moon could have an iron core about 600 km (400 miles) in diameter. Lunar Prospector was deliberately crashed into a crater in the south polar region on July 31, 1999, by using the last of its propellant. Telescopes on and around Earth watched for spectral signatures unique to water but found none.

DEEP SPACE 1

Deep Space 1 was a U.S. satellite designed to test technologies—including an ion engine, autonomous navigation, and miniature cameras and electronics—for use on future space missions. It was launched on Oct. 24, 1998, and entered an orbit around the sun. On November 11, part of its mission—flybys of an asteroid and a comet—was threatened when the ion engine, which used electrical charges to repel its exhaust fluid, shut down unexpectedly only minutes after it was powered up for a test. Engineers soon determined what the problem was —apparently a common self-contamination effect—and started long-duration burns on November 24. On July 29, 1999, Deep Space 1 flew past asteroid Braille. Although the probe was pointed in the

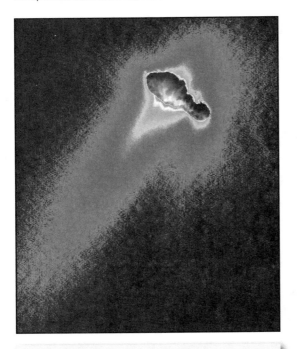

A composite of images taken by the Deep Space 1 spacecraft shows Comet Borrelly's nucleus, dust jets, and coma (its hazy, dusty atmosphere). The nucleus (off-centre) is about 8 km (5 miles) long. The main jet of dust escaping from the nucleus extends to the bottom left. The comet's nucleus is the brightest part of the image. The other features are anywhere from about a tenth to a thousandth as bright as the nucleus. NASA/JPL

successfully navigated its way past Comet Borrelly. This provided excellent views of the ice particles, dust, and gas leaving comets. The spacecraft came within 2,200 km (1,400 miles) of the roughly 8 × 4-km (5 × 2.5-mile) cometary nucleus. It sent back images that showed a rough surface terrain, with rolling plains and deep fractures—a hint that the comet may have formed as a collection of icy and stony rubble rather than as a coherent solid object. From the amount of reflected light, only about 4 percent, the surface appeared to be composed of very dark matter. Cosmochemists proposed that the surface was most likely covered with carbon and substances rich in organic compounds.

NOZOMI

Nozomi (Japanese: "Hope") was an unsuccessful Japanese space probe that was designed to measure the interaction between the solar wind and the Martian upper atmosphere. Nozomi was launched on July 4, 1998, from Kagoshima Space Center, making Japan the third country —after the Soviet Union and the United States—to send a probe to Mars. Nozomi made two flybys of the Moon in August and December 1998 and one flyby of Earth in December 1998 to reshape its trajectory for arrival in a highly elliptical Mars orbit in October 1999. Unfortunately, a defective thrust valve prevented Nozomi from gaining sufficient velocity from the Earth flyby. Two subsequent

wrong direction and did not obtain the high-resolution images scientists wanted, the mission was an overall success.

The primary mission of Deep Space 1 ended on Sept. 18, 1999, with a flyby of asteroid 1992 KD. Nevertheless, it was kept operational, and on Sept. 22, 2001, it

course corrections used more fuel than was originally planned, and Japan's Institute of Space and Astronomical Science, which was in charge of the Nozomi project, had to alter the spacecraft's trajectory for a December 2003 arrival at Mars. When Nozomi came close to Mars, problems with its propulsion system prevented it from being put into orbit, and the craft ended up in an orbit around the Sun.

Mars Polar Lander

The unsuccessful U.S. space probe Mars Polar Lander was designed to study the polar regions of Mars. Its loss in late 1999 badly stung NASA, forcing the agency to reassess its Mars exploration strategy.

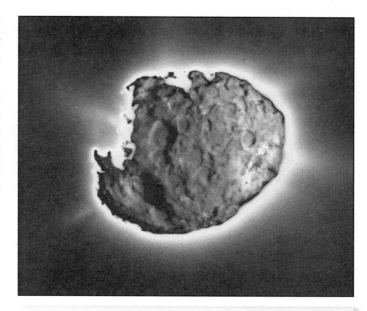

The Stardust spacecraft took this composite image of Comet Wild 2's nucleus during a flyby in 2004. It combines a short-exposure image that resolved surface detail and a long-exposure image that captured jets of gas and dust streaming away into space. NASA/JPL-Caltech

The Mars Polar Lander was launched on Jan. 3, 1999, from Cape Canaveral, Florida. In addition to the main probe, which was to land near the Martian south pole, the mission also carried the Deep Space 2 microprobes. These were to be dropped from the spacecraft during landing and penetrate about 60 cm (2 feet) into the ground. The Mars Polar Lander was to land on Dec. 3, 1999, but contact was lost during atmospheric entry and was never reestablished. In March 2000, investigators reported that, because of a software fault, the onboard computer probably interpreted the jolt from the extension of the landing legs as the landing signal itself and shut off the engines prematurely, when the craft was still more than 40 metres (132 feet) above the surface. The probe then would have crashed to the surface. Following this debacle, NASA restructured its unmanned Mars exploration program and decided to fly simpler missions based on the air-bag lander and rover technology from the highly successful Mars Pathfinder and Sojourner mission of 1997. The exploration of the polar regions of Mars was

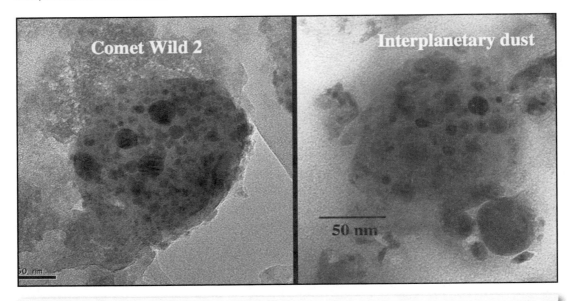

Microscopic components of dust particles collected from the vicinity of Comet Wild 2 (left) and interplanetary space (right) by the Stardust mission and returned to Earth. Both components consist of glass with embedded rounded grains of metal and sulfides. They may be preserved interstellar grains that were incorporated into bodies of the early solar system. NASA

finally accomplished in 2008 by the Phoenix lander.

STARDUST/NExT

The U.S. space probe Stardust/NExT captured and returned dust grains from interplanetary space and from a comet. Stardust was launched on Feb. 7, 1999. It flew past the asteroid Annefrank on Nov. 2, 2002, and the comet Wild 2 on Jan. 2, 2004. A sample capsule containing the dust grains returned to Earth and landed in the Utah desert on Jan. 15, 2006. The main space probe was redesignated NExT (New Exploration of Tempel 1) and

on Feb. 14, 2011, is scheduled to fly by Comet Tempel 1, which was visited by the U.S. space probe Deep Impact in 2005.

The most significant instrument in the Stardust probe is the Stardust Sample Collection Apparatus, consisting of two arrays of aerogel mounted on opposite sides of a common plate. Aerogel is an inert silica-based substance that has the lowest density (2 mg per cubic cm [0.001 ounce per cubic inch]) of any solid. It is designed to capture particles by gently slowing and then stopping them in the aerogel matrix. One side was 3 cm (1 inch) thick for collection of heavier cometary dust particles. The other side was thinner, just 1 cm (0.3 inch), for collection of inter-planetary dust. The collecting area of each plate is 1,000 square cm (155 square inches). The arrays were enclosed during the mission and only exposed during the collecting phases in space. A major find-ing is that the dust in comets is from the early solar system. The dust includes Inti (named for the Inca god of the sun), a calcium-aluminum inclusion mineral common in meteorites. These and other aspects indicate that the dust grains in comets were forged in the hot, young inner solar system and then swept to the outer solar system where they were grad-ually incorporated into the icy material that became comets.

Other instruments on the Stardust probe include the Imaging and Navigation Camera, which is used to help fine-tune the approach to target bodies and then to produce high-resolution images during the flyby. However, two years into the mission, the filter wheel became stuck in the white-light position, thus precluding the collection of images at other wavelengths. Contamination on the outside optical element also causes a slight halo effect on all images. The Cometary and Interstellar Dust Analyzer detects the mass of dust particles after they scatter off a small silver target. The Dust Flux Monitor Instrument is basi-cally a sophisticated large-area microphone that measures particle impact rates and mass distribution. It is built as a shield to protect the spacecraft from fast-moving dust.

Far Ultraviolet Spectroscopic Explorer

The U.S. satellite observatory Far Ultraviolet Spectroscopic Explorer (FUSE) observed the universe in far-ul-traviolet light (wavelengths between 90.5 and 119.5 nanometres, or 3 to 4 feet). FUSE was launched on June 24, 1999. One of its main aims was the study of hydrogen-deuterium (H-D) ratios in intergalactic clouds and interstellar clouds unaffected by star formation in an effort to determine the H-D ratio as it was shortly after the Big Bang. Such a measurement allows the determination of the amount of bary-ons (heavy subatomic particles, which include protons and neutrons) in the universe. In its observations of the Milky Way Galaxy, FUSE discovered molecular nitrogen in the interstellar medium. NASA shut down FUSE on Oct. 18, 2007, after eight years of operation, because it was running out of fuel needed for accu-rate pointing.

Chandra X-ray Observatory

The Chandra X-ray Observatory is one of the NASA fleet of "Great Observatories" satellites and is designed to make high-resolution images of celestial X-ray sources. In operation since 1999, it was named in honour of Subrahmanyan Chandrasekhar, a pioneer of the field of stellar evolution.

Chandra was preceded by two X-ray satellites, the U.S. Einstein Observatory

(1978–81) and the multinational Röntgensatellit (1990–99), which produced surveys across the entire sky of sources emitting at X-ray wavelengths. Chandra (originally known as the Advanced X-Ray Astrophysics Facility) was designed to study individual sources in detail. Following deployment by the space shuttle *Columbia* on July 23, 1999, a solid-rocket stage boosted the observatory into a highly elliptical orbit with an apogee of 140,000 km (87,000 miles) and a perigee of 10,000 km (6,200 miles). This allowed it to remain above the worst interference by Earth's radiation and to provide long periods of uninterrupted study of almost any part of the sky.

In effect, Chandra is to X-ray astronomy what the Hubble Space Telescope is to optical astronomy. It focuses X-rays using four pairs of nested iridium mirrors, with an aperture of 1.2 metres (4 feet) and a focal length of 10 metres (33 feet), and is capable of unprecedented spatial resolution. A transmission grating can be inserted into the optical path before the camera to create a high-resolution spectrum in the energy range of 0.07–10 keV (kiloelectron volts, or thousand electron volts) to investigate the characteristics of sources in this range and measure the temperatures, densities, and composition of the glowing plasma clouds that pervade space.

As a "high-energy" facility, Chandra's primary focus is black holes, supernova remnants, starburst galaxies, and the panoply of exotic objects at the farthest reaches of the universe. Much of a starburst galaxy's luminosity is produced outside of the core region, and Chandra found that these galaxies have a proportionally higher number of intermediate-size black holes that sink to the centre, where they merge with each other. In following up on the Hubble Space Telescope's "deep field" study of the earliest period of galaxy formation, Chandra found evidence that giant black holes were much more active in the past than now, so that after an initial period of extreme activity they appear to grow quiescent. (Supermassive black holes in the cores of galaxies are believed to have been responsible for the quasar phase of a galaxy's life.) By detecting emissions from infalling material, Chandra confirmed that there is a quiescent supermassive black hole at the centre of the Milky Way Galaxy. In addition, Chandra found direct proof of the existence of dark matter in the merging of two galaxy clusters. The hot gas (which is ordinary visible matter) was slowed by the drag effect of one cluster passing through the other, while the mass was not, showing that most of the mass is dark matter. Observations of four other galaxy clusters showed that dark energy, the dominant component of the universe, has not changed greatly over time, suggesting that the universe's expansion might continue indefinitely.

Chandra was later complemented in December 1999 by Europe's X-ray Multi-Mirror Mission (XMM-Newton, named for Sir Isaac Newton), which carries a cluster of coaligned X-ray telescopes, and in July 2005 by the joint U.S.-Japanese Suzaku satellite, which carries five X-ray telescopes. These later facilities have larger mirrors and are sensitive to higher energies, but—because there is an inherent trade-off in mirror design—their larger light-collecting area has been secured at the expense of higher-resolution imaging.

Chandra is managed by the Chandra X-ray Observatory Center, which is located at the Harvard-Smithsonian Center for Astrophysics in Cambridge, Mass.

THE 2000S AND BEYOND

One of the astronomical highlights of the first decade of the 21st century was the Spitzer Space Telescope, the final telescope of NASA's Great Observatories program. In this decade, China and India launched their first satellites (Chang'e 1 and Chandrayaan-1, respectively) beyond Earth orbit. These two probes, along with Japan's Kaguya and the U.S.'s Lunar Reconnaissance Orbiter, were part of a resurgence of interest in the Moon prior to the proposed return of astronauts in 2015. Satellites continued to explore every aspect of the universe, from the strength of gravity on Earth to the soil on Mars to the origin of gamma-ray bursts near the beginning of time.

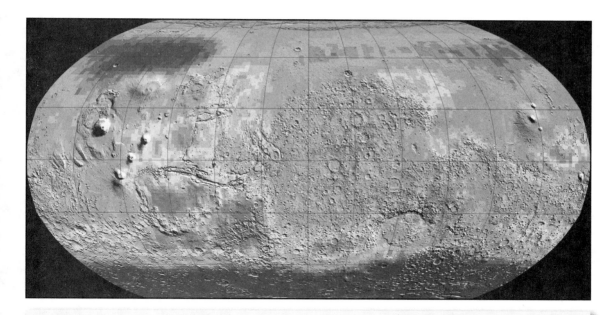

Global map of Mars in epithermal (intermediate-energy) neutrons created from data collected by the 2001 Mars Odyssey spacecraft. Odyssey mapped the location and concentrations of epithermal neutrons knocked off the Martian surface by incoming cosmic rays. Deep blue areas at the high latitudes mark the lowest levels of neutrons, which scientists have interpreted to indicate the presence of high levels of hydrogen. The hydrogen enrichment, in turn, is suggestive of large reservoirs of water ice below the surface. NASA/JPL/University of Arizona/Los Alamos National Laboratories

MARS ODYSSEY

The U.S. 2001 Mars Odyssey spacecraft studied Mars from orbit and served as a communication relay for the Mars Exploration Rovers and Phoenix. It was launched from Cape Canaveral, Florida, on April 7, 2001, and was named after the science fiction film *2001: A Space Odyssey* (1968).

On Oct. 23, 2001, Mars Odyssey entered Mars orbit, where it spent the next several weeks using the Martian atmosphere as a brake to reshape its orbit for a 917-day mapping mission. Visible-light, infrared, and other instruments collected data on the mineral content of the surface and on radiation hazards in the orbital environment. Its instruments also included a neutron detector designed to map the location of intermediate-energy neutrons knocked off the Martian surface by incoming cosmic rays. The maps revealed low neutron levels in the high latitudes, which was interpreted to indicate the presence of high levels of hydrogen. The hydrogen enrichment, in turn, suggested that the polar regions above latitude 60° contain huge sub-surface reservoirs of water ice. The total amount of water detected was estimated to be 10,000 cubic km (2,400 cubic miles), nearly the amount of water in Lake Superior. Odyssey's instruments, however, could not detect water lying at depths much greater than 1 metre (3.3 feet), so the total amount could be vastly larger.

Mars Odyssey discovered caves on a volcano by using its infrared cameras to show that the temperatures of the cave entrances, which appeared as dark circular features—did not change as much as the surrounding surface.

WILKINSON MICROWAVE ANISOTROPY PROBE

The U.S. satellite Wilkinson Microwave Anisotropy Probe (WMAP) was launched on June 30, 2001, and was designed to map irregularities in the CMB.

WMAP uses microwave radio receivers pointed in opposite directions to map the unevenness—anisotropy—of the background. WMAP is named in tribute to American physicist David Todd Wilkinson, who died in 2002 and who was a contributor to both WMAP and WMAP's predecessor, the Cosmic Background Explorer.

WMAP was positioned near the second Lagrangian point (L2), a gravitational balance point between Earth and the sun and 1.5 million km (0.9 million miles) opposite the sun from Earth. The spacecraft moves in a controlled Lissajous pattern around L2 rather than "hovering" there. This orbit isolates the spacecraft from radio emissions from Earth and the Moon without having to place it on a more distant trajectory that would complicate tracking. WMAP was initially planned to operate for two years, but its mission was extended to September 2009.

A full-sky map produced by the Wilkinson Microwave Anisotropy Probe (WMAP) showing cosmic background radiation, a very uniform glow of microwaves emitted by the infant universe more than 13 billion years ago. Colour differences indicate tiny fluctuations in the intensity of the radiation, a result of tiny variations in the density of matter in the early universe. According to inflation theory, these irregularities were the "seeds" that became the galaxies. WMAP's data support the big bang and inflation models. NASA/WMAP Science Team

The spacecraft carries a pair of microwave receivers that observe in nearly opposite directions through 1.4 × 1.6-metre (4.6 × 5.2-foot) reflecting telescopes. These reflectors resemble a home satellite "dish" antenna. The receivers measure the relative brightness of opposite points in the universe at frequencies of 23, 33, 41, 61, and 94 gigahertz and are cooled to eliminate internal noise. The spacecraft is protected from the sun by a shield that is deployed with the solar arrays and is permanently pointed at the sun. The spacecraft rotates so the two reflectors scan a circle across the sky. As WMAP orbits the sun with the L2 point and Earth, the scanned circle precesses so that the entire sky is mapped every six months. When Jupiter passes through the field of view, it is used as a calibration source.

Data from WMAP show temperature variations of 0.0002 K caused by intense sound waves echoing through the dense, early universe, about 380,000 years after the big bang. This anisotropy hints at density variations where matter would later coalesce into the stars and galaxies that form today's universe. WMAP also measured the composition of the early, dense universe, showing that it started at 63 percent dark matter, 12 percent atoms, 15 percent photons, and 10 percent neutrinos. As the universe expanded, the composition shifted to 23 percent dark matter and 4.6 percent atoms. The contribution of photons and neutrinos became negligible, while dark energy—a poorly understood field that accelerates the expansion of the universe—is now 72 percent of the content. Although neutrinos are now a negligible component of the universe, they form their own cosmic background, which was discovered by WMAP. WMAP also showed that the first stars in the universe formed half a billion years after the big bang.

Genesis

The U.S. spacecraft Genesis returned particles of the solar wind to Earth in 2004. Genesis was launched on Aug. 8, 2001. The spacecraft spent 884 days orbiting the first Lagrangian point, 1.5 million km (930,000 miles) from Earth, and capturing 10–20 micrograms of solar wind particles on ultrapure collector arrays. The intent was to determine directly the composition of the sun in order to provide more certain results than those obtained by means of spectral data from telescopic observations. In addition, the collected particles were expected to provide clues to the composition of the original nebula that formed the solar system.

However, the mission ended as a near-total failure when the Genesis spacecraft crashed into the Utah desert on Sept. 8, 2004. Genesis was to have been recovered by helicopter as it parachuted to Earth. The parachutes did not deploy, apparently because, as investigations later suggested, drawings for the craft's gravity sensors were reversed. Despite damage to the sample capsule, the Genesis science team was able to salvage some specimens.

Odin

The Swedish–French–Canadian–Finnish satellite Odin carried a 1.1-metre (43-inch) radio telescope as its main instrument. On Feb. 20, 2002, Odin was launched from Svobodny, Russia. It is named after the ruler of the Norse gods. Using two separate operating modes, the dual-mission craft was designed to study ozone-depletion mechanisms in Earth's atmosphere and to observe radiation from a variety of molecular species in order to elucidate star formation processes in deep space. Odin typically switches from astronomical to atmospheric observations every third day, when it turns to scan Earth's atmosphere. Odin achieved one of its primary goals when it discovered molecular oxygen in a star-forming cloud.

Gravity Recovery and Climate Experiment

Gravity Recovery and Climate Experiment (GRACE) is a U.S.-German Earth-mapping mission consisting of twin spacecraft, GRACE 1 and 2 (nicknamed Tom and Jerry after the cartoon characters). GRACE 1 and 2 were launched on March 17, 2002. By tracking the precise distance between the two spacecraft and their exact altitude and path over Earth, scientists could measure subtle variations in Earth's gravitational field and detect mass movements due to such natural activity as sea level changes, glacial motions, and ice melting. GRACE observed an accelerating loss of ice in Greenland and Antarctica and the change in the gravitational field caused by the Sumatran earthquake responsible for the 2004 Indian Ocean tsunami.

INTERNATIONAL GAMMA-RAY ASTROPHYSICS LABORATORY

The ESA–Russian–U.S. satellite observatory International Gamma-ray Astrophysics Laboratory (Integral) was designed to study gamma rays emitted from astronomical objects. Integral was launched by Russia from the Baikonur Cosmodrome in Kazakhstan on Oct. 17, 2002. It carried a gamma-ray imager and spectrometer to study the most energetic events in the universe. An onboard X-ray monitor and an optical camera were used to provide precise locations of the sources discovered by the gamma-ray instruments. It mapped the sky in the 511 kilo-electron-volt emission line that arises from electron-positron annihilation and found that the emission is concentrated toward the centre of the Milky Way Galaxy. Integral also found a population of faint

gamma-ray bursts that are concentrated toward nearby superclusters.

HAYABUSA

The Japanese spacecraft Hayabusa was launched on May 9, 2003, from the Kagoshima Space Center, landed on the asteroid Itokawa in November 2005, and is scheduled to return to Earth with a landing near Woomera, Austl., in June 2010. Hayabusa ("Falcon") has experienced several technical problems but has returned much valuable scientific data on Itokawa.

Since injection into an interplanetary transfer orbit, the spacecraft has been propelled by four small ion engines. However, a large solar flare, in November 2003, reduced the electrical output of the solar arrays. Thus the thrust that the engines could provide to Hayabusa. This delayed the planned rendezvous from June 2005 to Sept. 12, 2005, when Hayabusa achieved a station-keeping position that effectively was nearly stationary relative to the asteroid. The spacecraft had also suffered thruster leaks and battery and equipment failures that made operations exceptionally challenging.

Instruments on board the Hayabusa include the Asteroid Multi-band Imaging Camera (AMICA), infrared and X-ray spectrometers, and a light detection and ranging (lidar) system. AMICA took images during the inbound approach to identify the asteroid's rotational axis and then mapped Itokawa as it rotated under the spacecraft. The spectrometers assayed the chemical and physical properties of the surface. The lidar system that was used mapped the asteroid's topography. Hayabusa also carried a small robot called MINERVA (MIcro/Nano Experimental Robot Vehicle for Asteroid) that was designed to move across Itokawa's surface by hopping from place to place.

On Nov. 4, 2005, a landing rehearsal was started but then aborted by a bad data signal. In a second rehearsal on November 12, Hayabusa came within 55 metres (180 feet) of Itokawa's surface. However, after Hayabusa ascended from near Itokawa, MINERVA was accidentally released and cast into space. Hayabusa made two landings and ascents from the asteroid surface on November 19 and 25. Neither went as planned, and scientists expect that only a gram or so of asteroid dust was collected by the spacecraft as it fired a tantalum pellet into the surface to stir up dust for capture. Hayabusa is scheduled to return to Earth in 2010. Upon its return, it is designed to eject a capsule covered with a heat shield to protect the asteroid dust within from the heat of reentry into Earth's atmosphere. The dust will be returned to Japan for analysis.

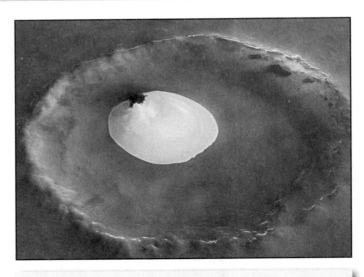

A patch of water ice sheltered on the floor of a crater located on Vastitas Borealis, as seen by Mars Express. ESA/DLR/FU Berlin

MARS EXPRESS

Mars Express was a European spacecraft that mapped the surface of Mars. The ESA's Mars Express was launched on June 2, 2003, from the Baikonur Cosmodrome in Kazakhstan and went into Mars orbit on Dec. 25, 2003. Mars Express carried a colour stereo camera, an energetic neutral atoms analyzer to study how the solar wind erodes the atmosphere, a mineralogical mapping spectrometer, and atmospheric and radio science experiments.

It also carried a British lander, named Beagle 2 after HMS *Beagle*, the ship that carried Charles Darwin on his epoch-making voyage around the world. The

33-kg (73-pound) lander was equipped with a robotic arm to acquire soil and rock samples for X-ray, gamma-ray, and mass spectroscopy analysis. Beagle 2 was to have descended by parachute and air-bag cushions to a site in Isidis Planitia, a sedimentary basin that may have been formed by water. It was released from Mars Express on Dec. 19, 2003, and likely reached the Martian surface on December 25, but no radio contact was ever established.

Meanwhile, the orbiter started return-ing a series of striking images of the Martian surface after settling into its oper-ational orbit on Jan. 28, 2004. Data from onboard instruments indicated the pres-ence of trace quantities of methane over an area containing water ice. This finding was taken as a possible sign of microbial life on Mars. The Mars Express orbiter also

deployed the Mars Advanced Radar for Subsurface and Ionosphere Sounding instrument, which used microwave pulses to search for radar signatures of subsur-face water. An ultraviolet spectrometer was used to discover aurorae on Mars.

MARS EXPLORATION ROVER

The Mars Exploration Rovers are a pair of U.S. robotic vehicles that explored the surface of Mars beginning in January 2004. The mission of each rover was to study the chemical and physical composition of the surface at various locations in order to help determine whether water had ever existed on the planet and to search for other signs that the planet might have supported some form of life.

The twin rovers, Spirit and Oppor-tunity, were launched on June 10 and July 7, 2003, respec-tively. Spirit touched down in Gusev crater on Jan. 3, 2004. Three weeks later, on January 24, Opportunity landed in a crater on the equatorial plain called Meridiani Planum on the opposite side of the planet. Both six-wheeled 18-kg (40-pound) rovers were equipped with cameras and a suite of instruments that included a microscopic imager, a rock-grinding tool, and infrared, gamma-ray, and alpha-particle spectrometers that analyzed

Artist's conception of Mars Exploration Rover. NASA Jet Propulsion Laboratory

The promontory called "Cape Verde" on the rim of Victoria crater as seen by Opportunity, a Mars Exploration Rover. This cliff of layered rocks, about 50 metres (165 feet) away from the rover, is about 6 metres (20 feet) tall. NASA/JPL/Cornell

the rocks, soil, and dust around their landing sites.

The landing sites had been chosen because they appeared to have been affected by water in Mars's past. Both rovers found evidence of past water. Perhaps the most dramatic was Opportunity's discovery of rocks that appeared to have been laid down at the shoreline of an ancient body of salty water.

Each rover was designed for a nominal 90-day mission but functioned so well that operations were extended several times. NASA finally decided to continue operating the two landers until they failed to respond to commands from Earth. In August 2005, Spirit reached the summit of Husband Hill, 82 metres (269 feet) above the Gusev crater plain. Spirit and Opportunity continued to work even after a significant Martian dust storm in 2007 coated their solar cells. Opportunity entered Victoria crater, an impact crater roughly 800 metres (2,600 feet) in diameter and 70 metres (230 feet) deep, on

Sept. 11, 2007, on the riskiest trek yet for either of the rovers. On Aug. 28, 2008, Opportunity emerged from Victoria crater and set off on a 12-km (7-mile) journey to the much larger (22 km [14 miles] in diameter) Endeavour crater. As of 2009, Spirit had traveled more than 7.7 km (4.8 miles) and Opportunity more than 15.8 km (9.8 miles).

Microvariability and Oscillations of Stars (MOST)

Microvariability and Oscillations of Stars (MOST) is a Canadian orbiting telescope that studies physical processes in stars and properties of extrasolar planets. MOST was launched on June 30, 2003, from Plestek, Russia. It is a small spacecraft that weighs about 60 kg (130 pounds) and carries a telescope 15 cm (6 inches) in diameter. It discovered that the planet orbiting HD 209458 has a very low albedo—that is, it does not reflect much of its star's light.

SPITZER SPACE TELESCOPE

The U.S. Spitzer Space Telescope satellite, the fourth and last of the NASA fleet of "Great Observatories" satellites, was designed to study the cosmos at infrared wavelengths. In operation since 2003, the Spitzer observatory is expected to spend at least six years gathering information on the origin, evolution, and composition of planets and smaller bodies, stars, galaxies, and the universe as a whole. It was named in honour of Lyman Spitzer, Jr., an American astrophysicist who, in a seminal 1946 paper, foresaw the power of astronomical telescopes operating in space.

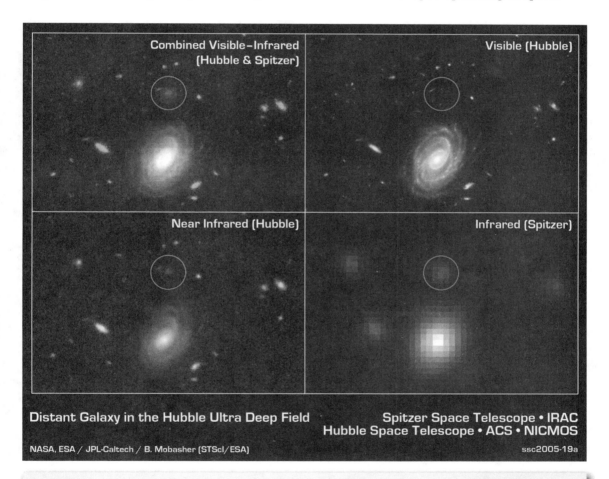

Distant galaxy HUDF-JD2 (enclosed in circles) as seen by the Spitzer Space Telescope in the infrared (bottom right), by the Hubble Space Telescope in visible light (top right) and in the near-infrared (bottom left), and in a combination of the Hubble and Spitzer images (top left). NASA, ESA—JPL-Caltech/B. Mobasher (STScI/ESA)

The Spitzer observatory was launched on Aug. 25, 2003, by a Delta II rocket. To remove the spacecraft from Earth's thermal radiation effects, it was placed into a heliocentric, or solar, orbit with a period of revolution that causes it to drift away from Earth at a rate of 0.1 astronomical unit (15 million km, or 10 million miles) per year. This orbit differs radically from the low Earth orbits used by Spitzer's sister Great Observatories, the Hubble Space Telescope, the Compton Gamma Ray Observatory, and the Chandra X-ray Observatory. The satellite is a little over 4 metres (13 feet) tall and weighs about 900 kg (2,000 pounds). It was built around an all-beryllium 85-cm (33-inch) primary mirror that focuses infrared light on three instruments—a general-purpose near-infrared camera, a spectrograph sensitive to mid-infrared wavelengths, and an imaging photometer taking measurements in three far-infrared bands. Together, the instruments cover a wavelength range of 3 to 180 micrometres. These instruments exceed those flown in previous infrared space observatories by using, as their detectors, large-format arrays with tens of thousands of pixels.

To reduce interference caused by thermal radiation from the environment and from their own components, infrared space observatories require cryogenic cooling, typically to temperatures as low as 5 K (-268°C, or -450°F). Spitzer's solar orbit simplifies the satellite's cryogenic system by taking it away from the heat of Earth. Much of the satellite's own heat is radiated into the cold vacuum of space, so that only a small amount of precious liquid helium cryogen is needed to maintain the telescope at its operating temperature of 5–15 K (-268 to -258°C, or -450 to -432°F).

The most striking results from Spitzer's observations concern extrasolar planets. Since the central stars around which these planets revolve heat the planets to some 1,000 K (700°C, or 1,300°F), the planets themselves produce enough infrared radiation that Spitzer can easily detect them. Spitzer has determined the temperature and the atmospheric structure, composition, and dynamics of several extrasolar planets.

Spitzer has also detected infrared radiation from sources so far away that, in effect, it has looked almost 13 billion years back in time to when the universe was less than 1 billion years old. Spitzer has shown that, even at this early epoch, some galaxies had already grown to the size of present-day galaxies and that they must have formed within a few hundred million years of the Big Bang that gave birth to the universe some 13.7 billion years ago. Such observations can provide stringent tests of theories of the origin and growth of structure in the evolving universe.

Astronomers continued to use all of Spitzer's capabilities until May 2009, when the liquid helium cryogen was depleted. Even without the helium, however, Spitzer's unique thermal design and its solar orbit will ensure that the telescope and instruments reach a new equilibrium at a temperature of only 30 K

(-243°C, or -405°F). At this temperature, Spitzer's shortest-wavelength-detector arrays should continue to operate without any loss of sensitivity. Spitzer's 5.5-year cryogenic mission will thus be followed by a "warm Spitzer" mission that will continue until the satellite is expected to move out of convenient communication range in 2014.

SMALL MISSIONS FOR ADVANCED RESEARCH AND TECHNOLOGY-1

Small Missions for Advanced Research and Technology-1 (SMART-1) was the first lunar probe of the ESA. It was launched on Sept. 27, 2003. The 367-kg (809-pound) probe had a xenon-ion engine that generated only 7 grams (0.2 ounce) of thrust, but it was sufficient to nudge SMART-1 from its first stop—the first Lagrangian point between Earth and the sun—into lunar orbit on Nov. 15, 2003. Once there, SMART-1 scanned the Moon for signs of water in polar craters and mapped the lunar terrain. When its mission ended, it was crashed into the Moon on Sept. 3, 2006, and telescopes on Earth observed the impact in order to study the lunar surface.

ROSETTA

The ESA spacecraft Rosetta is designed to collect samples from a cometary nucleus. Rosetta was launched on March 2, 2004, by an Ariane 5 rocket from Kourou, French Guiana, on a 10-year mission to obtain sample materials from Comet Churyumov-Gerasimenko. The expectation was that, like the Rosetta Stone, the craft would help decode ancient history—in this case, the history of the solar system. Before Rosetta arrives at the comet in 2014, its 654-million-km (406-million-mile) cruise will have involved three gravity-assisted flybys of Earth (in 2005, 2007, and 2009) and one of Mars (in 2007), as well as flybys of the asteroids Steins (in 2008) and Lutetia (in 2010). Rosetta will then deploy a 100-kg (220-pound) probe, Philae (named after a Nile River island on which was found an obelisk that helped in the deciphering of the Rosetta Stone), that will use two harpoons to anchor itself to the surface of the comet. Data will be collected by an alpha-particle spectrometer and a set of six panoramic cameras, and a drill will be used to extract samples for chemical analysis. Rosetta will eventually orbit Comet Churyumov-Gerasimenko.

GRAVITY PROBE B

The U.S. spacecraft Gravity Probe B was launched into polar orbit on April 20, 2004. It was designed to test Einstein's general theory of relativity. Specifically, it would prove or disprove the frame-dragging effect—a very subtle phenomenon in which the rotation of a body (in this case, Earth) slowly drags the space-time continuum with it. It carried four gyroscopes of ultraprecision 4-cm (1.6-inch) polished quartz spheres spinning in liquid helium. The mission of Gravity Probe B ended on Sept. 25, 2005, when the last of its

Artist's impression of the Messenger spacecraft at the planet Mercury. NASA/Johns Hopkins University Applied Physics Laboratory/Carnegie Institution of Washington

liquid helium coolant ran out. Data from Gravity Probe B are still being analyzed, and final results are expected in 2010.

MERCURY SURFACE, SPACE ENVIRONMENT, GEOCHEMISTRY, AND RANGING

The U.S. spacecraft Mercury Surface, Space Environment, Geochemistry, and Ranging—better known as Messenger—was designed to study the surface and environmental properties of Mercury. The name was selected in honour of ancient Greek observers who perceived Mercury in its 88-day orbit of the sun and named it for the messenger of the gods—Hermes, known to the Romans as Mercury.

Messenger was launched on Aug. 3, 2004, by a Delta II rocket from Cape

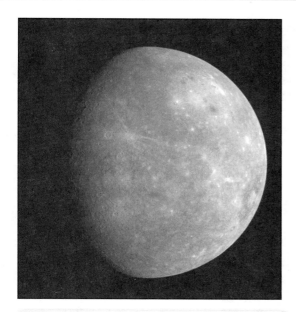

Mercury as seen by the Messenger probe, Jan. 14, 2008. This image shows half of the hemisphere missed by Mariner 10 in 1974–75 and was snapped by Messenger's Wide Angle Camera when it was about 27,000 km (17,000 miles) from the planet. NASA/Johns Hopkins University Applied Physics Laboratory/Carnegie Institution of Washington

Canaveral, Florida. Its first flybys were of Earth, on Aug. 2, 2005, and of Venus, on Oct. 24, 2006, and June 5, 2007. The first two Mercury flybys happened on Jan. 14 and Oct. 6, 2008, and a third was scheduled for Sept. 29, 2009. During the fourth encounter, on March 18, 2011, a thruster maneuver is scheduled to insert Messenger into a 200 × 15,193-km (124 × 9,420-mile) orbit around Mercury. Over the next Mercury year (88 Earth days),

Messenger's orbit is expected to be adjusted by solar tidal effects until two final burns trim the orbit to 200 km high and 12 hours long. The nominal mission then would last one year. Messenger was the first mission to Mercury since the flybys of Mariner 10 in 1974.

Instruments on Messenger include a laser altimeter to profile the surface of Mercury and a dual-imaging system with wide-angle and telephoto optics and filters that span wavelengths from violet light to the near infrared. Other instruments are designed to measure particles in Mercury's magnetosphere, X-rays and gamma rays produced by cosmic ray collisions with the surface, and magnetic fields.

Messenger's first flyby of Mercury revealed that the planet's craters are only half as deep as those of the Moon. Mercury's Caloris impact basin, one of the youngest and largest impact features in the solar system, was found to have evidence of volcanic vents. Messenger also discovered lobate scarps, which are huge cliffs at the top of crustal faults. These structures indicate that the planet, as it cooled early in its history, shrank by a third more than what had previously been believed.

SWIFT

The U.S. satellite observatory Swift was designed to swing into the proper orientation to catch the first few seconds of gamma-ray bursts. It was launched on Nov. 20, 2004. Swift has a gamma-ray telescope that makes the first detection

A camera aboard the Deep Impact spacecraft captured this image of the nucleus of Comet Tempel 1 and the flash of light that was produced by the high-speed collision with an impactor probe. NASA/JPL-Caltech/UMD

Earth. One event, GRB 080319B, detected on March 19, 2008, was so powerful that it could have been observed with the naked eye, even though it was 7.5 billion light-years away. Swift also recorded, for the first time, the precise location of a relatively short-lived gamma-ray burst, GRB 050509B, detected on May 9, 2005. On the basis of its position, this event was shown to have arisen in a relatively nearby galaxy (2.7 billion light-years away), which meant that the luminosity of the event was approximately a thousand times less than those of long-lived gamma-ray bursts detected from distant galaxies. Some astronomers thought that short bursts arose from the merger of compact objects—for example, when two neutron stars coalesced and produced jets of high-energy particles and radiation. Swift also made the first observation of a supernova in the act of exploding.

of a gamma-ray burst. The spacecraft is moved so that the gamma-ray burst can be observed by an X-ray telescope and an ultraviolet-optical telescope. Sixty seconds after the first gamma-rays are observed, the X-ray telescope produces a better position for the burst, and within 200 seconds the ultraviolet-optical telescope produces the most accurate position of all. As of 2009, Swift had detected more than 450 gamma-ray bursts. The most distant of these, GRB 090423, detected on April 23, 2009, exploded about 13 billion light-years from

DEEP IMPACT/EPOXI

In 2005, the U.S. space probe Deep Impact studied cometary structure by shooting a 370-kg (810-pound) mass into the nucleus of the comet Tempel 1 and then analyzing the debris and crater. In 2007, Deep Impact was renamed EPOXI and given two new missions, Extrasolar Planet Observation and Characterization (EPOCh) and Deep Impact Extended Investigation (DIXI).

Deep Impact was launched on Jan. 12, 2005, on a solar orbit to rendezvous with Comet Tempel 1. The spacecraft had two primary sections, the impactor and the flyby spacecraft. The impactor was built around a copper and aluminum mass with a small, guided propulsive stage. The comet's constituents could be identified from the spectral makeup of the vaporized ejecta. The mass and velocity would allow scientists to deduce the structure of the comet from the crater that was formed. The Impactor Targeting Sensor doubled as an experiment camera during final approach. The flyby spacecraft carried two primary instruments, high- and medium-resolution imagers, with the radio system used as a third experiment to measure possible velocity changes due to the comet's mass or atmospheric drag. The imagers had filters to highlight diatomic carbon and cyanogen molecules in the debris. An infrared spectrometer was designed to detect water, carbon monoxide, and carbon dioxide.

The impactor was released on July 3, 2005, and struck the comet 24 hours later at a speed of 37,000 km (23,000 miles) per hour. The flyby spacecraft flew to within 500 km (300 miles) of Comet Tempel 1. The nucleus of Comet Tempel 1 was found to be highly porous. The impact was observed by telescopes on Earth, as well as from satellite observatories such as the Hubble and Spitzer space telescopes.

Avalanches near Mars's north pole in an image taken by the Mars Reconnaissance Orbiter, Feb. 19, 2008. Science@NASA

The primary mission ended in August 2005. The extended mission, for which Deep Impact was renamed EPOXI, has cruise and hibernation phases, the latter to conserve propellant and funding (mainly for operations on Earth). In the DIXI mission, EPOXI was to fly past Comet Boethin, but this comet had not been seen since 1986, so EPOXI was retargeted for Comet Hartley 2, with a flyby scheduled for Oct. 11, 2010. Retargeting was accomplished by trimming the trajectory during EPOXI's flyby of Earth on Dec. 31, 2007. In the EPOCh part of the EPOXI mission, the high-resolution imager is used to observe the transits of three extrasolar planets and to search for other planets around those stars.

SUZAKU

Suzaku (or Astro-EII) is a Japanese-U.S. satellite observatory designed to observe celestial X-ray sources. Suzaku was launched on July 10, 2005, from the Uchinoura Space Center and means "the vermilion bird of the south" in Japanese. It was designed to complement the U.S. Chandra X-ray Observatory and Europe's XMM-Newton spacecraft. Suzaku was equipped with X-ray instruments to study hot plasmas that occur in star clusters, around black holes, and in other regions. Among Suzaku's discoveries was a white dwarf star that emits pulses of X-rays like a pulsar and evidence that cosmic rays are accelerated by magnetic fields in supernova remnants.

MARS RECONNAISSANCE ORBITER

The U.S. satellite Mars Reconnaissance Orbiter (MRO) orbited Mars and studied its geology and climate. The MRO was launched on Aug. 12, 2005, and carried instruments for studying the atmosphere of Mars and for searching for signs of water on the planet. Its shallow subsurface radar was designed to probe the surface to a depth of 1 km (0.6 mile) to detect variations in electrical conductivity that might be caused by water. On March 10, 2006, MRO entered Mars orbit and—to reduce fuel requirements—gradually reached its operational orbit over the next six months by using atmospheric drag for aerobraking. It achieved its final operational orbit on Sept. 12, 2006.

Among the first photos showing the capabilities of the MRO were images of the Viking landers and the Mars Exploration Rovers on the Martian surface. The subsurface radar detected buried glaciers tens of kilometres in extent. The MRO photographed avalanches tumbling down a slope near the north pole and a repeating pattern in sedimentary rock layers that may indicate a regular change in Mars' rotational axis.

VENUS EXPRESS

The ESA spacecraft Venus Express orbited the planet Venus. The design of Venus Express was based on that of the earlier Mars Express. It was launched on

The European Space Agency's Venus Express launch rocket prior to liftoff from the Baikonur Cosmodrome in Kazakhstan. The craft launched on Nov. 9, 2005, and arrived at Venus on April 11, 2006. ESA/Starem—S. Corvaja

Nov. 9, 2005, by a Russian Soyuz-Fregat rocket and went into orbit around Venus on April 11, 2006. Near-infrared and other instruments studied the structure and composition of the middle and upper Venusian atmosphere. Venus Express observed small amounts of water and a large ratio of deuterium to hydrogen, both of which could be explained by the presence of oceans early in Venus's history. Radio waves characteristic of lightning in Venus's clouds were also discovered.

Venus Express completed its originally planned mission on July 24, 2007, but the mission was extended through December 2009. Venus Express also made observations of Earth in the hope of finding spectroscopic signatures of life that could possibly be seen on extrasolar planets.

Artist's rendering of the New Horizons spacecraft approaching Pluto and its three moons. NASA/Johns Hopkins University Applied Physics Laboratory/ Southwest Research Institute

NEW HORIZONS

New Horizons is a U.S. space probe designed to fly by the dwarf planet Pluto and its largest moon, Charon, in July 2015. It would be the first space probe to visit Pluto.

New Horizons was launched from Cape Canaveral, Florida, on Jan. 19, 2006, and flew past Jupiter on Feb. 28, 2007, for a gravitational boost on its long journey.

During the flyby, the spacecraft made observations of Jupiter and its moons and ring system. Detailed images of the ring system did not reveal any embedded moonlets larger than about 1 km (0.6 mile). Astronomers expected to see such objects if the ring system had been formed from the debris of shattered moons. The spacecraft's route took it along the tail of Jupiter's magnetosphere, and New Horizons found pulses of energetic particles flowing along the tail modulated by Jupiter's 10-hour rotation rate. The spacecraft also studied a major volcanic eruption on the moon Io, found global changes in Jupiter's weather, observed the formation of ammonia clouds in the atmosphere, and—for the first time—detected lightning in the planet's polar regions.

After New Horizons flew past Jupiter, it entered a period of electronic hibernation, during which it transmitted information on its status once a week. New Horizons will begin studying the Pluto-Charon system five months before its closest approach. (About 10 weeks before its closest approach, images taken by New Horizons will be of better resolution than those taken with the Hubble Space Telescope.) The onboard instruments were designed to study in detail the atmosphere and the surface of both Pluto and Charon. An extended mission has been proposed, in which the spacecraft, after its flyby of Pluto, would encounter one or two other Kuiper belt objects.

AKARI

The Japanese satellite observatory Akari (also called Astro-F) carried a 67-cm (26-inch) near- to far-infrared telescope. On Feb. 22, 2006, Akari ("Light" in Japanese) was launched from the Uchinoura Space Center in Japan. Its mission was to produce an infrared map of the entire sky that would improve on the map made by IRAS, nearly 25 years earlier. In making its all-sky map, Akari detected three times as many sources as IRAS had. For its operation, the telescope needed to be cooled by liquid helium, and the spacecraft carried a supply that lasted until Aug. 26, 2007.

HINODE

Hinode (or Solar-B,) is a Japanese-U.S.-U.K. satellite that carries a 50-cm (20-inch) solar optical telescope, a 34-cm (13-inch) X-ray telescope, and an extreme ultraviolet imaging spectrometer to observe changes in intense solar magnetic fields that are associated with solar flares and coronal mass ejections. It was launched on Sept. 23, 2006, from Japan's Uchinoura Space Center by an M-5 rocket into a Sun-synchronous Earth orbit that kept the satellite continuously in sunlight. The name is the Japanese word for "sunrise." Hinode discovered magnetic waves in the solar chromosphere that drive the solar wind.

SOLAR TERRESTRIAL RELATIONS OBSERVATORY

Solar Terrestrial Relations Observatory (STEREO) comprises two U.S. spacecraft that were designed to observe the sun from separate locations in space and thus provide a stereoscopic view of solar activities. The STEREO mission was launched on Oct. 25, 2006, by a Delta II rocket from Cape Canaveral, Florida. The Moon's gravity was used to pitch the satellites into different places along Earth's orbit, where one would orbit the sun ahead of Earth and the other following Earth. After two years, the two spacecraft formed a 90° angle with the sun. Each spacecraft carried an ultraviolet telescope, a coronagraph, and other instruments. In addition to making stereoscopic images of the sun, STEREO also detected the heliosheath, the place before the heliopause where solar wind particles decelerate when they encounter the interstellar medium.

TIME HISTORY OF EVENTS AND MACROSCALE INTERACTIONS DURING SUBSTORMS

Time History of Events and Macroscale Interactions During Substorms, commonly known as THEMIS, comprises five U.S. satellites that studied variations in the aurora. The spacecraft were launched by NASA on Feb. 17, 2007. By following elliptical orbits whose orientation shifted relative to Earth, the sun, and Earth's radiation belts, they helped unravel the origin of disturbances in Earth's magnetosphere—called substorms—that cause

Artist's conception of the Phoenix space probe collecting soil samples near the north polar ice cap of Mars. NASA/JPL (NASA photo # PIA07247)

spectacular auroral displays. The mission also involved an array of ground stations. THEMIS found that substorms occur about 120,000 km (75,000 miles) from the surface of Earth when magnetic field lines break and release energy after they reconnect.

AERONOMY OF ICE IN THE MESOSPHERE

The U.S. satellite Aeronomy of Ice in the Mesosphere (AIM) was designed to study noctilucent clouds. AIM was launched on April 25, 2007, by a Pegasus XL rocket that was dropped from an airplane. Noctilucent clouds are faint ice-bearing clouds that form at a height of about 80 km (50 miles) in the layer of the atmosphere called the mesosphere. These clouds were first seen in 1885 and have grown brighter since then. AIM carries experiments designed to study ice particles, chemicals, and interplanetary dust in the upper atmosphere, in order to determine how noctilucent clouds form and why their brightness is changing. AIM is managed by Hampton University, making it the first satellite to be managed by a historically black university.

PHOENIX

The U.S. space probe Phoenix was launched by NASA on Aug. 4, 2007. It landed on May 25, 2008, in the north polar region of Mars. Phoenix's main objective was to collect and analyze soil samples in order to provide answers to the questions of whether the Martian arctic can support life, what the history of water is at the landing site, and how Martian climate is affected by polar dynamics.

Phoenix more closely resembled the Viking landers of the 1970s than the twin rovers Spirit and Opportunity, which landed on Mars in 2004 and roamed their respective landing sites for years. Like the Viking landers, Phoenix was slowed in its descent to the Martian surface by thrusters rather than air bags, which were used by the twin rovers. Phoenix stayed at a single location in the Martian arctic and drilled for rock samples with a 2.35-metre (7.7-foot) robotic arm, the arm placing the samples for analysis in a small self-contained chemistry laboratory. Other instruments included a small weather station and a camera.

One of Phoenix's most important discoveries was the existence of water ice beneath the surface of Mars. Phoenix's robotic arm dug a trench that uncovered a white material that sublimed directly into the atmosphere and was, therefore, water ice. Minerals, such as calcium carbonate, that form in the presence of water were found. The soil at the landing site was found to be alkaline with a pH between 8 and 9. (Earlier missions to Mars had detected acidic soil.) Compounds containing the perchlorate ion (ClO_4^-) were also discovered. Phoenix ceased transmitting to Earth on Nov. 2, 2008, as its solar panels received

less and less light in the gathering Martian winter.

KAGUYA

Japan's second unmanned mission to the Moon, Kaguya, was launched by the Japan Aerospace Exploration Agency (JAXA) in September 2007. Its proper name, Selene (Selenological and Engineering Explorer), was derived from the ancient Greek goddess of the Moon. Kaguya, chosen from among many suggestions received from the Japanese public, is the name of a legendary princess who spurns earthly suitors and returns to the Moon. Kaguya comprised three spacecraft launched together and then deployed once in lunar orbit: the Selene orbiter proper, the Ouna (Very Long Baseline Interferometry) Radio (VRAD) satellite, and the Okina radio relay satellite. (Okina and Ouna are the elderly couple who adopt Kaguya in the legend.)

Kaguya was launched into Earth orbit on Sept. 14, 2007, from the Tanegashima Space Center on Tanegashima Island, Kagoshima prefecture. Following two maneuvers, it entered a translunar injection orbit that lasted almost five days. Before Kaguya entered lunar orbit, Okina and then Ouna were released into elliptical polar orbits. The main 1,984-kg (4,374-pound) spacecraft then entered a circular polar orbit roughly 100 km (60 miles) high that was lowered to 40–70 km (25–43 miles) in early 2009. Operations started on Oct. 20, 2007. Okina and

Ouna were used to ensure continuous communication between Earth and Selene and to help map gravity variations in the Moon as mass variations accelerate and decelerate the craft—causing the frequency of Okina and Ouna's radio signals to shift according to the Doppler effect. Okina impacted on the Moon on Feb. 12, 2009.

The three spacecraft supported 13 scientific experiments. The most notable was a high-definition television (HDTV) camera with wide-angle and telephoto lenses and 2.2-megapixel imagers. Early in the mission, it returned stunning images of Earth rising above the lunar horizon. Selene had three other major scientific imaging experiments that had resolutions as small as 10 metres (33 feet) at the lunar surface and cover wavelengths from the visible through the near-infrared. One of these experiments, the Terrain Camera, had forward- and aft-looking components for stereo imaging. Other instruments measured particles, magnetic fields, and radiation scattered back into space (in order to assay the surface chemistry). Kaguya impacted the lunar surface near the south pole on June 10, 2009.

CHANG'E 1

Chang'e 1 was the first lunar probe launched by the China National Space Administration. The satellite is named for a goddess who, according to Chinese legend, flew from Earth to the Moon. Chang'e 1's mission included stereoscopic imaging of the lunar surface, assaying the chemistry of the surface, and testing technologies that could be used in expanding the Chinese national space program to the Moon. A Long March 3A rocket launched Chang'e 1 into an elliptical Earth orbit on Oct. 24, 2007. An upper stage injected it toward the Moon, and it entered lunar orbit on Nov. 5, 2007. Two days later, it settled into a 200-km (120-mile) near polar orbit. After nearly 16 months in lunar orbit, Chang'e 1 was crashed into the Moon on March 1, 2009.

Chang'e 1 carried eight instruments. A stereo camera and a laser altimeter developed a three-dimensional map of the surface, with the camera tilting forward, down, and aft to illuminate three charge-coupled device (CCD) arrays. The interferometer spectrometer imager used a special lens system to project light onto an array of CCDs. X-ray and gamma-ray spectrometers measured radiation emitted by naturally decaying heavy elements or produced in response to solar radiation. This spectral data helped quantify the amounts of minerals on the lunar surface. The microwave radiometer detected microwaves emitted by the Moon itself and measured the thickness of the debris layer, or regolith, that fills the huge basins called maria. One aim of the regolith investigations was to help scientists understand how much helium-3 may be on the Moon. Helium-3 is a trace element in the solar wind, and the lunar surface has absorbed larger quantities of helium-3 than have been found on Earth. If mining on the moon were ever practical, helium-3 would be a valuable fuel for nuclear fusion power. Other instruments monitored the solar wind and space environment.

Dawn

The U.S. satellite Dawn was designed to orbit the large asteroid Vesta and the dwarf planet Ceres. Dawn was launched Sept. 27, 2007, and flew past Mars on Feb. 17, 2009, to help reshape its trajectory toward the asteroid belt. Dawn is scheduled to arrive at Vesta in September 2011 and to orbit Vesta until June 2012, when it will leave for Ceres. It will arrive at Ceres in February 2015. Vesta and Ceres exemplify planetary evolution from early in the history of the solar system.

Dawn is powered by three xenon-ion thrusters that are based on those of the U.S. Deep Space 1 satellite and that continuously produce 92 millinewtons (0.021 pound) of thrust. The xenon thrusters provide the cruise thrust to get the spacecraft from Earth to Ceres and Vesta, but more powerful hydrazine thrusters will be used for orbital insertion and departure.

The primary science instruments are two identical 1,024 × 1,024-pixel cameras, which were provided by four German agencies and universities. A filter wheel can pass white light or select one of seven bands from the near-ultraviolet to the near-infrared. A series of imaging tests using star fields as targets has demonstrated that the cameras operate as planned.

The Visible and Infrared Mapping Spectrometer, provided by the Italian National Institute of Astrophysics, is based on an earlier instrument that is on board the ESA satellite Rosetta. This spectrometer will analyze minerals and other chemicals on Vesta and Ceres, based on what they absorb from incident sunlight. The Gamma Ray/Neutron Spectrometer developed by the U.S. Los Alamos National Laboratory will also study surface chemistry by measuring radiation from the sun that is scattered back into space. In particular, it will measure abundances of oxygen, silicon, iron, titanium, magnesium, aluminum, and calcium—all key to the makeup of planetary bodies—and of trace elements such as uranium and potassium.

Fermi Gamma-ray Space Telescope

The U.S. Fermi Gamma-ray Space Telescope, launched June 11, 2008, was designed to study gamma-ray-emitting sources. These sources are the universe's most violent and energetic objects and include gamma-ray bursts, pulsars, and high-speed jets emitted by black holes. NASA is the lead agency, with contributions from France, Germany, Japan, Italy, and Sweden.

Fermi carries two instruments, the Large Area Telescope (LAT) and the Gamma-ray Burst Monitor (GBM). These work in the energy range of 10 keV to 300 GeV (10,000 to 300 billion electron volts)

Artist's conception of the Chandrayaan-1 lunar probe.
Doug Ellison

The GBM consists of 12 identical detectors, each containing a thin, single-crystal disk of sodium iodide positioned as a face of an imaginary dodecahedron. An incident gamma ray causes the crystal to emit flashes of light that are counted by light-sensitive tubes. The same flash may be seen by up to half of the detectors but at different intensities, depending on the detector's angle to the source. This process allows the calculation of a gamma-ray burst's location so the spacecraft can then be oriented to point the LAT at the source for detailed observations.

CHANDRAYAAN-1

Chandrayaan-1 was the first lunar space probe of the Indian Space Research Organisation (ISRO). Launched on Oct. 22, 2008, Chandrayaan-1 (*chandrayaan* is Hindi for "moon craft") was designed to map the Moon in infrared, visible, and X-ray light from lunar orbit for two years and to use reflected radiation to prospect for various elements, minerals, and ice.

A Polar Satellite Launch Vehicle launched the 590-kg (1,300-pound) Chandrayaan-1 from the Satish Dhawan Space Centre on Sriharikota Island, Andhra Pradesh state. The probe then was boosted into an elliptical polar orbit around the Moon, 504 km (312 miles) high at its closest to the lunar surface,

and are based on highly successful predecessors that flew on the CGRO in the 1990s. Unlike visible light or even X-rays, gamma rays cannot be focused with lenses or mirrors. Therefore, the main detectors of the LAT are made of silicon and tungsten strips set at right angles to each other. Gamma rays produce electron-positron pairs that then ionize material in the strips. The ionized charge is proportional to the strength of the gamma ray. The arrangement of the strips helps determine the direction of the incoming radiation. Cosmic rays are far more common than gamma rays, but the LAT has materials that interact with cosmic rays only and with both cosmic rays and gamma rays, so cosmic rays can be distinguished and ignored. In its first 95 hours of operation, the LAT produced a map of the entire sky. CGRO took years to produce a similar map.

and 7,502 km (4,651 miles) at its farthest. After checkout, it descended to a 100-km (60-mile) orbit for two years of operations. On Nov. 14, 2008, Chandrayaan-1 launched a small probe that was designed to land on the Moon's surface and study the thin lunar atmosphere, but the probe did not survive the landing.

The principal instruments from ISRO—the Terrain Mapping Camera, the HyperSpectral Imager, and the Lunar Laser Ranging Instrument—can produce images of the lunar surface with high spectral and spatial resolution, including stereo images with a 5-metre (16-foot) resolution and global topographic maps with a resolution of 10 metres (33 feet). The Chandrayaan Imaging X-ray Spectrometer, developed by ISRO and the European Space Agency (ESA), can detect magnesium, aluminum, silicon, calcium, titanium, and iron by the X-rays they emit when exposed to solar flares. This is done in part with the Solar X-ray Monitor, which measures incoming solar radiation.

NASA contributed two instruments, the Moon Mineralogy Mapper (M^3) and the Miniature Synthetic Aperture Radar (Mini-SAR), which will seek ice at the poles. Mini-SAR can broadcast polarized radio waves at the north and south polar regions. Changes in the polarization of the echo measure the dielectric constant and porosity, which are related to the presence of water ice. M^3 will study the lunar surface in wavelengths from the visible to the infrared to isolate signatures of different minerals on the surface.

The ESA has two other planned experiments, an infrared spectrometer and a solar wind monitor. The Bulgarian Aerospace Agency will provide a radiation monitor.

A Chandrayaan-2 mission with a small surface rover is planned for 2011.

OMĪD

Omīd was the first satellite orbited by Iran. Omīd (Farsi for "hope") was launched on Feb. 2, 2009, by a Safīr rocket from a site near Semnan. It was a cube 40 cm (16 inches) on a side and had a mass of 27 kg (60 pounds). Its orbit had a perigee of 245 km (152 miles) and an apogee of 378 km (235 miles). It carried a GPS receiver and an instrument that studied the space environment. Omīd's mission lasted seven weeks.

KEPLER

Kepler is a U.S. satellite designed to detect extrasolar planets by watching— from orbit around the sun—for a slight dimming during transits as these bodies pass in front of their stars. One important objective of Kepler's mission is to determine the percentage of planets that are in or near their stars' habitable zones—that is, the distances from the stars at which liquid water—and therefore possibly life— could exist.

Detecting the transit of an extrasolar planet is very challenging. For example, the diameter of Earth is only 1/109th that of the sun, so that, for an outside observer of the solar system, the passage of Earth would dim the output of the sun by only 0.008 percent. In addition, a planet's orbital plane must be aligned to pass in front of the star. Continuous observation without atmospheric distortion or day-night cycles—not possible from Earth—is essential to the mission. Kepler was placed in a heliocentric orbit with a 372.5-day period so it gradually trails Earth, thus avoiding effects from the magnetosphere that might interfere with the mission. Operations started about a month after its March 6, 2009, launch.

The spacecraft carries a single 95-cm (37-inch) telescope that will stare at the same patch of sky (105 square degrees) for at least four years. The selected region is in the constellation Cygnus, which is out of the plane of the solar system to avoid fogging by light scattered by interplanetary dust or reflected by asteroids. Charge-coupled devices (CCDs) operate as light sensors, rather than as imagers, in order to capture small changes in star brightness during the mission. The scene is out of focus so that each star covers several pixels. If the stars were not defocused, pixels in the CCDs would become saturated and reduce the precision of the observations. Stars fainter than visual magnitude 14 are rejected, but this will leave more than 100,000 stars in the field of view. For a star with an Earth-like planet, scientists estimate that the probability of Kepler's observing that planet eclipsing its star is about 0.47 percent. If Earth-like planets do exist, Kepler is likely to observe them.

HERSCHEL

Herschel is an ESA space telescope, launched on May 14, 2009, that is designed to study infrared radiation from astronomical objects. It is named in honour of German-born British astronomer Sir William Herschel, who discovered infrared radiation in 1800. Herschel was launched on an Ariane 5 rocket that also carried Planck, a satellite that will study the cosmic microwave background.

Herschel is the largest telescope launched into space. Its primary mirror is 3.5 metres (11.5 feet) across. Herschel has three instruments: a high-resolution spectrometer that operates in two bands to observe light with wavelengths from 157 to 212 and from 240 to 625 micrometres (1 micrometre = 10^{-6} metre), a combined camera-spectrometer that sees infrared radiation between 55 to 210 micrometres, and another combined camera-spectrometer that can observe three wavelength bands at 250, 350, and 500 micrometres. Galaxies forming in the early universe, the interstellar medium in other galaxies, and nascent planetary systems are some of the objects that Herschel is particularly well suited to study.

Like WMAP, Herschel was positioned about two months after launch near the second Lagrangian point (L2), a gravitational balance point between Earth and the sun and 1.5 million km (0.9 million miles) opposite the sun from Earth. The spacecraft will move in a controlled Lissajous pattern around L2 that keeps it at an average distance of 800,000 km (500,000 miles) from L2. This isolates the spacecraft from infrared emissions from Earth and the Moon. The spacecraft will be shielded from the sun by a sunshade. Herschel's mission will last about three and a half years, at which time observations will become impossible because it will run out of its supply of liquid helium coolant. The coolant minimizes the thermal interference that the instruments receive from the rest of the telescope.

PLANCK

Launched on May 14, 2009, Planck is an ESA satellite that was designed to measure the cosmic microwave background (CMB)—the residual radiation left over from the big bang—at a much greater sensitivity and resolution than was provided by the U.S. Wilkinson Microwave Anisotropy Probe (WMAP). It is named in honour of German physicist Max Planck, a pioneer in quantum physics and in the theory of blackbody radiation. The satellite was launched on an Ariane 5 rocket that also carried Herschel, an infrared space telescope.

Like Herschel, Planck—in position near L2—will move in a controlled Lissajous pattern around L2, rather than "hovering" there. This isolates the spacecraft from radio emissions from Earth and the Moon without having to place it on a more distant trajectory that would complicate tracking. The spacecraft spins once per minute and shifts its rotational axis every 15 minutes to shield itself from the sun. Two complete scans of the sky will be made in the planned 15-month mission.

Planck's instruments can cover radio emissions from 30 to 857 gigahertz and are able to measure temperature fluctuations in the CMB with a precision of about 2 parts per million at an angular resolution of about 10 minutes of arc. Temperature fluctuations in turn indicate density fluctuations from which the first

Artist's conception of the Planck satellite, showing the path that microwaves follow through the satellite. AOES Medialab—ESA

Planck satellite. ESA

galaxies formed. The high angular resolution and the polarization of the instruments allow Planck to observe gravitational lensing in the CMB and to measure the Sunyaev-Zeldovich effect, a distortion of the CMB caused by galaxy clusters.

LUNAR RECONNAISSANCE ORBITER

The U.S. Lunar Reconnaissance Orbiter (LRO) spacecraft was designed to map the surface of the Moon and to help select ideal sites for unmanned and eventually manned lunar landers. It launched on June 17, 2009, from Cape Canaveral, Florida, on an Atlas rocket that will also launch the Lunar Crater Observation and Sensing Satellite, which is designed to seek water at the lunar south pole. The transfer from Earth orbit to lunar orbit took four days. LRO was placed in an elliptical, polar commissioning orbit for up to 60 days and then used onboard thrusters to lower its orbit to a height of 50 km (30 miles) for one year of operations. An extended five-year mission at a higher altitude orbit may be added.

NASA has given highest priority to characterization of the radiation environment in lunar orbit since this is a major health consideration for space crews on future missions of the manned Constellation program. To that end, the Cosmic Ray Telescope for the Effects of Radiation will carry two special silicon and plastic detectors, one aimed toward the lunar surface and the other spaceward. These detectors were designed to absorb radiation in the same way as human bone and muscle tissue.

The Lunar Reconnaissance Orbiter Camera will map most of the surface (including regions covered by Apollo and other missions) in order to determine crater formation rates and hazards, as well as smaller features that may be hazardous to spacecraft landing on the Moon. Sites suitable for in situ resource utilization have the highest importance. Data from the Lunar Orbiter Laser Altimeter will be used to produce topographic maps with a vertical accuracy of 1 metre (3 feet).

Three instruments will be used in the search for water for future lunar bases. The Lyman-Alpha Mapper looks for the ultraviolet glow specific to hydrogen in permanently shadowed regions. The Diviner Lunar Radiometer charts how surface materials heat and cool during lunar day and night, and the Lunar Exploration Neutron Detector measures neutrons scattered back to space by hydrogen nuclei.

JAMES WEBB SPACE TELESCOPE

The James Webb Space Telescope (JWST) is a U.S.-ESA-Canadian satellite observatory proposed as the successor to the Hubble Space Telescope (HST) and is scheduled for launch by an Ariane 5 rocket in 2014. The JWST will have a mirror 6.5 metres (21.3 feet) in diameter, seven times larger than that of the HST, and will orbit the sun in a Lissajous orbit around the second Lagrangian point—about 1.5 million km (930,000 miles) from Earth on the planet's night side. The telescope was designed primarily to observe light in the infrared in order to observe sources such as the first galaxies and protostars that radiate at those wavelengths. Since infrared satellite observatories must be protected from thermal radiation, a sunshield about 150 square metres (1,600 square feet) in area will be deployed to protect the telescope. Since there is no rocket wide enough to hold the JWST, both the sunshield and the mirror will be launched folded up and will unfold when the telescope reaches its proper orbit.

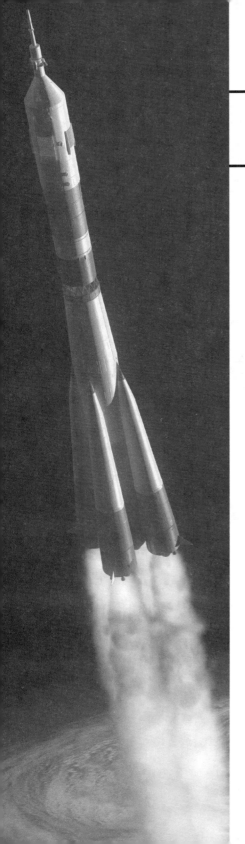

CHAPTER 4

SCIENCE IN SPACE

In the decades following the first Sputnik and Explorer satellites, the ability to put their instruments into outer space gave scientists the opportunity to acquire new information about the natural universe—information that in many cases would have been unobtainable any other way. Space science added a new dimension to the quest for knowledge, complementing and extending what had been gained from centuries of theoretical speculations and ground-based observations.

After Gagarin's 1961 flight, space missions involving human crews carried out a range of significant research, from on-site geologic investigations on the Moon to a wide variety of observations and experiments aboard orbiting spacecraft. In particular, the presence in space of humans as experimenters and, in some cases, as experimental subjects facilitated studies in biomedicine and materials science. Nevertheless, most space science was, and continues to be, performed by robotic spacecraft in Earth orbit or on missions to various bodies in the solar system. In general, such missions are far less expensive than those involving humans and can carry sophisticated automated instruments to gather a wide variety of relevant data.

In addition to the United States and the Soviet Union, several other countries achieved the capability of developing and operating scientific spacecraft and carrying out their own space science missions. Many other countries became involved in space activities through the participation of their

WEIGHTLESSNESS

Objects in space are said to be weightless. (The term zero gravity is also used.) Weightlessness is what objects experience when they are in free fall. A body is in free fall if it moves freely in any manner in the presence of gravity. The planets, for example, are in free fall in the gravitational field of the sun. Newton's laws show that a body in free fall follows an orbit such that the sum of the gravitational and inertial forces equals zero. This explains why an astronaut in a spacecraft orbiting Earth experiences a condition of weightlessness. Earth's gravitational pull is equal and opposite to the inertial—in this case, centrifugal—force because of the motion of the vehicle. Gravitational forces are never uniform, and therefore only the centre of mass is in free fall. All other points of a body are subject to tidal forces because they move in a slightly different gravitational field. Earth is in free fall, but the pull of the Moon is not the same at Earth's surface as at its centre. The rise and fall of ocean tides occur because the oceans are not in perfect free fall.

In unmanned spaceflight, scientists have investigated the impact of weightlessness on cell metabolism, circadian rhythms, spiderweb formation, and root growth and orientation in plants. Experiments have also been conducted to determine the influence of gravity and the effects of its absence in physical, chemical, and metallurgical processes. The mixing of alloys and chemical reagents without the stratification that occurs on Earth, the mixing of gases and metals to produce foam metals of unusual properties, and the formation of large perfect crystals illustrate a few of the possibilities of zero-gravity technology.

scientists in specific missions. Bilateral or multilateral cooperation between various countries in carrying out space science missions grew to be the usual way of proceeding.

Scientific research in space can be divided into five general areas: (1) solar and space physics, including study of the magnetic and electromagnetic fields in space and the various energetic particles also present, with particular attention to their interactions with Earth, (2) exploration of the planets, moons, asteroids, comets, meteoroids, and dust in the solar system, (3) study of the origin, evolution, and current state of the varied objects in the universe beyond the solar system, (4) research on nonliving and living materials, including humans, in the very low gravity levels of the space environment, and (5) study of Earth from space.

SOLAR AND SPACE PHYSICS

The first scientific discovery made with instruments orbiting in space was the existence of the Van Allen radiation belts, by Explorer 1 and other spacecraft in 1958. Subsequent space missions investigated Earth's magnetosphere, the surrounding region of space in which the planet's magnetic field exerts a controlling effect. Of particular and ongoing interest has been the interaction of the flux of charged particles emitted by the sun, called the solar wind, with the magnetosphere. Early space science investigations showed, for example, that luminous atmospheric displays known as auroras are the result of this interaction, and scientists came to understand that the magnetosphere is an extremely complex phenomenon.

The focus of inquiry in space physics was later extended to understanding the characteristics of the sun—both as an average star and as the primary source of energy for the rest of the solar system—and to exploring space between the sun and Earth and other planets. The magnetospheres of other planets, particularly Jupiter with its strong magnetic field, also came under study. Scientists sought a better understanding of the internal dynamics and overall behaviour of the sun, the underlying causes of variations in solar activity, and the way in which those variations propagate through space and ultimately affect Earth's magnetosphere and upper atmosphere. The concept of space weather was advanced to describe the changing conditions in the sun-Earth region of the solar system. Variations in space weather can cause geomagnetic storms that interfere with the operation of satellites and even systems on the ground such as power grids.

To carry out the investigations required for addressing these scientific questions, the United States, Europe, the Soviet Union, and Japan developed a variety of

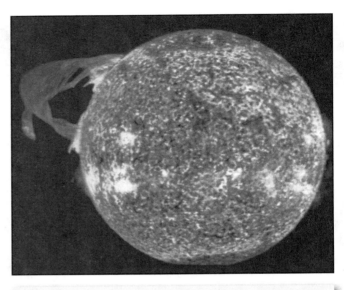

A spectacular flare on the sun, photographed in extreme ultraviolet light on Dec. 19, 1973, by the third astronaut crew aboard the U.S. space station Skylab. NASA

space missions, often in a coordinated fashion. In the United States, early studies of the sun were undertaken by a series of Orbiting Solar Observatory satellites (launched 1962–75) and the astronaut crews of the Skylab space station in 1973–74, using that facility's Apollo Telescope Mount. These were followed by the Solar Maximum Mission satellite (launched 1980). The ESA developed the Ulysses mission (1990) to explore the sun's polar regions. Solar-terrestrial interactions were the focus of many of the Explorer series of spacecraft (1958–75) and the Orbiting Geophysical Observatory satellites (1964–69). In the 1980s, NASA, the ESA, and Japan's Institute of Space and Astronautical Science undertook a cooperative venture

SOLAR AND HELIOSPHERIC OBSERVATORY

The Solar and Heliospheric Observatory (SOHO) satellite, managed jointly by the ESA and NASA, is equipped with a battery of novel instruments to study the sun.

SOHO was launched by NASA on an Atlas rocket on Dec. 2, 1995. In order to provide continuous observations, it was maneuvered to orbit the first Lagrangian point (L1)—a point some 1.5 million km (900,000 miles) from Earth toward the sun where the gravitational attraction of Earth and the sun combine in such a way that a small body remains approximately at rest relative to both. SOHO's suite of 11 instruments included three to conduct helioseismological investigations of the structure and dynamics of the solar interior, from the core out to the surface; five to study the means by which the corona is heated; and three to study where and how the solar wind is accelerated away from the sun. The goal was to start observations near the minimum of the solar cycle in order to monitor the buildup to the next maximum.

In monitoring the corona, SOHO caught a surprisingly large number of comets (one every few weeks) diving into the sun. More than 1,600 comets have been found in SOHO images, making it the top "discoverer" of comets of all time.

After an incorrect command on June 25, 1998, caused SOHO to spin out of control, the spacecraft was slowly nursed back to life. In December 2000—when the sun was at its most active—SOHO undertook solar wind studies in coordination with Ulysses, which was then flying high in solar orbit over the sun's southern polar region, in order to construct three-dimensional maps.

Among its many achievements, SOHO found that sunspots are shallow and that a hurricane-like structure at their base keeps them stable. Helioseismological data were used to make images of the far side of the sun. Sunspot activity on the far side of the sun could also be monitored by observing how the ultraviolet light emitted by the sunspots interacts with nearby hydrogen gas. SOHO also determined that the solar wind flows outward by waves in vibrating magnetic field lines.

Artist's conception of the Solar and Heliospheric Observatory (SOHO) spacecraft. ESA

to develop a comprehensive series of space missions—named the International Solar-Terrestrial Physics Program—that would be aimed at full investigation of the sun-Earth connection. This program was responsible for the U.S. Wind (1994) and Polar (1996) spacecraft, the European Solar and Heliospheric Observatory (SOHO; 1995) and Cluster (2000) missions, and the Japanese Geotail satellite (1992).

SOLAR SYSTEM EXPLORATION

From the start of space activity, scientists recognized that spacecraft could gather scientifically valuable data about the various planets, moons, and smaller bodies in the solar system. Both the

Developed to explore polar regions of the Sun, the Ulysses spacecraft unexpectedly crossed the tail of Comet Hyakutake in 1996, an event immortalized in this artist's conception. ESA, David A. Hardy

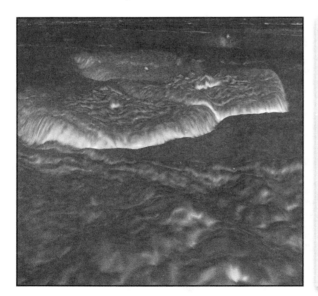

Merged pancake domes on the eastern edge of the Alpha Regio highland area of Venus, in an oblique view generated by computer from radar data gathered by the Magellan spacecraft. The volcanic features, each about 25 km (15 miles) in diameter and about 750 metres (0.5 mile) high, are thought to have been formed from the extrusion of extremely viscous lava onto the surface. The vertical scale of the image is exaggerated to bring out topological detail. Photo NASA/JPL/Caltech

United States and the U.S.S.R. attempted to send robotic missions to the Moon in the late 1950s with the Pioneer and Luna missions.

In the 1960s, the United States became the first country to send a spacecraft to the vicinity of other planets with the Mariner missions. Among significant accomplishments of planetary missions in succeeding decades were the U.S. Viking landings on Mars in 1976 and the Soviet Venera explorations of the atmosphere and surface of Venus from the mid-1960s to the mid-1980s. In the years since, the United States has continued an active program of solar system exploration, as did the Soviet Union until its dissolution in 1991. Japan launched missions to the Moon, Mars, and Halley's Comet. After the turn of the 21st century, Europe sent missions to the Moon and Mars and an orbiter-lander to a comet.

Early on, scientists planned to conduct solar system exploration in three stages: initial reconnaissance from spacecraft flying by a planet, comet, or asteroid; detailed surveillance from a spacecraft orbiting the object; and on-site research after landing on the object or, in the case of the giant gas planets, by sending a probe into its atmosphere. By the start of the 21st century, all three of those stages had been carried out for the Moon, Venus, Mars, Jupiter, and a near-Earth asteroid. Several Soviet and U.S. robotic spacecraft have landed on Venus and the Moon, and the United States has landed spacecraft on the surface of Mars. Among the rocky inner planets, only Mercury has remained relatively neglected, with the exception of the U.S. Mariner 10 probe, which made three flybys in 1974–75.

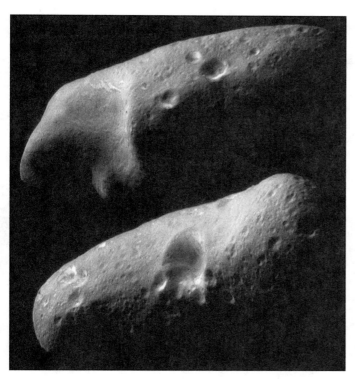

Opposite hemispheres of the asteroid Eros, shown in a pair of mosaics made from images taken by the U.S. Near Earth Asteroid Rendezvous (NEAR) Shoemaker spacecraft on February 23, 2000, from orbit around the asteroid. Johns Hopkins University/Applied Physics Laboratory/NASA

As of 2009, the exploration of the other giant gas planets—Saturn, Uranus, and Neptune—remained at the first or second stage. The Pioneer and Voyager missions—followed later by the U.S. Cassini spacecraft and European Huygens probe—were all launched with the intent of exploring these planets further. Therefore, every significant body in the solar system except the dwarf planet Pluto and its largest moon, Charon, has been visited at least once by a spacecraft. However, the U.S. New Horizons spacecraft will arrive at Pluto in 2015.

These exploratory missions sought information on the origin and evolution of the solar system and on the various objects that it comprises, including chemical composition; surface topography; data on magnetic fields, atmospheres, and volcanic activity; and—particularly for Mars and perhaps eventually for Jupiter's moon Europa and Saturn's moon Titan—evidence of water or other liquids in the present or past and perhaps even of extraterrestrial life in some form.

What has been learned to date confirms that Earth and the rest of the solar system formed at about the same time from the same cloud of gas and dust surrounding the sun. The four outer giant gas planets are roughly similar in size and chemical composition, but each has a set of moons that differ widely in their characteristics. In some ways, they and their satellites resemble miniature solar systems. The four rocky inner planets had a common origin but followed very different evolutionary paths and today have very different surfaces, atmospheres, and internal activity. Ongoing comparative study of the evolution of Venus, Mars,

VOYAGER

Voyager 1 and 2 were a pair of robotic U.S. interplanetary probes launched to observe and to transmit information to Earth about the giant planets of the outer solar system and the farthest reaches of the sun's sphere of influence.

Voyager 2 was launched first, on Aug. 20, 1977; Voyager 1 followed some two weeks later, on September 5. The twin-spacecraft mission took advantage of a rare orbital positioning of Jupiter, Saturn, Uranus, and Neptune that permitted a multiplanet tour with relatively low fuel requirements and flight time. The alignment allowed each spacecraft, following a particular trajectory, to use its fall into a planet's gravitational field to increase its velocity and alter its direction enough to fling it to its next destination. Using this gravity-assist, or slingshot, technique, Voyager 1 swung by Jupiter on March 5, 1979, and then headed for Saturn, which it reached on Nov. 12, 1980. It then adopted a trajectory to take it out of the solar system. Voyager 2 traveled more slowly and on a longer trajectory than its partner. It sped by Jupiter on July 9, 1979, and passed Saturn on Aug. 25, 1981. It then flew past Uranus on Jan. 24, 1986, and Neptune on Aug. 25, 1989, before being hurled toward interstellar space. Voyager 2 is the only spacecraft to have visited Uranus and Neptune.

Data and photographs collected by the Voyagers' cameras, magnetometers, and other instruments revealed previously unknown details about each of the giant planets and their moons. For example, close-up images from the spacecraft charted Jupiter's complex cloud forms, winds, and storm systems and discovered volcanic activity on its moon Io. Saturn's rings were found to have enigmatic braids, kinks, and spokes and are accompanied by myriad "ringlets." At Uranus Voyager 2 discovered a substantial magnetic field around the planet and 10 additional moons. Its flyby of Neptune uncovered three complete rings and six hitherto unknown moons as well as a planetary magnetic field and complex, widely distributed auroras.

On Feb. 17, 1998, Voyager 1 overtook the space probe Pioneer 10 to become the most distant human-made object in space. By 2004, both Voyagers were well beyond the orbit of Pluto. They were expected to remain operable through the first or second decade of the 21st century, periodically transmitting data on the heliopause, the outer limit of the sun's magnetic field and solar wind. Each craft carried a greeting to any form of extraterrestrial intelligence that might eventually find it. A gold-plated copper phonograph record—accompanied by a cartridge, needle, and symbolic instructions for playing it—contained images and sounds chosen to depict the diversity of life and culture on Earth.

and Earth could provide important insights into Earth's future and its continued ability to support life.

The question of whether life has ever existed elsewhere in the solar system continues to intrigue both scientists and the general public. When the United States sent two Viking spacecraft to land on the surface of Mars in 1976, each contained three experiments intended to search for traces of organic material that might indicate the presence of past or present life-forms. None of the experiments produced positive results. Twenty years later, a team of scientists studying a meteorite of Martian origin found in Antarctica announced the discovery of possible microscopic fossils resulting from past organic life. Their claim was not universally accepted, but it led to an accelerated program of Martian exploration focused on the search for evidence of the action of liquid water—thought necessary for life to have evolved. A major goal of this program is to return samples of the Martian surface to Earth for laboratory analysis.

The Galileo mission provided images and other data related to Jupiter's moon Europa that suggest the presence of a liquid water ocean beneath its icy crust. The Cassini mission observed geysers of water vapour on Saturn's moon Enceladus. Future missions will seek to confirm the existence of these oceans and search for evidence of organic or biological processes in them.

SPACE OBSERVATORIES

Until the dawn of spaceflight, astronomers were limited in their ability to observe objects beyond the solar system

Solar Maximum Mission (SMM) satellite observatory, photographed above Earth during a U.S. space shuttle mission in 1984 to conduct in-orbit repairs of the satellite. Launched in 1980 near the most active part of the solar cycle, the SMM observatory carried several instruments to study solar flares and the solar atmosphere across a range of wavelengths from visible light to gamma rays. An astronaut wearing a space suit with a maneuvering backpack is visible in the upper left of the image. **NASA**

Beginning in the 1960s, the space agencies of the United States and several other countries, independently and in cooperation, developed satellite observatories specifically instrumented to explore cosmic phenomena in the gamma-ray, X-ray, ultraviolet, visible, and infrared regions. The IUE studied faint objects in the ultraviolet region, and the IRAS mapped the sky in the infrared region, finding hundreds of thousands of new stars and galaxies.

More recently, space-based radio astronomy has been pursued with the launches of the Great Observatories: the Hubble Space Telescope, the Compton Gamma Ray Observatory, the Chandra X-ray Observatory, and the Spitzer Space Telescope. Europe and Japan have also been active in space-based astronomy and astrophysics. Although most observatories in space orbit Earth, the Solar and Heliospheric Observatory (SOHO) and the Spitzer Space Telescope were both placed in orbit around the sun.

The results of these space investigations have made major contributions to an understanding of the origin, evolution, and likely future of the universe, galaxies, stars, and planetary systems. The U.S. Cosmic Background Explorer (COBE) satellite mapped the microwave background radiation left over from the early universe,

to those portions of the electromagnetic spectrum that can penetrate Earth's atmosphere. These portions include the visible region, parts of the ultraviolet and infrared regions, and most of the radio-frequency region. The ability to place instruments on a spacecraft operating above the atmosphere opened the possibility of observing the universe in all regions of the spectrum. Even operating in the visible region, a space-based observatory could avoid the problems caused by atmospheric turbulence and airglow.

HUBBLE SPACE TELESCOPE

The Hubble Space Telescope (HST) is the most sophisticated optical observatory ever placed into orbit around Earth. Earth's atmosphere obscures ground-based astronomers' view of celestial objects by absorbing or distorting light rays from them. A telescope stationed in outer space is entirely above the atmosphere, however, and receives images of much greater brightness, clarity, and detail than do ground-based telescopes with comparable optics.

After the U.S. Congress authorized its construction in 1977, the Hubble Space Telescope was built under the supervision of NASA and was named after Edwin Hubble, the foremost American astronomer of the 20th century. The HST was placed into orbit about 600 km (370 miles) above Earth by the crew of the space shuttle Discovery on April 25, 1990.

The HST is a large reflecting telescope whose mirror optics gather light from celestial objects and direct it into two cameras, two spectrographs, and an infrared instrument that has both a camera and a spectrograph. The HST has a 2.4-metre (94-inch) primary mirror, a smaller secondary mirror, and various recording instruments that can detect visible, ultraviolet, and infrared light. The most important of these instruments, the wide-field planetary camera, can take either wide-field or high-resolution images of the planets and of galactic and extragalactic objects. This camera is designed to achieve image resolutions 10 times greater than that of even the largest Earth-based telescope. A high-resolution spectrograph receives distant objects' ultraviolet light that cannot reach Earth because of atmospheric absorption.

About one month after launch, it became apparent that the HST's large primary mirror had been ground to the wrong shape due to faulty testing procedures by the mirror's manufacturer. The resulting optical defect, spherical aberration, caused the mirror to produce fuzzy images. The HST also developed problems with its gyroscopes and with its solar-power arrays. On Dec. 2–13, 1993, a mission of the NASA space shuttle Endeavour sought to correct the telescope's optical system and other problems. In five space walks, the shuttle astronauts replaced the HST's wide-field planetary camera and installed a new device containing 10 tiny mirrors to correct the light paths from the primary mirror to the other three scientific instruments. The mission proved an unqualified success, and the HST soon began operating at its full potential, returning spectacular photographs of various cosmic phenomena.

Three subsequent space shuttle missions in 1997, 1999, and 2002 repaired the HST's gyroscopes and added new instruments including a near-infrared spectrometer and a wide-field camera. The final space shuttle mission to service the HST, which installed a new camera and an ultraviolet spectrograph, was launched in 2009. The HST is scheduled to remain operational until 2014, when it is expected to be replaced by the James Webb Space Telescope, equipped with a mirror seven times larger than that of the HST.

The HST's discoveries have revolutionized astronomy. Observations of Cepheid variables in nearby galaxies allowed the first accurate determination of Hubble's constant, which is the rate of the universe's expansion. The HST photographed young stars with disks that will eventually become planetary systems. The Hubble Deep Field, a photograph of about 1,500 galaxies, revealed galactic evolution over nearly the entire history of the universe.

providing strong support for the theory of the big bang. The striking images of cosmic objects obtained by the Hubble Space Telescope not only have added significantly to scientific knowledge but also have shaped the public's perception of the cosmos—perhaps as significantly as did the astronomer Galileo's observations of the Moon and Jupiter nearly four centuries earlier. Working as complements to ground-based observatories of increasing sensitivity, space-based observatories have helped create a revolution in modern astronomy.

OBSERVING EARTH

Satellites, space stations, and space shuttle missions have provided a new perspective for scientists to collect data about Earth itself. In addition to practical applications, Earth observation from space has made significant contributions to fundamental knowledge. One early and continuing example is the use of satellites to make various geodetic measurements, which has allowed precise determinations of Earth's shape, internal structure, and rotational motion and the tidal and other periodic motions of the oceans. Fields as diverse as archaeology, seismology, and oceanography likewise have benefited from observations and measurements made from orbit.

Scientists have begun to use observations from space as part of comprehensive efforts in fields such as oceanography and ecology to understand and model the

SPACE DEBRIS

What happens to an unmanned satellite that is no longer functional? It becomes space debris (or space junk). This material can be as large as a discarded rocket stage or as small as a microscopic chip of paint. Much of the debris is in low Earth orbit, within 2,000 km (1,200 miles) of Earth's surface. However, some debris can be found in geostationary orbit 35,785 km (22,236 miles) above Earth's equator. As of 2009, the U.S. Space Surveillance Network was tracking over 9,500 pieces of space debris larger than 10 cm (4 inches) across. It is estimated that there are about 200,000 pieces between 1 and 10 cm (0.4 and 4 inches) across and that there could be millions of pieces smaller than 1 cm. How long a piece of space debris takes to fall back to Earth depends on its altitude. Objects below 600 km (375 miles) orbit for several years before reentering Earth's atmosphere. Objects above 1,000 km (600 miles) orbit for centuries.

Because of the high speeds (up to 8 km [5 miles] per second) at which objects orbit Earth, a collision with even a small piece of space debris can damage a spacecraft. Space shuttle windows must often be replaced because of damage by a collision with man-made debris smaller than 1 mm (0.04 inch). When in orbit, the space shuttle flies tail-forward to protect the forward crew compartment.

The amount of debris in space is growing and threatens both manned and unmanned spaceflight. The risk of a catastrophic collision of a space shuttle with a piece of space debris is 1 in 300.

(For missions to the Hubble Space Telescope, with its higher and more debris-filled orbit, the risk is 1 in 185.) On July 24, 1996, the first collision between an operational satellite and a piece of space debris took place when a fragment from the upper stage of a European Ariane rocket collided with Cerise, a French microsatellite. Cerise was damaged but continued to function. The first collision that destroyed an operational satellite happened on Feb. 10, 2009, when Iridium 33—a communications satellite owned by the American company Motorola—collided with Cosmos 2251, an inactive Russian military communications satellite, about 760 km (470 miles) above northern Siberia. Both satellites shattered.

The worst space-debris event happened on Jan. 11, 2007, when the Chinese military destroyed the Fengyun-1C weather satellite in a test of an antisatellite system, creating nearly 2,800 fragments, or more than 25 percent of all space debris. Within two years, these fragments had spread out from Fengyun-1C's original orbit to form a cloud of debris that completely encircled Earth and that would not reenter the atmosphere for decades.

With the increasing amount of space debris, there are fears that collisions such as that between Iridium 33 and Cosmos 2251 could set off a chain reaction in which the resulting space debris would destroy other satellites and so on, with the result that low Earth orbit would become unusable. To forestall such a buildup in debris, space agencies have begun taking steps to mitigate the problem, such as burning up all the fuel in a rocket stage so it does not explode later or saving enough fuel to deorbit a satellite at the end of its mission. Satellites in geostationary orbit that are near the end of their missions are sometimes moved to a "graveyard" orbit 300 km (200 miles) higher.

causes, processes, and effects of global climate change—including the influence of human activities. The goal is to obtain comprehensive sets of data over meaningful time spans about key physical, chemical, and biological processes that are shaping the planet's future. This is a coordinated international effort, in which the United States, Europe, and Japan are providing satellites to obtain the needed observations.

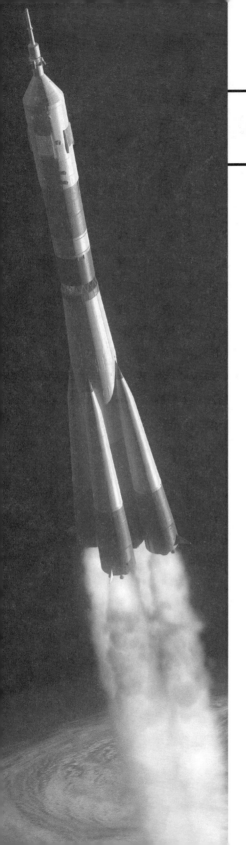

CHAPTER 5

SPACE APPLICATIONS

S pace visionaries in the early 20th century recognized that putting satellites into orbit could furnish direct and tangible benefits to people on Earth. Arthur C. Clarke in 1945 described a way in which three satellites in orbit about 35,800 km (22,250 miles) above the equator could relay communications around the globe. In this orbit, called a geostationary orbit, the satellites would have an orbital period equal to Earth's rotational period and thus appear from the ground to be stationary in the sky. In 1946, a report for the U.S. Army Air Forces by Project RAND (the predecessor of the RAND Corporation) identified the benefits of being able to observe Earth from space, which included distinguishing the impact sites of bombs dropped by U.S. aircraft and improved weather forecasting.

Space development, the practical application of the capabilities of spacecraft and of the data collected from space, has evolved in parallel with space exploration. There are two general categories of space applications. One provides benefits that are considered public goods—cannot easily be marketed to individual purchasers—and are therefore usually provided by governments, using public funds. Examples of public-good space applications include meteorology; navigation, position location, and timing; and military and national security uses. The other category of applications provides goods or services that can be sold to purchasers at a profit. These applications are the basis for the commercial development of space by the private sector. Examples of existing commercial space applications include various forms of telecommunications via satellites, remote sensing of Earth's surface, and commercial space transportation. Other applications, such as space-based power generation, the manufacture of high-value materials in a microgravity environment, and the commercial development of extraterrestrial resources, may appear in the future.

Many space applications have both civilian and military uses, and, thus, similar systems have been developed by both sectors. How to manage and use these dual-purpose systems effectively is a continuing policy issue.

PUBLIC-GOOD APPLICATIONS

Some of the applications of spaceflight are public goods that are useful to all. The farmer plowing a field, the fan on the way to a baseball game, and the builder starting construction all rely on the information about future weather provided by meteorological satellites. The accurate satellite data of where one is on Earth, which was once available only to those in uniform, now comes with many cars. The armed forces that protect our national security rely on satellites for communication and intelligence.

METEOROLOGY

Meteorologists initially thought that satellites would be used primarily to observe cloud patterns and provide warnings of impending storms. They did not expect space observations to be central to improved weather forecasting overall. Nevertheless, as the technology of space-based instrumentation became more sophisticated, satellites were called upon to provide three-dimensional profiles of additional variables in the atmosphere, including temperature, moisture content, and wind speed. These data have become critical to modern weather forecasting.

Meteorological satellites are placed in one of two different kinds of orbit. Satellites in geostationary orbit provide continuous images of cloud patterns over large areas of Earth's surface. From changes in those patterns, meteorologists can deduce wind speeds and locate developing storms. Satellites in lower orbits aligned in a north-south direction, called polar orbits, can obtain more detailed data about changing atmospheric conditions. They also provide repetitive global coverage as Earth rotates beneath their orbit. In the United States, military and civilian agencies each have developed independent polar-orbiting meteorological satellite systems. China, Europe, and the Soviet Union have also deployed their own polar-orbiting satellites. The United States, Europe, the Soviet Union, India, and Japan have orbited geostationary meteorological satellites.

Although the research and development activity needed to produce meteorological satellites has been carried out by various space agencies, control over satellite operation usually has been handed over to organizations with general responsibility for weather forecasting. In the United States, the National Oceanographic and Atmospheric Administration (NOAA) operates geostationary and polar-orbiting satellites for short- and long-term forecasting. The Department of Defense (DOD) also has developed similar satellites for military use. Operation of U.S. civilian and military polar satellite programs have been combined under joint NOAA-DOD management. In Europe, an intergovernmental organization called Eumetsat was created in 1986 to operate Europe's meteorological satellites and provide their observations to national weather services. Agencies around the world cooperate in the exchange of data from their satellites. Meteorological satellites are an excellent example of both the ability of space systems to provide extremely valuable benefits to humanity and the need for international cooperation to maximize those benefits.

POSITIONING, NAVIGATION, AND TIMING

In 1957, scientists tracking the first satellite, Sputnik 1, found that they could plot the satellite's orbit very precisely by analyzing the Doppler shift in the frequency of its transmitted signal with respect to a fixed location on Earth. They understood that if this process could be reversed—if the orbits of several satellites were precisely known—it would be possible to identify one's location on Earth by using information from those satellites.

This realization, coupled with the need to establish the position of submarines carrying ballistic missiles, led the United States and the Soviet Union each to develop satellite-based navigation systems in the 1960s and early '70s. Those systems, however, did not provide highly accurate information and were unwieldy to use. The two countries then developed second-generation products—the U.S. Navstar Global Positioning System (GPS) and the Soviet Global Navigation Satellite System (GLONASS)—that did much to solve the problems of their predecessors. The original purpose of the systems was the support of military activities, and, at the start of the 21st century, they continued to operate under military control.

GPS requires a minimum of 24 satellites, with four satellites distributed in each of six orbits. Deployment of the full complement of satellites was completed in 1994 and included provision for continual replenishment and updating and the maintenance of several spare satellites in orbit. Each satellite carries four atomic clocks accurate to one nanosecond. Because the satellites' orbits are maintained very precisely by ground controllers and the time signals from each satellite are highly accurate, users with a GPS receiver can determine their distance from each of a minimum of four satellites and, from this information, pinpoint their exact location in three dimensions with an accuracy of approximately 18 metres (59 feet) horizontally and 28 metres (92 feet) vertically. GLONASS, which became operational in

1996, functions on the same general principles as GPS. A fully deployed system would consist of 24 satellites distributed in three orbits. Because of Russia's economic difficulties, however, GLONASS has not been well maintained, and replacement satellite deployment has been slow.

Notwithstanding, the military origin of GPS and GLONASS, civilian users have multiplied. They range from wilderness campers, farmers, golfers, and recreational sailors to surveyors, car-rental firms, bus and truck fleets, and the world's airlines. The timing information from GPS satellites is also used by the Internet and other computer networks to manage the flow of information. Users have found ways to increase the accuracy of position location to a few centimetres by combining GPS signals with ground-based enhancements, and affordable GPS receivers make the system widely accessible. The United States regards GPS as a global utility to be offered free of charge to all users, and it has stated its intent to maintain and upgrade the system into the indefinite future. Concern has been expressed, however, that important worldwide civilian activities such as air traffic control should not depend on a system controlled by one country's military forces. In response, Europe began, in the late 1990s, to develop its own navigation satellite system, called Galileo, to be operated under civilian control. In the early 21st century, China also began to develop its own global navigation system, called Compass.

MILITARY AND NATIONAL SECURITY USES OF SPACE

Those countries and organizations with armed forces deployed abroad were quick to recognize the great usefulness of space-based systems in military operations. The United States, the Soviet Union, the United Kingdom, the North Atlantic Treaty Organization (NATO), and, to a lesser degree, other European countries and China have deployed increasingly sophisticated space systems—including satellites for communications, meteorology, and positioning and navigation—that are dedicated to military uses. In addition, the United States and the Soviet Union have developed satellites to provide early warning of hostile missile launches. Many of these satellites have been designed to meet unique military requirements, such as the ability to operate in a wartime environment, when an opponent may try to interfere with their functioning.

To date, military space systems have served primarily to enhance the effectiveness of ground-, air-, and sea-based military forces. Commanders rely on satellites to communicate with troops on the front lines, and, in extreme circumstances, national authorities could use them to issue the commands to launch nuclear weapons. Meteorological satellites assist in planning air strikes, and positioning satellites are used to guide weapons to their targets with high accuracy.

Despite the substantial military use of space, no country has deployed a space system capable of attacking a satellite in orbit or of delivering a weapon to a target on Earth. Nevertheless, as more countries acquire military space capabilities and as regional and local conflicts persist around the world, it is not clear whether space will continue to be treated as a weapons-free sanctuary.

In addition to recognizing the value of space systems in warfare, national leaders in the United States and the Soviet Union realized early on that the ability to gather information about surface-based activities—such as weapons development and deployment and troop movements—would assist them in planning their own national security activities. As a result, both countries deployed a variety of space systems for collecting intelligence. They include reconnaissance satellites that provide high-resolution images of Earth's surface in close to real time for use in identifying threatening activities, planning military operations, and monitoring arms-control agreements. Other satellites collect electronic signals such as telephone, radio, and Internet messages and other emissions, which can be used to determine the type of activities that are taking place in a particular location. Most national-security space activity is carried out in a highly secret manner. As the value to national security of such satellite systems has become evident, other countries, such as France, China, India, and Israel, have developed similar capabilities, and still others have begun planning their own systems.

COMMERCIAL APPLICATIONS

Since the beginning of the space age, some aspects of spaceflight have branched out from the province of governments to become profitable businesses. Billions rely on communications satellites to connect with those in other nations. The study of Earth and its features from space is a vital part of our agricultural and mining industries. The building of launch vehicles themselves employs thousands.

SATELLITE TELECOMMUNICATIONS

Although some early space experiments explored the use of large orbiting satellites as passive reflectors of signals from point to point on Earth, most work in the late 1950s and early '60s focused on the technology by which a signal sent from the ground would be received by satellite. It was then electronically processed and relayed to another ground station. American Telephone and Telegraph, recognizing the commercial potential of satellite communications, in 1962, paid NASA to launch its first Telstar satellite. Because that satellite, which operated in a fairly low orbit, was in range of any one receiving antenna for only a few minutes, a large network of such satellites would have been necessary for an operational system. Engineers from the American firm Hughes Aircraft, led by Harold Rosen, developed a design for a satellite that would operate in geostationary orbit. Aided by research support

Telstar 1, launched July 10, 1962, relayed the first transatlantic television signals. NASA

from NASA, the first successful geostationary satellite, Syncom 2, was launched in 1963. It demonstrated the feasibility of the Hughes concept prior to commercial use.

The United States also took the lead in creating the organizational framework for communications satellites. Establishment of the Communications Satellite Corporation (Comsat) was authorized in 1962 to operate American communications satellites. Two years later, an international agency— the International Telecommunications Satellite Organization (Intelsat)—was formed at the proposal of the United States to develop a global network. Comsat, the original manager of Intelsat, decided to base the Intelsat network on geostationary satellites. The first commercial communications satellite, Intelsat 1, also known as Early Bird, was launched in 1965. Intelsat completed its initial global network with the stationing of a satellite over the Indian Ocean in mid-1969, in time to televise the first Moon landing around the world.

The original use of communications satellites was to relay voice, video, and data from one relatively large antenna to a second, distant one, from which the communication then would be distributed over terrestrial networks. This point-to-point application introduced international communications to many new areas of the world, and in the 1970s, it also was employed domestically within a number of countries, especially the United States. As undersea fibre-optic cables improved in carrying capacity and signal quality, they became competitive with communications satellites. The latter responded with comparable technological advances that allowed these space-based systems to meet the challenge. A number of companies in the United States and Europe manufacture communications satellites and vie for customers on a global basis.

Other space-based communications applications have appeared, the most prominent being the broadcast of signals—primarily television programming—directly to small antennas serving individual households. A similar emerging use is the broadcast of audio programming to small antennas in locations ranging from rural villages in the developing world to individual automobiles. International private satellite networks have emerged as rivals to the government-owned Intelsat, which in 2001 was itself transformed into a private-sector organization.

Yet another service that has been devised for satellites is communication with and between mobile users. In 1979, the International Maritime Satellite Organization (Inmarsat) was formed to relay messages to ships at sea. Beginning in the late 1990s, with the growth of personal mobile communications such as cellular telephone services, several attempts were made to establish satellite-based systems for this purpose. Typically employing constellations of many satellites in low Earth orbit, they experienced difficulty competing with ground-based cellular systems. At the start of the 21st century, the outlook for their economic viability was not good, but other satellite-based personal communication systems—including some based on geostationary satellites—were under development.

The first commercial space application was satellite communications, and that remained the most successful one. One estimate of revenues associated with the industry for the year 2007 included $12 billion for satellite manufacturing, $34 billion for the associated ground systems, and $74 billion from the users of satellite revenues—for a total of $120 billion. As of 2009, there were more than 300 commercial geostationary communications satellites around the world, operated by almost 60 different owners.

REMOTE SENSING

Remote sensing is a term applied to the use of satellites to observe various characteristics of Earth's land and water surfaces in order to obtain information valuable in mapping, mineral exploration, land-use planning, resource management, and other activities. Remote sensing is carried out from orbit with multispectral sensors. Observations are made in several discrete regions of the electromagnetic spectrum that include visible light and usually other wavelengths. From multispectral imagery, analysts are able to derive information on such varied areas of interest as crop condition and type, pollution patterns, and sea conditions.

Because many applications of remote sensing have a public-good character, a commercial remote-sensing industry has been slow to develop. In addition, the secrecy surrounding intelligence-gathering satellites during the Cold War era set stringent limits on the capabilities that could be offered on a commercial basis. The United States launched the first remote-sensing satellite, NASA's Landsat 1 (originally called Earth Resources Technology Satellite), in 1972. The goals of the Landsat program, which by 1999 had included six successful satellites, were to demonstrate the value of multispectral observation and to prepare the system for transfer to private operators. Despite two decades of attempts at such a transfer, Landsat remained a U.S. government program at the start of the 21st century. In 1986 France launched the first of its SPOT remote-sensing satellites and created a marketing organization, Spot Image, to promote use of its imagery. Both Landsat's and SPOT's multispectral images offered a moderate ground resolution of 10–30 metres (about 33–100 feet). Japan and India also launched multispectral remote-sensing satellites.

In the 1990s, with the end of the Cold War, some of the technology used in reconnaissance satellites was declassified. This allowed several American firms to begin developing high-ground-resolution (less than one metre [3.3 feet]) commercial remote-sensing satellites. The first commercial high-resolution satellite, called Ikonos 1, was launched by the Space Imaging Company in 1999. Among major customers for high-resolution imagery are governments that lack their own reconnaissance satellites. The global availability of imagery previously available only to the leaders of a few countries is troubling to some observers, who express concern that it could lead to increased military activity. Others suggest that this widespread availability will contribute to a more stable world.

Remote sensing from space has yet to develop into a viable commercial business. Nevertheless, as users become more familiar with the benefits of combining space-derived data with other sources of geographic information, the possibility of commercial success could improve.

COMMERCIAL SPACE TRANSPORTATION

The prosperity of the communications satellite business was accompanied by a willingness of the private sector to pay substantial sums for the launch of its satellites. As growth in the business slowed at the turn of the 21st century, so did growth in commercial space transportation, because there were few other commercial spacecraft needing access to orbit. Initially, most commercial communications satellites went into space on

LANDSAT

The Landsat U.S. scientific satellites were designed primarily to collect information about Earth's natural resources, including the location of mineral deposits and the condition of forests and farming regions. They were also equipped to monitor atmospheric and oceanic conditions and to detect variations in pollution level and other ecological changes. The first three Landsat satellites were launched in 1972, 1975, and 1978. All three satellites carried various types of cameras, including those with infrared sensors. Landsat cameras provided images of surface areas 184 km (115 miles) square; each such area could be photographed at 18-day intervals. These pictures were the basis of a far more comprehensive survey than could be made from airplanes. A fourth Landsat satellite was launched in 1982 and a fifth in 1984. In 1985, Landsat was transferred to a private commercial operator, the Earth Observation Satellite Company (EOSAT). In 1992, the U.S. government again assumed control of the program. The newer models contained two sensors: a multispectral scanner and a thematic mapper, which provides 30-metre (100-foot) spatial resolution in seven spectral bands. Landsat 6 failed to achieve orbit after its launch in 1993. Landsat 7 was launched successfully in 1999. Because Landsat 5 and 7 are nearing the end of their operational lifetimes, a new satellite, the Landsat Data Continuity Mission, is planned for launch in December 2012.

U.S.-government-operated vehicles. When the space shuttle was declared operational in 1982, it became the sole American launch vehicle providing such services. After the 1986 *Challenger* accident, however, the shuttle was prohibited from launching commercial payloads. This created an opportunity for the private sector to employ existing expendable launch vehicles such as the Delta, Atlas, and Titan as commercial launchers. In the 1990s, an American commercial space transportation industry emerged. Whereas the Titan was not a commercial success, the other two vehicles found commercial customers for a number of years.

Europe followed a different path to commercial space transport. After deciding in the early 1970s to develop the Ariane launcher, it created under French leadership a marketing organization called Arianespace to seek commercial launch contracts for the vehicle. In the mid-1980s, both the U.S.S.R. and China initiated efforts to attract commercial customers for their launch vehicles. As the industry developed in the 1990s, the United States initiated joint ventures with Russia and Ukraine to market their launchers. Europe also created a similar alliance with Russia. China continued to market its Long March series of launch vehicles for commercial use, and other countries hoped to market their indigenous launchers on a commercial basis.

In the first years of the 21th century, only 20 commercial launches were conducted per year on average, although the launch capacity worldwide was significantly greater.

NEW COMMERCIAL APPLICATIONS

Space advocates have identified a number of possible opportunities for the future commercial use of space. For their economic feasibility, many depend on lowering the cost of transportation to space—an objective that has eluded both governments and private entrepreneurs. Access to low Earth orbit continues to cost thousands of dollars per kilogram of payload—a significant barrier to further space development.

As an alternative to existing sources of energy, suggestions have been made for space-based systems that capture large amounts of solar energy and transmit it in the form of microwaves or laser beams to Earth. Achieving this objective would require the deployment of a number of large structures in space and the development of an environmentally acceptable form of energy transmission to create a cost-effective competitor to Earth-based energy-supply systems.

Resources available on the Moon and other bodies of the solar system represent additional potential objectives for commercial development. For example, over billions of years, the solar wind has deposited large amounts of the isotope helium-3 in the soil of the lunar surface. Scientists and engineers have suggested that helium-3 could be extracted and transported to Earth, where it is rare, for use in nuclear fusion reactors. In addition, there is evidence to suggest that the Moon's polar regions contain ice, which could supply a manned lunar outpost with drinking water, breathable oxygen, and hydrogen for spacecraft fuel. Significant quantities of potentially valuable resources such as water, carbon, and nitrogen may also exist on some asteroids, and space mining of those resources has been proposed.

ISSUES FOR THE FUTURE

Space exploration and development have been stimulated by a complex mixture of motivations, including scientific inquiry, intense competition between national governments and ideologies, and commercial profit. Scientists will continue to seek answers to leading questions about the physical and biological universe through the deployment of increasingly advanced instruments on orbiting satellites and space probes. The principal space-faring countries appear willing to continue their substantial support for space science. The availability of government funding will set the pace of scientific progress.

The various applications of space capability hold the greatest promise for significant change. If other commercial ventures equal or surpass the success of the satellite communications sector, space could become a major centre of business activity. If governments decide to expand the activity in space of their armed forces, space could become another major military theatre—like the land, sea, and air on Earth—for waging war and deploying weapons. If observing Earth from space becomes crucial for

Space Law

The evolution of space law began with U.S. Pres. Dwight D. Eisenhower's introduction of the concept into the United Nations in 1957, in connection with disarmament negotiations. Following the successful launchings of the Soviet satellite Sputnik 1 in 1957 and the U.S. satellite Explorer 1 in 1958, both the United States and the U.S.S.R. took an active interest in the development of international space policy. It was established that traditional laws of sovereignty that allow any nation to claim for itself uninhabited and uncivilized lands are not viable in space territories, and that countries cannot extend the boundaries of their dominion indefinitely into the space regions above them. In 1959, a permanent Outer Space Committee was formed for the purpose of maintaining the United Nations Charter and other international law in space, which opened the way for peaceful exploration. In 1963, the Nuclear Test Ban Treaty was signed, followed by an Outer Space Committee resolution to prohibit nuclear weapons testing in space. Later that same year, a UN General Assembly declaration acknowledged a free international interest in space development and outlined rules assigning each nation individual responsibility for dealing with transgressions of international law and for any resulting destruction. International cooperation was recommended for the safeguarding of all astronauts in crisis situations.

In 1967, an Outer Space Treaty was ratified by 63 participants in the United Nations. This agreement reasserted all earlier guidelines for international space conduct. In addition, it banned certain military activities, such as the deployment of weapons of mass destruction in space and on celestial bodies. It also established each state's ownership of and responsibility for its space projectiles and components, urged common participation in the protection of space and terrestrial environments, and provided for the open observation and inspection of each state's activities and installations by others. This treaty was followed in 1968 by an Agreement on the Rescue and Return of Astronauts and the Return of Objects Launched into Space. This agreement reinforced international commitment to the safety of humans in space, assigned economic responsibility to each country for the recovery of its equipment, and confirmed the control of each space power over the vehicles that it launches. Another important treaty, the 1972 Convention on International Liability for Damage Caused by Space Objects, set out detailed rules regarding the recovery of damages for losses caused by space objects.

Although international diplomacy continues to play an active role in the codification of acceptable space conduct, several issues remain the subjects of debate. Because nations are prohibited from laying claim to space territories, for instance, there is a need to establish regulations governing the apportionment of usable resources that space may eventually provide. A method for determining the extent of each country's control over the air above remains to be agreed upon.

The development of space for a growing array of government and private activities also poses significant challenges for space law. The agreements on which space law is based were formulated at a time when governments dominated space activities and commercial space ventures were just beginning. Whether these agreements remain adequate and appropriate for the 21st century requires review.

effective planetary management, an assortment of increasingly varied and specialized observation satellites could be launched. Thus, outer space could become a much busier area of human activity in the 21st century than in the first four decades of endeavour there. At some point, it even may become necessary to establish a space traffic-control system analogous to traffic-control systems on Earth.

The development of space as an arena for multiple government and private activities will pose significant policy and legal challenges. The legal framework for space activities is based on the 1967 Outer Space Treaty and four subsequent United Nations treaties implementing its provisions. These agreements were negotiated at a time when governments were the principal players in space and commercial space activities were in their infancy. Whether they form an adequate and appropriate framework for current and future space activities requires review.

Under the terms of the Outer Space Treaty, the parties are prohibited from placing nuclear arms or other weapons of mass destruction in orbit, on the Moon, or on other bodies in space. Nations cannot claim sovereignty over the Moon or other celestial bodies. Nations are responsible for their activities in space, are liable for any damage caused by objects launched into space from their territory, and are bound to assist astronauts in distress. Their space installations and vehicles shall be open, on a reciprocal basis, to representatives of other countries, and all parties agree to conduct outer-space activities openly and in accordance with international law. This document has been noted as a landmark in the development of international space law. Like most subsequent space-law agreements generated by the United Nations, it remains in effect today among participating countries.

Other treaties have limited some military activities in space, but there is no general framework regulating the military uses of space. The wisdom of developing space weapons—or, alternatively, of limiting their development and keeping space a weapons-free environment—is an issue for discussion and debate.

To date, the benefits of space exploration and development have accrued mainly to those countries that have financed space activities. The contributions of space to the economic and social development of large regions of Earth have been limited. The Outer Space Treaty identifies space as "the common heritage of mankind." How to ensure that the benefits of this common heritage are more equitably distributed will be a continuing challenge.

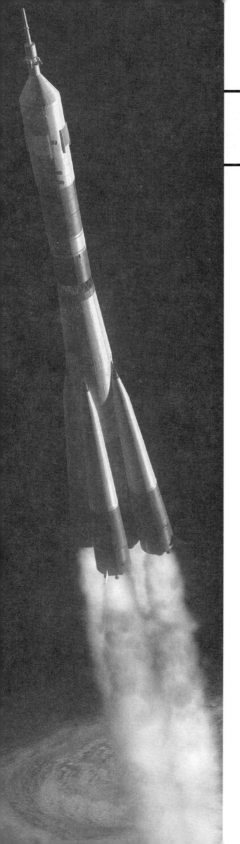

CHAPTER 6

SPACE AGENCIES

M uch of unmanned spaceflight has happened under the aegis of national (and sometimes) international space agencies. The most prominent agencies and their histories are described below.

EUROPEAN SPACE AGENCY

The European Space Agency (ESA) is a space and space-technology research organization founded in 1975 from the merger of the European Launcher Development Organisation (ELDO) and the European Space Research Organisation (ESRO), both established in 1964. Members include Austria, Belgium, the Czech Republic, Denmark, Finland, France, Germany, Greece, Ireland, Italy, Luxembourg, The Netherlands, Norway, Portugal, Spain, Sweden, Switzerland, and the United Kingdom. In 1981, Canada signed a special cooperative agreement, which enables it to participate in some ESA projects. The ESA has also cooperated with NASA on many projects. Headquarters of the agency are in Paris.

Representatives of ESA's member nations form the agency's policy-making council. A science program committee established by convention deals with matters related to the mandatory science program; other such bodies may be formed by the council to assist in decision making. The chief executive and legal representative of the ESA is the director

European Space Operations Centre, Darmstadt, Ger. © J. Mai/ESA

Antennas at the European Space Agency's Redu ground station, Ardennes, Belg. © A. Gonin/ESA

general, assisted by an inspector general and the directors of various departments.

The principal components of the organization are (1) the European Space Research and Technology Centre (ESTEC), located in Noordwijk, Netherlands, which houses the satellite project teams and testing facilities and is the agency's main space science and technological research centre, (2) the European Space Operations Centre (ESOC), located in Darmstadt, Germany, which is concerned with satellite control, monitoring, and data retrieval, (3) the European Space Research Institute (ESRIN), located in Frascati, Italy, which supports the ESA Information Retrieval Service and the Earthnet program, the system by which remote sensing images are retrieved and distributed, (4) the European Astronaut Centre (EAC), located in Cologne, Germany, which is a training centre, and (5) the European Space Astronomy Centre (ESAC), located in Villafranca del Castillo, Madrid, Spain, which holds scientific operations centres as well as archives. The ESA also operates the Guiana Space Centre (CSG), a launch base in French Guiana.

European Space Agency officials tracking Mars Express and Beagle 2 from the main control room of the European Space Operations Centre, Darmstadt, Ger. © J. Mai/ESA

NATIONAL AERONAUTICS AND SPACE ADMINISTRATION

The National Aeronautics and Space Administration (NASA) is an independent U.S. governmental agency established in 1958 for the research and development of vehicles and activities for the exploration of space within and outside of Earth's atmosphere.

The organization is composed of four mission directorates program offices: Aeronautics Research and Space Technology, for the development of equipment to improve America's air transportation; Exploration Systems, for the exploration of the Moon and Mars; Science, for understanding the origin, structure, and evolution of the universe, the solar system, and Earth; and Space Operations, in charge of manned spaceflight, specifically the space shuttle and the International Space Station. A number of additional research centres are affiliated, including the Goddard Space Flight Center in Greenbelt, Maryland.; the Jet Propulsion Laboratory in Pasadena, California; the Lyndon B. Johnson Space Center in Houston, Texas; and the Langley Research Center in Hampton, Virginia. Headquarters of NASA are in Washington, D.C.

NASA was created largely in response to the Soviet launching of Sputnik in 1957. It was organized around the National Advisory Committee for Aeronautics (NACA), which had been created by Congress in 1915. NASA's organization was well underway by the early years of

Liftoff of the first U.S. space shuttle, April 12, 1981, from John F. Kennedy Space Center, Cape Canaveral, Florida. NASA

Pres. John F. Kennedy's administration, when Kennedy proposed that the United States put a man on the Moon by the end of the 1960s. To that end, the Apollo program was designed, and in 1969, the U.S. astronaut Neil Armstrong became the first man on the Moon. Later unmanned programs—such as Viking, Mariner, Voyager, and Galileo—explored other bodies of the solar system.

NASA was also responsible for the development and launching of a number of satellites with Earth applications, such as Landsat , a series of satellites designed to collect information on natural resources and other Earth features; communications satellites; and weather satellites. It also planned and developed the space shuttle, a reusable vehicle capable of carrying out missions that cannot be conducted with conventional spacecraft.

SOVIET AND RUSSIAN SPACE AGENCIES

In contrast to the United States, the Soviet Union had no separate, publicly acknowledged space agency. For 35 years after Sputnik, various design bureaus—state-controlled organizations that actually conceived and developed aircraft and space systems—had great influence within the Soviet system. Rivalry between those bureaus and their heads, who were known as chief designers, was a constant reality and posed an obstacle to a coherent Soviet space program. Space policy decisions were made by the Politburo of the Central Committee of the Communist Party, as well as the Soviet government's Council of Ministers. After 1965, the government's Ministry of General Machine Building was assigned responsibility for managing all Soviet space and missile programs. The Ministry of Defense was also quite influential in shaping space efforts. A separate military branch, the Strategic Missile Forces, was in charge of space launchers and strategic missiles. Various institutes of the Soviet Academy of Sciences, particularly the Institute for Space Research (IKI), proposed and managed scientific missions.

Only after the dissolution of the U.S.S.R. did Russia create a civilian organization for space activities. Formed in February 1992, the Russian Space Agency acted as a central focus for the country's space policy and programs. Although it began as a small organization that dealt with international contacts and the setting of space policies, it quickly took on increasing responsibility for the management of nonmilitary space activities and, as an added charge, aviation efforts. It later was renamed the Russian Federal Space Agency, or Roskosmos.

EUROPE

In 1961—within four years of the launch of the first U.S. and Soviet satellites—the government of France created a space agency, the Centre National d'Études

Spatiales (CNES), which became the largest national organization of its kind in Europe. Gradually, other European countries formed government or government-sponsored organizations for space, among them the German Aerospace Center (DLR), the British National Space Centre (BNSC), and the Italian Space Agency (ASI). Still others included space as part of their science or technology ministries.

JAPANESE SPACE AGENCIES

In Japan, the University of Tokyo created an Institute of Space and Astronautical Science (ISAS) in 1964. This small group undertook the development of scientific spacecraft and the vehicles needed to launch them. It launched Japan's first satellite, Ōsumi, in 1970. In 1981, oversight of ISAS was transferred to the Japanese Ministry of Education. In 1969, the Japanese government founded a National Space Development Agency (NASDA), which subsequently undertook a comprehensive program of space technology and satellite development and built a large launch vehicle—called the H-II—for those satellites. In 2001, both ISAS and NASDA came under the control of the Japanese Ministry of Education, Culture, Sports, Science and Technology. In 2003, ISAS, NASDA, and the National Aerospace Laboratory were merged into a new organization, the Japan Aerospace Exploration Agency (JAXA).

CHINESE SPACE AGENCIES

China's space program evolved largely in secret, under the joint control of the Chinese military and the Commission on Science, Technology, and Industry for the National Defense. After the communist takeover of 1949, Qian Xuesen, who had worked at GALCIT in the 1940s and helped found JPL, returned to China, where he became the guiding figure in the development of Chinese missiles and launch vehicles—both originally derived from a Soviet ICBM. China developed a family of Long March boosters, which are used domestically and serve as competitors in the international commercial space launch market. Its space development has concentrated on applications, such as communications satellites and Earth-observation satellites for civilian and military use. In 1993, the Ministry of Aerospace Industry was split into an independent Chinese Aerospace Corporation to oversee most Chinese space-equipment manufacturers and the China National Space Administration, which is the Chinese space agency.

INTERNATIONAL ORGANIZATIONS

A number of international organizations are involved in space activities as well. The United Nations General Assembly established a Committee on the Peaceful Uses of Outer Space in 1959 to discuss scientific, technical, and legal issues related to international space activities. Sixty-one countries were members of the committee in 2001. The committee has provided the forum for the development of five treaties and a number of declarations of principles related to space activities. The most important of them is the 1967 Outer Space Treaty. Other parts of the UN system, most notably the International Telecommunications Union (ITU), are engaged in space-related concerns. The ITU is responsible for allocation of radio frequencies and orbital locations for various satellites providing public and commercial services.

At the initiative of the United States, an International Telecommunications Satellite Organization (Intelsat) was founded in 1964 to develop and operate a global system of communications satellites. By 1969, the organization had established a system of satellites with global coverage. In the late 1980s, it provided services to more than 200 countries and territories. Intelsat membership grew to 144 countries before a decision was made in 1999 to change the ownership of the organization from national governments to the private sector. A similar consortium, the International Maritime Satellite Organization (Inmarsat), was established as an intergovernmental organization in 1979 to supply maritime and other mobile communications services via satellite. It also was later transformed into a privately owned entity. In addition, a number of regional organizations have been created to operate communication and meteorologic satellites.

CHAPTER 7

SPACEFLIGHT LEADERS AND PIONEERS

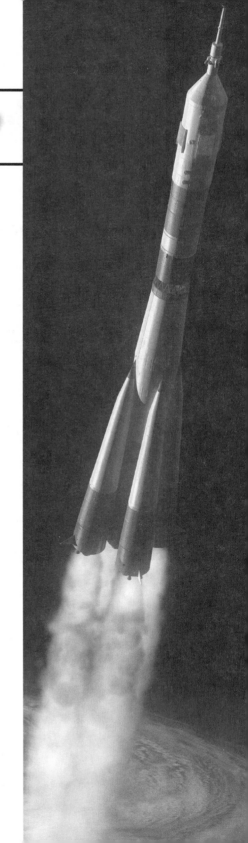

The history of unmanned spaceflight has required bold action and penetrating thought on the part of scientists, engineers, and government leaders. Below are biographies of some of those who made the dream of space travel a reality.

HUGH DRYDEN

(b. July 2, 1898, Pocomoke City, Md., U.S.—d. Dec. 2, 1965, Washington, D.C.)

U.S. physicist Hugh Latimer Dryden was deputy administrator of NASA for seven years. Educated at Johns Hopkins University (Baltimore) in 1920, Dryden was named chief of the aerodynamics section of the National Bureau of Standards, Washington. He made pioneering studies in the aerodynamics of high speed and some of the earliest studies of air flow around wing surfaces at the speed of sound. In 1934, he became chief of the mechanics and sound division. During World War II, he headed the Washington Project of the National Defense Research Committee, which developed the Bat radar-homing missile—the first successful U.S. guided missile. This missile was used by the navy against the Japanese during World War II. For his part in the project, he was awarded the Presidential Certificate of Merit in 1948.

Dryden resigned from the National Bureau of Standards in 1947 and became director of aeronautical research of the

National Advisory Committee for Aeronautics (NACA). Two years later, he became director of NACA, and under his leadership, the organization gained widespread recognition for its advanced aeronautical research and development. In 1958, he became deputy administrator of NASA, and, in 1962, led negotiations for joint U.S.–Soviet space projects. He was instrumental in achieving the exchange of weather-satellite data and operation of cooperative communications satellite tests.

VALENTIN GLUSHKO
(b. Aug. 20 [Sept. 2, New Style], 1908, Odessa, Ukr., Russian Empire—d. Jan. 10, 1989, Moscow, Russia, U.S.S.R.)

Soviet rocket scientist Valentin Petrovich Glushko was a pioneer in rocket propulsion systems and a major contributor to Soviet space and defense technology.

After graduating from Leningrad State University in 1929, Glushko headed the design bureau of Gas Dynamics Laboratory in Leningrad and began research on electrothermal, solid-fuel, and liquid-fuel rocket engines. Working together from 1932 to 1966, Glushko and renowned rocket designer Sergey Pavlovich Korolyov achieved their greatest triumphs in 1957 with the launching of both the first intercontinental ballistic missile in August and Sputnik 1 in October. In 1974, he was named chief designer of the Soviet space program, in which he oversaw the development of the

Mir space station. Glushko received numerous official honours, including the Lenin Prize (1957) and election to the U.S.S.R. Academy of Sciences (1958).

DANIEL GOLDIN
(b. July 23, 1940, New York, N.Y., U.S.)

American engineer Daniel Saul Goldin was the longest-serving NASA administrator (1992–2001). He brought to the U.S. space agency a new vision and a concentration on "faster, better, cheaper" programs to achieve that vision.

Goldin received a B.S. in engineering from the City College of New York in 1962 and joined NASA's Lewis Research Center in Cleveland, where he worked on

Daniel Saul Goldin. NASA

advanced propulsion technology. He left NASA in 1966 to join the TRW Space and Technology Group in Redondo Beach, California, where for 25 years he primarily worked on classified national security space programs and became TRW vice president and general manager of the group.

Goldin became NASA administrator on April 1, 1992, with an explicit mandate to reform what the White House had concluded was an excessively bureaucratic and technologically stagnant space agency. He combined an intense, sometimes abrasive, management style with a strong commitment to the values of space exploration. In addition to his emphasis of the "faster, better, cheaper" approach to scientific spacecraft, Goldin was a leader in the 1993 redesign of the space station program and the invitation to Russia to become a central partner in that program. He stressed the need to develop and use new capabilities in areas such as biotechnology, nanotechnology, and information technology in the planning of future space programs. Goldin left NASA in 2001. He was selected in 2003 as president of Boston University, but a conflict in views between Goldin and the university's board led to his contract being terminated just prior to his inauguration. He turned to private-sector consulting related to cutting-edge technological innovation, joined various corporate boards, and became president of Intellisis Corporation, a company that developed products based on cognitive computing.

SAMUEL HOFFMAN
(b. April 15, 1902, Williamsport, Penn., U.S.—d. June 26, 1995, Santa Barbara, Calif.)

American propulsion engineer Samuel Kurtz Hoffman led U.S. efforts to develop rocket engines for space vehicles. An aeronautical-design engineer from 1932 to 1945, Hoffman later became professor of aeronautical engineering at Pennsylvania State University, University Park. In 1949, he joined North American Aviation, Inc. (later North American Rockwell Corp.), as chief of the Propulsion Section of the Aerophysics Department. There, he helped develop a 34,000 kilogram (75,000-pound) thrust rocket engine for an intercontinental missile.

Under Hoffman's leadership, North American developed and completed in 1950 one of the first high-thrust rocket engines. This engine was a prototype of the Jupiter-C, which launched the first U.S. satellite and placed the first American astronauts in space. His work was also essential to the early development of the intercontinental Atlas and the intermediate-range Thor and Jupiter ballistic missiles.

In 1955, Hoffman was placed in charge of North American's Rocketdyne Division, which developed new high-pressure pumps and improved techniques for rocket maneuvering. Rocketdyne pioneered in the use of highly volatile fuels and liquid oxidizers of extremely low temperatures. In 1958, Hoffman took charge of the development of the rocket engines that were used in the Saturn launch vehicles, which eventually carried American astronauts to the Moon. He was president of Rocketdyne in 1960–70 and thereafter served as aerospace consultant to the firm.

THEODORE VON KÁRMÁN
(b. May 11, 1881, Budapest—d. May 6, 1963, Aachen, W.Ger.)

Hungarian-born American research engineer Theodore von Kármán was best known for his pioneering work in the use of mathematics and the basic sciences in aeronautics and astronautics. His laboratory at the California Institute of Technology later became NASA's Jet Propulsion Laboratory.

Von Kármán was the third of five children of Maurice and Helene von Kármán. His father was a professor at the University of Budapest and commissioner of the Ministry of Education. He reformed the secondary-school system of the country and founded the Minta (Model) Gymnasium, which his son attended—as did the atomic physicists George de Hevesy and Leo Szilard. Von Kármán showed a natural mathematical facility at an early age and was well on his way to becoming a child prodigy when his father, fearing that he would become a mathematical freak, guided him toward engineering.

On completing his undergraduate studies in 1902 at the Royal Polytechnic University in Budapest, von Kármán decided to pursue his engineering career in the academic world. This would enable him to fulfill his wide scientific interests and to practice the art of teaching, which his father had inspired in him. In later years, he was delighted when engineers to whom he had imparted his scientific attitude and methodological approach acknowledged him as their teacher.

Between 1903 and 1906, von Kármán served on the faculty of the Polytechnic University and as consultant to the principal Hungarian engine manufacturer. The research that he conducted on the strength of materials paved the way for important later contributions to the design of aircraft structures. He was awarded a two-year fellowship to the University of Göttingen, Germany, in order to obtain a doctor's degree. But before completing it, von Kármán went to the University of Paris. There, after an all-night party, a friend suggested that, instead of going to sleep, they watch the French aviation pioneer Henri Farman fly his machine. Farman successfully completed a 2-km (1.25-mile) course, unknowingly providing the inspiration for the young man who was to become a founder of the aeronautical and astronautical sciences.

Shortly thereafter, Ludwig Prandtl, a pioneer of modern fluid mechanics, invited von Kármán to return to Göttingen as his assistant on dirigible research and to complete his degree. The environment at the university was admirably suited to develop von Kármán's talents. He responded, in particular, to the school of the eminent mathematician Felix Klein, which stressed the fullest use of mathematics and of the basic sciences in engineering to increase technological efficiency. In 1911, he made an analysis of the alternating double row of vortices behind a bluff body (one having a broad, flattened front) in a fluid stream, now famous as Kármán's Vortex Street. The use of his analysis to explain the collapse, during high winds, of the Tacoma Narrows Bridge in the state of Washington, in the United States, in 1940, is one of the most striking examples of its value.

In 1912, after a short stay at the College of Mining Engineering in Hungary, he became director of the Aeronautical Institute at Aachen (Aix-la-Chapelle), Germany, at the age of 31, remaining until 1930. In World War I, von Kármán was called into military service and, while at the Military Aircraft Factory at Fischamend in Austria, led the development of the first helicopter tethered to the ground that was able to maintain hovering flight. After the war, as his international reputation grew, so did that of the institute. Students came from many countries, attracted by the intellectual and social atmosphere he had created. To help reestablish contacts and friendships broken by the war, he was instrumental in calling an international congress on aerodynamics and hydrodynamics at Innsbruck, Austria, in 1922. This meeting resulted in the formation of the International Applied Mechanics Congress Committee, which continues to organize quadrennial congresses. In 1946, this gave birth to the International Union of Theoretical and Applied Mechanics, with von Kármán as honorary president.

Von Kármán never married. His mother and his sister, Josephine, lived with him from 1923 onward in The Netherlands near Aachen and later in Pasadena, California. His sister was his manager and hostess until her death in 1951 in America. Brother and sister were devoted to each other, and her death plunged von Kármán into deep depression for several months, during which he was unable to work.

He began traveling widely in the 1920s as a lecturer and consultant to industry. After his first visit to the United States in 1926, von Kármán was invited in 1930 to assume the direction of the Guggenheim Aeronautical Laboratory at the California Institute of Technology (GALCIT) and of the Guggenheim Airship Institute at Akron, Ohio. His love for Aachen made him hesitate, but the darkening shadow of German Nazism caused him to accept. He never regretted his decision. When Pres. John F. Kennedy presented to him the first National Medal of Science in 1963, he "pledged his brain as long as it lasted" to the country of which he had become a citizen in 1936.

Shortly after his arrival at the California Institute of Technology, his laboratory became again a mecca of the world of the aeronautical sciences. Two years later, von Kármán became a founder of the U.S. Institute of Aeronautical Sciences, consultant to various American industries and to the government. His personal scientific work continued unabated with important contributions to fluid mechanics, turbulence theory, supersonic flight, mathematics in engineering, aircraft structures, and wind erosion of soil.

His open-mindedness was well demonstrated by his involvement in the development of astronautics. In 1936, in spite of the general disbelief in academic circles in the possibilities of rocket propulsion and its applications, he supported the interest of a group of his students in the subject. Within two years the U.S. Army Air Corps sponsored a project at his laboratory on the use of rockets to provide superperformance for conventional aircraft—especially to reduce their distance of takeoff from the ground and from naval aircraft carriers. In 1940, von Kármán, together with Frank J. Malina, showed for the first time since the invention of the black-powder rocket in China that it was possible to design a stable, long-duration, solid-propellant rocket engine. Shortly thereafter, the prototype of the famed jet-assisted takeoff (JATO) rocket was constructed. This became the prototype for rocket engines used in present-day long-range missiles, such as the Polaris, Minuteman, and Poseidon of the U.S. armed forces. In 1941, von Kármán participated in the founding of the Aerojet

General Corporation, the first American manufacturer of liquid- and solid-propellant rocket engines. In 1944, he became the cofounder of the present NASA Jet Propulsion Laboratory at the California Institute of Technology, when it undertook America's first governmental long-range missile and space-exploration research program for the U.S. Ordnance Department.

When he took leave from the institute in 1944 to establish in Washington, D.C., the Air Corps Scientific Advisory Group for General Henry H. Arnold (commander of the U.S. Army Air Forces in World War II), von Kármán could look back on his participation in a number of major contributions to rocket technology. These included America's first assisted takeoff of aircraft with solid- and liquid-propellant rockets, flight of an aircraft with rocket propulsion alone, and development of spontaneously igniting liquid propellants of the kind that were to be used in the Apollo Command and Lunar Excursion modules some 25 years later.

His dedication to international scientific cooperation led him in 1947 to propose to the United Nations the establishment of an international research centre for fluid and soil mechanics in the Middle East. This proposal, though unfulfilled, contributed to the development by UNESCO of the Arid Zone Research Project in 1950. Von Kármán conceived the idea of cooperation among aeronautical engineers of the member nations of the North Atlantic Treaty Organization

(NATO) and, in 1951, obtained approval to launch the Advisory Group for Aeronautical Research and Development (AGARD)—of which he was chairman until his death in 1963. In 1956, his efforts brought into being the International Council of the Aeronautical Sciences (ICAS) and, in 1960, the International Academy of Astronautics. One of the outstanding activities of the academy under his presidency was its sponsorship, in 1962, in Paris, of the First International Symposium on the Basic Environmental Problems of Man in Space. For the first time scientists from the United States and the Soviet Union, as well as other countries, exchanged information in this field. Between 1960 and 1963, von Kármán led NATO-sponsored studies on the interaction of science and technology.

During his lifetime, laboratories were named after von Kármán at the California Institute of Technology, the Arnold Engineering Development Center of the U.S. Air Force at Tullahoma, Tennessee, and the NATO institute for fluid dynamics at Sint-Genesius-Rode, Belgium. A crater on the Moon has carried his name since 1970.

An appreciation of von Kármán's personality must also take account of his nonscientific talents. He was much interested in poetry and literature and could always supply a story appropriate to any occasion. When the atmosphere became charged with tension in a scientific meeting, he was able to restore balance by drawing on his collection of anecdotes. He had a fantastic capacity for work and left behind him wherever he went a trail of bits of paper covered with calculations. He was an optimist and believed in the future, despite the prevailing difficulties in the world.

JAMES KILLIAN
(b. July 24, 1904, Blacksburg, S.C., U.S.—d. Jan. 29, 1988, Cambridge, Mass.)

American statesman and academic administrator James Rhyne Killian, Jr., was instrumental in the formation of NASA, both as chairman of the President's Science Advisory Committee and as presidential assistant to Dwight D. Eisenhower from 1957 to 1959.

In 1926, Killian earned a B.S. in engineering and business administration from the Massachusetts Institute of Technology (MIT). He served on the editorial staff of *Technology Review* (1926–39)—a scientific journal published by the MIT alumni association—before holding a series of administrative positions at MIT, including vice president (1945–48) and president (1948–59).

When the Soviets launched Sputnik, the first artificial Earth satellite, in 1957, the United States reevaluated its science policy. Eisenhower chose Killian to establish priorities in research and development. After Killian helped create NASA (1958), he resigned the post as presidential adviser but continued to serve as a member of the President's Science Advisory Committee until 1961. He worked as chairman of the Carnegie Commission on Educational Television (1965–67) and as chairman of the Corporation of Public Broadcasting (1973–74).

SERGEY KOROLYOV

(b. Jan. 12, 1907, [Dec. 30, 1906, Old Style], Zhitomir, Russia—d. Jan. 14, 1966, Moscow, Russia, U.S.S.R.)

Sergey Pavlovich Korolyov was the chief Soviet designer of guided missiles, rockets, and spacecraft. Educated at the Odessa Building Trades School, the Kiev Polytechnic Institute, and the Moscow N.E. Bauman Higher Technical School, Korolyov studied aeronautical engineering under the celebrated designers Nikolay Yegorovich Zhukovsky and Andrey Nikolayevich Tupolev. Becoming interested in rocketry, he and F.A. Tsander formed the Moscow Group for the Study of Reactive Motion. In 1933, the group launched the Soviet Union's first liquid-propellant rocket.

During World War II Korolyov was held under technical arrest but spent the years designing and testing liquid-fuel rocket boosters for military aircraft. After the war, he modified the German V-2 missile, increasing its range to about 426 miles (685 km). He also supervised the test firing of captured V-2 missiles at the Kapustin Yar proving ground in 1947. In 1953, he began to develop the series of ballistic missiles that led to the Soviet Union's first intercontinental ballistic missile. Essentially apolitical, he did not join the Communist Party until after Stalin's death in 1953.

Korolyov was placed in charge of systems engineering for Soviet launch vehicles and spacecraft. He directed the design, testing, construction, and launching of the Vostok, Voskhod, and Soyuz manned spacecraft, as well as of the unmanned spacecraft in the Cosmos, Molniya, and Zond series. He was the guiding genius behind the Soviet spaceflight program until his death, and he was buried in the Kremlin wall on Red Square. During his lifetime he was publicly known only as "the Chief Designer." In accordance with the Soviet government's space policies, his identity and role in his nation's space program were not publicly revealed until after his death.

HERMANN OBERTH

(b. June 25, 1894, Nagyszeben, Austria-Hungary [now Sibiu, Rom.]—d. Dec. 29, 1989, Nürnberg, W.Ger.)

German scientist Hermann Julius Oberth is considered to be one of the founders of modern astronautics.

The son of a prosperous physician, Oberth studied medicine in Munich, but his education was interrupted by service in the Austro-Hungarian army during World War I. After being wounded in the war, he found time to pursue his studies in astronautics. He performed experiments to simulate weightlessness and worked out a design for a long-range, liquid-propellant rocket that his commanding officer sent to the War Ministry. The design was rejected as a fantasy. After the war, Oberth sought a Ph.D. degree at the University of Heidelberg with a dissertation based on his rocket design. It was rejected by the university in 1922, but Oberth partially underwrote publishing expenses, and it appeared as *Die Rakete zu den Planetenräumen* (1923; "The Rocket into Interplanetary Space"). The book, which explained mathematically how rockets could achieve a speed that would allow them to escape Earth's gravitational pull, gained Oberth widespread recognition.

Until 1922, he was unfamiliar with the work of Robert Goddard in the United States and, until 1925, with that of Konstantin Tsiolkovsky in the Soviet Union. After corresponding with both men, he acknowledged their precedence in deriving the equations associated with space flight. Oberth's *Wege zur Raumschiffahrt* (1929; *Ways to Spaceflight*) won the first annual Robert Esnault-Pelterie–André Hirsch Prize of 10,000 francs, enabling him to finance his research on liquid-propellant rocket motors. The book anticipated by 30 years the development of electric propulsion and of the ion rocket. In 1931, Oberth received a patent for a liquid-propellant rocket from the Romanian Patent Office, and the first rocket was launched on May 7, 1931, near Berlin.

In 1938, Oberth joined the faculty of the Technical University of Vienna. He became a German citizen in 1940 and in 1941 transferred to the German rocket development centre at Peenemünde. There, he worked for Wernher von Braun, his former assistant.

In 1943, he was sent to another location to work on solid-propellant antiaircraft rockets. He spent a year in Switzerland after the war as a rocket consultant, and in 1950, he moved to Italy, where he worked on solid-propellant antiaircraft rockets for the Italian navy. In the United States from 1955, he did advanced space research for the army until he retired to West Germany in 1958.

Residing permanently in the town of Feucht, near Nürnberg, from 1962, Oberth spent his retirement engaged in theoretical studies. In 1959, he published *Stoff und Leben* ("Material and Life"). Oberth posited in this work that materialism, the philosophy on which communism is based—is incorrect and further that aspects of human life such as the soul could not be explained by material reason.

WILLIAM PICKERING

(b. Dec. 24, 1910, Wellington, N.Z.— d. March 15, 2004, La Cañada Flintridge, Calif., U.S.)

New Zealand-born American engineer and physicist William Hayward Pickering was head of the team that developed Explorer 1, the first U.S. satellite. He played a leading role in the development of the U.S. space program.

Pickering attended Canterbury University in New Zealand before moving to the United States in 1929. He became a U.S. citizen in 1941. He studied at the California Institute of Technology in Pasadena (B.S. 1932, M.S. 1933, Ph.D. 1936) and joined the staff of the institute in 1936. Working under the American physicist Robert A. Millikan, Pickering developed cosmic-radiation-detection gear for high-altitude balloon flights. In 1944, he became a section chief of the Jet Propulsion Laboratory, where he developed the first telemetry system used in U.S. rockets. He was manager of the Corporal rocket project, which brought about important early advances in guidance and communication techniques.

In 1951, Pickering became chief of the division of guided-missile electronics, and three years later, he was appointed director of the Jet Propulsion Laboratory. He was in charge of the development of the Explorer 1 satellite and the modification of the Jupiter-C launch vehicle.

Among the laboratory's other important projects were the Ranger and Surveyor spacecraft, the Mariner spacecraft, and numerous other unmanned probes into the solar system.

Pickering retired from the Jet Propulsion Laboratory in 1976 and served for two years as director of the research institute of the University of Petroleum and Minerals in Saudi Arabia. He then returned to Pasadena to establish a private consulting practice. Pickering's numerous awards include an honorary knighthood (1976) from Queen Elizabeth II and the National Medal of Science (1976).

GLOSSARY

aerogel A manufactured material with the lowest density of any known solid. It can support a great deal of weight and can be used to capture tiny dust particles.

albedo The measurement of the extent to which an object reflects light from the sun.

apogee The point, in an elliptical Earth orbit, where an object is farthest from Earth.

atmosphere A layer of gases that may surround a material body of sufficient mass, kept there by gravity.

bipropellant systems Propulsion system wherein oxidizer and fuel are tanked separately and mixed in the combustion chamber.

black hole A region of space in which the gravitational field is so powerful that nothing, including light, can escape its pull.

cartography The study and practice of making geographical maps.

combustion A complex sequence of chemical reactions in the presence of a fuel and an oxidant, resulting in the production of heat or light.

concomitant Accompanying, connected with.

drop tower A structure used to produce a controlled period of weightlessness for an object under study.

force A push or pull that can cause an object with mass to change its velocity.

gravity well The field of gravitational potential around a massive body.

heliosheath The comet-like tail behind the sun.

heliosphere The teardrop-shaped region around the sun that is filled with solar magnetic fields and the outward-moving solar wind.

kinetic energy The extra energy that an object gains while in motion.

launchpad The area and facilities where rockets or spacecraft take off.

launch vehicle A rocket used to carry a payload from Earth's surface into outer space.

magnetosphere A highly magnetized region around and possessed by an astronomical object.

mascons A region of excess gravitational attraction on the surface of the Moon.

mass driver A proposed method of non-rocket space launch, using electromagnets to accelerate and catapult payloads up to high speeds.

mesosphere The layer of Earth's atmosphere that is above the stratosphere and below the thermosphere.

multiple staging A launch technique where a launch vehicle carries a second rocket as its payload, to be fired after the burnout of the first stage. This minimizes the size of the takeoff vehicle.

nozzle A mechanical device designed to control the characteristics of a fluid flow as it exits (or enters) an enclosed chamber or pipe.

orbit The curved path of one object around a point or another body.

perigee The point, in an elliptical Earth orbit, where an object is closest to Earth.

propellant A substance used to move an object, often through a chemical reaction.

quasar Any class of rare, bright galaxies that often have strong radio emission that is observed at great distances.

redshift The increase in the wavelength of electromagnetic radiation received by a detector compared with the wavelength emitted by the source.

satellite An object that has been placed into orbit by human endeavor.

sidereal day The rotational period of Earth measured against the fixed stars, used as a way to keep track of the direction in which telescopes need to be pointed to view any given star in the night sky.

sounding rocket An instrument-carrying rocket designed to take measurements and perform scientific experiments during its suborbital flight.

Space Race An informal competition between the United States and the Soviet Union to see who could make the furthest advancements into space first.

supernova A violently exploding star whose luminosity after eruption suddenly increases to many times its normal level.

thermal energy Internal energy present in a state of thermodynamic equilibrium.

turbojet A turbine-driven compressor that draws in and compresses air, forcing it into a combustion chamber into which fuel is injected.

velocity The quantity that designates how fast and in what direction a point is moving.

FOR FURTHER READING

Andrews, James T. *Red Cosmos: K.E. Tsiolkovkii, Grandfather of Soviet Rocketry*. College Station, TX: TAMU Press, 2009.

Bell, Jim, and Jacqueline Mitton, eds. *Asteroid Rendezvous: NEAR Shoemaker's Adventures at Eros*. New York, NY: Cambridge University Press, 2002.

Brzezinski, Matthew. *Red Moon Rising: Sputnik and the Hidden Rivalries that Ignited the Space Race*. New York, NY: Henry Holt & Company, 2007.

Butrica, Andrew J. *Single Stage to Orbit: Politics, Space Technology, and the Quest for Reusable Rocketry*. Baltimore, MD: Johns Hopkins University Press, 2003.

Capderou, Michel. *Satellites: Orbits and Missions*. New York, NY: Springer, 2005.

Dickson, Paul. *Sputnik: The Shock of the Century*. New York, NY: Walker & Co., 2007.

Elbert, Bruce R. *Introduction to Satellite Communication*. Norwood, MA: Artech House, Inc., 2008.

Gorn, Michael. *NASA: The Complete Illustrated History*. London, England: Merrell, 2008.

Gruntman, Michael. *Blazing the Trail: The Early History of Spacecraft and Rocketry*. Reston, VA: American Institute of Aeronautics and Astronautics, 2004.

Harland, David M. *Cassini at Saturn: Huygens Results*. New York, NY: Springer Praxis, 2007.

Harra, Louise K., and Keith O. Mason, eds. *Space Science*. London, England: Imperial College Press, 2004.

Harvey, Brian. *China's Space Program: From Conception to Manned Spaceflight*. New York, NY: Springer, 2009.

Hunley, J. D. *U.S. Space Launch-Vehicle Technology: Viking to Space Shuttle*. Gainesville, FL: University Press of Florida, 2008.

Maini, Ani Kumar. *Satellite Technology: Principles and Applications*. West Sussex, England: John Wiley & Sons, 2007.

Neufeld, Michael. *Von Braun: Dreamer of Space, Engineer of War*. New York, NY: Random House, 2008.

Roddy, Dennis. *Satellite Communications*. Columbus, OH: McGraw-Hill Companies, 2006.

Rogers, Lucy. *It's ONLY Rocket Science: An Introduction in Plain English*. New York, NY: Springer, 2008.

Russell, C. T. *2001 Mars Odyssey*. New York, NY: Springer, 2004.

Ulivi, Paolo, and David M. Harland. *Robotic Exploration of the Solar System, Part I: The Golden Age 1957–1982*. New York, NY: Springer, 2007.

Zimmerman, Robert. *The Universe in a Mirror: The Saga of the Hubble Space Telescope and the Visionaries Who Built It*. Princeton, NJ: Princeton University Press, 2008.

INDEX